MENCKEN ON MENCKEN

MENCKEN ON
MENCKEN

A New Collection of Autobiographical Writings

EDITED BY S. T. JOSHI

LOUISIANA STATE UNIVERSITY PRESS

BATON ROUGE

Published by Louisiana State University Press
Copyright © 2010 by Louisiana State University Press
All rights reserved
Manufactured in the United States of America

LSU Press Paperback Original

DESIGNER: *Amanda McDonald Scallan*
TYPEFACE: *Whitman, text; BlairMdITC TT , display*

Library of Congress Cataloging-in-Publication Data

Mencken, H. L. (Henry Louis), 1880–1956.
  Mencken on Mencken : a new collection of autobiographical writings / edited by S.T. Joshi.
    p.   cm.
  Includes bibliographical references and index.
  ISBN 978-0-8071-3592-1 (pbk. : alk. paper)
  1. Mencken, H. L. (Henry Louis), 1880–1956. 2. Authors, American—20th century—Biography.
I. Joshi, S. T., 1958– II. Title.
  PS3525.E43Z4675 2010
  818'.5209—dc22
  [B]

                                                                                          2009022308

CONTENTS

MENCKEN ON MENCKEN

INTRODUCTION

The publication of H. L. Mencken's autobiographies—*Happy Days* (1940), *Newspaper Days* (1941), and *Heathen Days* (1943)—may well have saved his reputation. By the late 1930s, Mencken was no longer the fiery, dynamic iconoclast who had done yeoman's work in purging American culture of the masses of intellectual and aesthetic rubbish that had cluttered it as it emerged out of the nineteenth century. His championing of Mark Twain, Theodore Dreiser, Sinclair Lewis, Willa Cather, and Joseph Conrad were long in the past; his flaying of William Jennings Bryan and other religious fundamentalists at the Scopes trial of 1925 had receded from memory; and he seemed to have become a crotchety, mean-spirited reactionary who failed to understand the depths of misery that so many Americans faced in the wake of the depression and could therefore see nothing but tyranny or, worse, incompetence, in Franklin D. Roosevelt's admittedly improvisatory attempts to revive America from its economic doldrums. Mencken had become tiresome and repetitious—hardly surprising, given that by this time he had probably written about seven or eight million of the ten or fifteen million words he later estimated he had written in a lifetime—in books, magazine articles, and especially newspaper columns.

But the "Days" books came to his rescue. Written in a winsome, blandly cynical, and engagingly genial manner, they vividly evoked a bygone period more than half a century in the past. *Happy Days*—focusing on his boyhood memories from his birth up to the year 1892—also featured Mencken's recollections of local characters whose own lives and memories extended back to the Civil War and before; accordingly, the collective impressions of the "Days" books could justifiably be seen to constitute a full century of American life.

Happy Days appears to have been composed almost by accident. Mencken wrote two articles about his boyhood—"The Career of a Philosopher" and "Innocence in a Wicked World"—for the *New Yorker* in 1936, and in the autobiographical statement from that year that constitutes the epilogue to this book he expressed his desire to write an entire volume "about my early youth—say from the dawn of consciousness to adolescence"; but health problems and other preoccupations prevented him from undertaking extensive work on the task until 1939. In that year, nine more chapters appeared in the *New Yorker,* and the completed volume—containing twenty chapters—emerged in January 1940. Biographer Fred Hobson notes both its critical and popular success: "The reviews in early 1940 were almost unanimous in their praise, sales from the first five months totaled nearly 10,000 copies, and Mencken, urged by *The New Yorker* to undertake more sketches, immediately began work on a second volume of reminiscences, this one dealing with his days as a young newspaperman in Baltimore."[1] The result was *Newspaper Days,* of whose sixteen chapters nine first appeared in the *New Yorker. Heathen Days* appeared in 1943, with eight of its twenty chapters having previously appeared in either the *New Yorker* or *Esquire.*

What has not been widely known, even to Mencken scholars, is that Mencken continued to write reminiscent pieces for both the *New Yorker* and *Esquire* for the next several years. Although Hobson declares that after *Heathen Days* "Mencken would write no more books in this vein"[2]—he was at this point undertaking his two immense chronicles of his variegated work, *My Life as Author and Editor* and *Thirty-five Years of Newspaper Work,* designed for posthumous publication (they appeared in 1993 and 1994, respectively)—it seems difficult to imagine that he did not envision gathering these memoirs in book form at some point or other. In any event, Mencken had written many other pieces that could, and should, have been incorporated into his formal autobiographies— pieces that discuss everything from his recollections of Jamaica in 1900 to his work as war correspondent at Germany's eastern front in 1917, from his theory and practice of journalism to the principles that guided his editorship of such magazines as the *Smart Set* and the *American Mercury,* and from his beliefs on God and the afterlife to his views of the many national politicians, from Theodore Roosevelt to Franklin D. Roosevelt, he had known and covered over a half-century of newspaper writing. The present volume therefore seeks humbly to be the fourth of Mencken's "Days" books, including writings written over a period of nearly fifty years and focusing on numerous facets of his life and thought that the three earlier books address only glancingly or not at all.

The basic facts of Henry Louis Mencken's life are well known, if only because he has chronicled them so vividly himself and because he was so central a presence in American literature and culture for the entire first half of the twentieth century. Born in Baltimore on September 12, 1880, the grandson of a German immigrant whose father had established a prosperous cigar factory, Mencken attended Friedrich Knapp's academy and Baltimore Polytechnic. In 1896 he began a three-year stint at his father's factory, even though he himself wished to be either a poet or a chemist. His chance to escape a life of business emerged when his father died unexpectedly in 1899; a few days after the funeral Mencken showed up at the offices of the *Baltimore Herald* and was soon hired as a reporter.

Difficult as it is to imagine the future author of *The American Language* reporting on sewage problems in Baltimore or whether telephone wires should be on overhead poles or underground, this nuts-and-bolts work as a beat reporter for the *Herald* proved to be both a valuable and a thrilling experience for Mencken. *Newspaper Days* is entirely devoted to the seven-year period of his work for this newspaper, which he later declared to be the most "gaudy and gorgeous" years of his journalistic career. Possibly Mencken was seeing the period through rose-colored glasses, since in the early essay "Footnote on Journalism" (1901), written before he turned twenty-one, he seems unable to summon any great enthusiasm for the lofty calling of a reporter struggling to get by on fifteen dollars a week. Mencken was soon taken off the streets to become, successively, Sunday editor and city editor of the *Herald*, during which time he engaged in a stint of theater reviewing and also undertook to cover his first political conventions, reporting on both the Republican and the Democratic national conventions (in Chicago and St. Louis, respectively) in 1904. Of course, 1904 was made memorable by the great Baltimore fire—an event so devastating that the *Herald* had to be issued in a skeletonic edition from Washington, D.C. This period also saw the publication of Mencken's first books, the slim poetry volume *Ventures into Verse* (1903) and the treatise *George Bernard Shaw: His Plays* (1905), the first book-length study of Shaw.

The *Herald* collapsed in 1906, and Mencken had several choices in seeking his journalistic fortunes in Baltimore. In the event, he was wise to choose the *Baltimore Sun*, which had been in continuous operation since its founding in 1837. He was initially made Sunday editor, but also wrote a great many unsigned editorials, theoretically enunciating the paper's stand on significant issues of local and national importance—although many of his editorials were (by today's standards, at any rate) shockingly flippant and satirical, in particular poking repeated fun at the institution of marriage.

In 1908 Mencken began his long career as a book reviewer, being hired by the *Smart Set* to write a monthly book review column. He would continue the work uninterruptedly for twenty-five years, both in that magazine and later in the *American Mercury*. In 1910 Mencken and others, convinced that an evening newspaper was the wave of the future, established the *Baltimore Evening Sun*. Mencken and John Haslup Adams were the editors, and once again Mencken wrote a substantial number of unsigned editorials as well as other anonymous and signed work. He took to the work readily, since—as he notes in the essay I have titled "Twenty-five Years of the *Evening Sun*"—he was "busting with ideas in those days." He may have spoken better than he knew, for in May 1911 he began a regular signed column, "The Free Lance," that ran—with a few vacations—*six days a week for the next four and a half years*. This immense body of work, totaling perhaps a million and a half words, remains virtually uncollected, but in many ways it may be among Mencken's most vibrant newspaper writing. He took not only Baltimore but the entire nation and the world for his stage; indeed, his column came to an abrupt end in October 1915 because his unrelenting sympathy for Germany since the outbreak of the Great War so alienated readers that the owners of the *Evening Sun* felt it prudent to put a muzzle on their star editorial writer.

Mencken, for his part, had other fish to fry. In late 1914 he had become coeditor, with his longtime colleague George Jean Nathan, of the *Smart Set*, and for the next several years he was busy both editing and writing for the magazine—including a fair number of short stories and novelettes, all written under pseudonyms. His one foray into journalism was his ill-fated trip to the eastern front, beginning in late 1916. By early the next year, America's abrupt breaking off of diplomatic relations with Germany necessitated his departure, along with the American ambassador James Watson Gerard, in a circuitous route through Spain and then to Cuba. Arriving on the Caribbean island, he witnessed a miniature rebellion before finally returning stateside.

Mencken states that he resumed work with the *Sun* in 1918, but this work must have been editorial only, for no actual signed articles appeared until early 1920. It was at this point, however, that he began what could be termed his golden age as a journalist. His "Monday articles" were widely syndicated and established both him and his paper as a national institution. Not the least of his ventures was his quadrennial attendance of the national political conventions—then far less scripted than now, so that there was genuine suspense as to which of several political figures would emerge as the standard-bearer of his party. Mencken's unfailingly lively reports[3] (he attended every convention from 1920 to 1940) capture both the dynamism and the long stretches of boredom at these political festivals, and they went far in establishing him as the most acute political commentator of his day.

Meanwhile, his editorship of the *Smart Set* came to an abrupt end in 1923, when the owners of the magazine decided to make it a crassly popular organ devoted to pulp fiction and celebrity features. Mencken and Nathan, along with his longtime publisher Alfred A. Knopf, took the occasion to found the *American Mercury,* and they quickly made it one of the most scintillating journals of opinion in the nation. Just as he had helped to introduce such writers as F. Scott Fitzgerald and Eugene O'Neill in the pages of the *Smart Set,* so he used the *American Mercury* as the venue to launch the careers of James M. Cain, Gerald W. Johnson, Emily Clark, and others. His editorials, chiefly on political and social subjects, and his endless succession of reviews—now devoted less to novels and tales and more to serious works of scholarship—revealed Mencken at the top of his form.

But by the 1930s a certain weariness seems to have set in. Mencken declared that ten years was long enough for anyone to edit a magazine, and true to his word he resigned the editorship of the *American Mercury* at the end of 1933. His work for the *Evening Sun* continued, but it seemed to lack freshness and vigor. A lifelong Democrat, Mencken initially had high hopes for Franklin D. Roosevelt, but his generally libertarian stance in regard to both civil liberties and economic principles soon caused him to consider FDR a blundering tyrant whose "planned economy" was nothing more than disguised socialism—and inefficient socialism at that. The tirades that Mencken directed toward FDR throughout the 1930s make sad reading today. Mencken himself, a self-confessed prosperous bourgeois, failed to grasp that desperate times required desperate measures, and he could see in the Brain Trust nothing but a crude grab for all-encompassing power.

But if Mencken's professional life was not entirely satisfactory, the same could not be said for his personal life. To the surprise of his friends—not to mention the many readers who had for decades been reading his cynical comments on marriage—Mencken in 1930 married Sara Haardt, a southern teacher and writer whom he had known since 1923. Their marriage appeared to be the epitome of happiness and domestic contentment, but her early death of tubercular meningitis in 1935 shadowed his later years.

During his lustrum of marital stability Mencken chose to devote a substantial amount of his time and attention to books. However, such works as *Treatise on the Gods* (1930) and *Treatise on Right and Wrong* (1934)—unwontedly sober treatments of religion and ethics, respectively—were not received enthusiastically. Many readers and critics felt that Mencken was written out. But the exhaustively revised fourth edition (1936) of his *American Language* (1919)—the treatise that first exhibited Mencken's taste for and understanding of the racy vulgate spoken by the great majority of Americans—began the restoration of his reputation that the "Days" books completed. Mencken was, indeed, notably silent on political matters during the 1940s: whereas his siding with Germany during the morally ambiguous Great War may have had some justification, his tortured support of the land of his ancestors during World War II (in spite of his repeated assertions of disdain for Hitler) could not have been uttered in public with impunity. He wrote nothing for either the *Sun* or the *Evening Sun* from 1941 to 1948, and he only came out of virtual retirement in that latter year only to cover the presidential campaign, in which he no doubt hoped and expected that Thomas E. Dewey would triumph over the hated Truman. The title of the article he wrote after Truman's victory ("Truman's Election: Mencken Says Country Jolly Well Deserves It," *Sun*, October 26, 1948) tells the whole story. The massive stroke he suffered on November 23, 1948, incapacitated him, rendering him unable to read or write. He dragged out a cheerless life at his home on Hollins Street until he died peacefully on January 29, 1956.

It would be a considerable exaggeration to say that Mencken was self-obsessed, but it is striking how often he lapses into a reminiscent mood for no apparent reason. His love for his hometown is expressed with especial fervor in both his "Days" books and in the uncollected pieces in this volume. "I am glad I was born long enough ago to remember, now, the days when the town had genuine color, and life here was worth living," he states in "Baltimoriana" (1926). Indeed, what comes through most poignantly in these essays is the vividness of his recollections of his childhood—whether they be of the "dummies" (deaf and dumb students) at Knapp's academy, or of the thrill of his driving a horse on a harness, or of the piquant characters he encountered as a boy. His reminiscing began surprisingly early: well before he was twenty-five his article "The Passing of 'The Hill'" appeared in the *Herald* and displayed his nostalgia for the tokens of his boyhood that were no more.

The "Days" books themselves gain some of their inimitable flavor from Mencken's recounting of the eccentrics he encountered both during his childhood and during his early years as a reporter. The uncollected pieces follow suit, telling of the hapless street cleaner Jock, who, pursued by a predatory widow, departs one night for parts unknown and is never seen again; of Charlie and Irene, a loving couple who remain devoted to one another through a long series of Charlie's illnesses until finally Irene can't take it anymore and vanishes; and perhaps most pungent of all, of Leopold Bortsch, the professional mourner for a Baltimore brewery. To be sure, the town had "genuine color" in those days.

But Mencken is perhaps at his best in telling of the friends and colleagues he had known over a lifetime. The list includes not only newspapermen (they were all men) but literary colleagues such as the critic James Huneker, and the novelist Theodore Dreiser, with whom he would have a tortured relationship for decades. Huneker's prodigious knowledge of music (which, aside from writing, was Mencken's own greatest love) and the other arts caused Mencken to fall under his sway in the first decade of the twentieth century; and Mencken's observation that one of the chief characteristics of Huneker's style and temperament was a "capacity for gusto" suggests how this now little-known figure may have cast a significant influence upon the junior colleague who would fast eclipse him as America's leading literary and cultural critic.

It would appear that Mencken did not regard his formal autobiographies as forums for the expression of his philosophical, aesthetic, or political views. Even the chapter he devotes to the Scopes trial in *Heathen Days* says little about the sources of his irreligiosity and anticlericalism, although the chapter titled "First Steps in Divinity" (in *Happy Days*) delightfully recapitulates his early Sunday-school lessons. It is striking that Mencken never reprinted the significant essay "What I Believe" (1930), for it encapsulates his (anti)religious and political philosophy more pointedly than any other single document. For once, Mencken generally eschews the flippancy that can make it difficult to ascertain whether he is expressing a seriously held belief or merely teasing the reader with a deliberately outrageous utterance. He makes no bones about his disbelief in the inerrancy of the Bible and the consequences of this disbelief:

Is it a fact that the authors of the New Testament were inspired by God, and compiled a record that is innocent of error? It is not a fact. They were ignorant and credulous men, and they put together a narrative that is as discordant and preposterous, at least in material parts, as the testimony of six darkies in a police court. Is it a fact that believing that narrative is an act of merit, and that its reward is deliverance from hell and entrance upon an eternity of bliss? It is not a fact. More, it is not even an innocent fiction. For its necessary implication is that the test of a proposition is something unrelated to its truth—that lying is virtuous so long as it brings a reward.

Let us bypass the casual racism hinted at in the comment on "darkies": the bulk of Mencken's career makes it indubitable that his devotion to the cause of civil liberties for African Americans was unremitting; indeed, in another essay (not included here), he urges blacks to rid themselves of "hog-wallow theology"[4] in order to expedite their social and political advance. A passage like the above shows why Mencken felt that William Jennings Bryan and his fellow fundamentalists were so dangerous: it was not that they were content to believe in a preposterous theology themselves, it is that they wished to force it down everyone else's throats. This brutal truth makes us censure Mencken a bit less when he figuratively danced upon Bryan's grave in a series of obituaries following the latter's abrupt demise days after the end of the Scopes trial.

Mencken's journalism leaves us in no doubt that he regarded politicians with whole skepticism, but what such essays as "What I Believe" and "'Generally Political'" (a lecture delivered at Columbia University in early 1940) make clear is his skepticism in regard to the very principle of democracy, at least as it is practiced in the United States. Mencken of course had written exhaustively on the subject in *Notes on Democracy* (1926), but "'Generally Political'" boils down his arguments to their quintessence. His general point—that the corruption and hypocrisy that appears endemic to politicians is a direct result of the intellectual and moral weakness of the public that elects them—is made abundantly clear in his blandly euphemistic references to the "intellectually underprivileged." This stance also colors his theory of journalism, since he repeatedly stated that a newspaper cannot address its message to intellectuals (there are too few of them to support a major paper), but rather to the ill-informed and emotion-driven public at large. Mencken's repeated assertions that, under American democracy, no politician who has "honor" and "common decency" (two phrases that pepper his writing from beginning to end) can possibly be elected except by a miracle was based on decades of the closest examination of politicians, local and national, in the heat of campaign battles and in the halls of legislation.

Heathen Days, a kind of catch-all memoir discussing random events in his life from 1890 to 1936, has several chapters dealing with Mencken's far-flung travels, but it fails to cover a number of voyages, taken both for business and for pleasure, that granted him substantial familiarity with the more notable features of two or three continents. These travels began rather earlier than Mencken himself perhaps expected: in the summer of 1900 his doctor, Z. K. Wiley, troubled by Mencken's ongoing bronchitis and fearing that he might have contracted tuberculosis, recommended that he take time off from the *Herald* to spend a month in the Caribbean. Jamaica was his destination, and the result was a number of special articles for the *Herald* expressing wonderment at the beauties of that exotic tropical land.

Eight years later Mencken took his first trip to Europe, a brief excursion to England and Germany. In 1912 he voyaged there again, in the company of his *Herald* colleague A. H. McDannald, and we can gauge the success of this expedition from two splendid papers, "The Beeriad" and "At Large in London," both published in the *Smart Set* and both regaling us with the quality of the food and (especially) beer to be found in Munich and London. These essays served as the basis of Mencken's contributions to the collaborative work *Europe After 8:15* (1914), cowritten with George Jean Nathan and Willard Huntington Wright, Mencken's predecessor as editor of the *Smart Set*.

I have already mentioned Mencken's trip to Germany in 1916–17 as a war correspondent. Aside from a several-month European tour in 1922, Mencken did not cross the Atlantic again until 1932, when he and Sara went on a cruise to various Caribbean ports—Panama, Jamaica, Venezuela, Cuba, and elsewhere. This set the stage for their extensive Mediterranean cruise in February and March of 1934, with stops ranging from Gibraltar to Jerusalem. One literary result of this trip was a rather peculiar series of stream-of-consciousness jottings—almost as if they were being telegraphed back to the States—that Mencken published in the *New Yorker* under the heading "Foreign Parts." The nine installments of this series, each taking up exactly two columns of a *New Yorker* page, appear to record his first impressions of the places he was visiting (although they were published several months after his return) and in that sense have a certain biographical value not found in the more conventionally written pieces he submitted to the *Evening Sun*, not to mention the chapter entitled "Vanishing Act" in *Heathen Days*, covering the same trip. (Hobson points out that all Mencken's writings of his Mediterranean tour sound as if he were alone, and in some sense he was, for Sara, her health already failing, frequently had to stay in the hotel while Mencken toured the sites on his own.)[5] Upon his return Mencken's attention was drawn to a circular by the Hamburg-America Line advertising American tours for Germans, and he wrote up the matter in a whimsical article, "Our Footloose Correspondents," which the *New Yorker* ran (at Mencken's suggestion) under the odd pseudonym "M. R. C."[6] The piece has been included here largely as a curiosity, as it has never been reprinted and few even know of its authorship.

Another piece—"The Black Country" (*Chicago Sunday Tribune*, January 23, 1927)—has been included for another reason. This article, the original of his celebrated and notorious essay "The Libido for the Ugly" in *Prejudices: Sixth Series* (1927), is a scathing indictment of the architectural hideousness of the towns of western Pennsylvania, whose vileness he takes as only an extreme version of the American "libido for the ugly" that Europeans have somehow managed to eschew. Recently a local scholar has pointed to some possible errors in Mencken's dismal portrayal of these Pennsylvania backwaters,[7] but Mencken's general purpose was to emphasize the aesthetic failings of his countrymen by contrasting them with the soundness of European taste, where "there is scarcely an ugly village on the whole continent." Mencken, in spite of his championing of the American language and his rich enjoyment of the buffooneries of American political and social life, was in this sense a perfect embodiment of Nietzsche's "good European": one need only observe his pungent remark, in "What Is This Talk about Utopia?" (1928), that he is first and foremost a citizen of the Maryland Free State and only secondarily—and not, apparently, by free choice—a citizen of the United States.

Mencken's travel pieces reveal all the wonder and enthusiasm of a small boy coming upon the miraculous for the first time. His gorgeous description of a Jamaican sunset, his deadpan account of deceitful child beggars in Athens, the lyrical prose-poetry of his pub crawls in Munich and his wholesome admiration for the buxom barmaids who served him—these are indeed the impressions of a man with a "capacity for gusto," utterly belying the comment made elsewhere (in "Meditations at Vespers") that "[s]peaking generally, I am of a somber disposition and get very little happiness out of life." Like his idol Mark Twain, Mencken could perhaps shed his celebrity overseas and become merely a tourist—but a tourist whose knowledge of the long history of European culture allowed him to grasp the essence of what he was seeing far more astutely than the faux-naïf Twain could bring himself to do.

How reliable are Mencken's recollections, whether in the "Days" books or in these uncollected pieces? A definitive judgment is difficult to make. I have already pointed out what seems to be a discontinuity between the less than enthusiastic account of his *Herald* work in the early essay "Footnote on Journalism" and his later admissions that this was the most enjoyable period of his journalistic career. Trivial discrepancies of this sort can no doubt be found by the diligent student, but do they cast any doubt as to the overall historicity of the memoirs?

It does seem remarkable that Mencken, both as a child and adolescent and as a reporter, came into contact with such an array of colorful characters as he did, although no doubt it is precisely one of the skills of a good reporter to be able to unearth such distinctive eccentrics. But it is hard to deny that the piquancy of these accounts lies as much in the manner of their relation as in the actual events. Delightful turns of phrase meet us on every page: there was the ex-policeman and honky-tonk owner Julius Olsen, who made sure to exclude any women who "raised a suspicion of chastity"; there were the dry politicians who "got down so much alcohol that it was impossible to freeze them in Winter, even though they lay in the gutter outside a Washington speakeasy, with five feet of snow over them"; there was, after the frigidity of the German eastern front, the restorative warmth of the Spanish sun, which "glared down with all the hospitable ferocity of the gates of hell." For all that Mencken is, largely as a result of his prodigious output, occasionally given to repetitions of pet phrases, his writing remains remarkably fresh and vivid, especially when he is discussing himself or those around him. I repeat that Mencken should not be considered self-absorbed; indeed, one of the chief merits of his autobiographical writings is his ability to look upon himself with the same genial cynicism as he looks upon the characters and events he is relating. But there is no question that, in the course of a long life, he cast his mind back with increasing fondness and nostalgia to a time when the world he knew was a simpler, more naïve, and perhaps more intimate place than the mechanized, overpopulated land that his city and his country had become. Such reflections are perhaps the inevitable products of aging, and we should be grateful that they have been articulated in such an imperishable manner.

A NOTE ON THIS EDITION

This volume assembles Mencken's autobiographical writings from a wide variety of sources. (The Bibliography of Original Appearances provides full bibliographical information on the original appearances of all the articles in this book.) Within each section, the articles are arranged chronologically, not by date of publication but by reference to the events they relate. In the absence of typescripts, it is sometimes difficult to ascertain Mencken's specific preferences in matters of punctuation, capitalization, and other such elements; the articles, as originally published, embody considerable differences in these matters, and it is debatable which texts or publications should be considered authoritative. By and large, based upon a knowledge of the entire range of Mencken's writing, I have attempted to systematize certain minor stylistic points—e.g., the omission of the serial comma; the use of quotation marks rather than italics for book titles; certain spelling preferences, such as "practise" (as a verb)—throughout the texts. In general, texts published in the *Baltimore Evening Sun* and *American Mercury* appear to reflect Mencken's preferences most clearly, since these were the texts over which he had greatest editorial control.

I have, however, decided to eliminate the section divisions that are found in the *Evening Sun* pieces. Nearly all his "Monday articles" for this paper were divided somewhat mechanically into four roman-numeraled sections, at times interfering with the flow of the discussion. When Mencken reprinted some of these articles in his *Prejudices* volumes, he generally eliminated the section divisions, and I have adopted the same principle in these cases. In other essays, section divisions appear to have greater textual justification, but even here I have systematized their usage by adopting roman numerals throughout. In some cases I have amended Mencken's titles so that they more accurately reflect the subject of the given essay; in the "Bibliography of Original Appearances" my amended titles are given in brackets, with the published titles following.

I have sought to illuminate certain literary, historical, and other points by the use of notes. To reduce their number, I have (as in my previous compilations of Mencken's writings) prepared a glossary of names to provide information on the many authors, artists, historical figures, and other individuals mentioned in the texts. This methodology generally allows for a more substantial discussion of the figures in question; in particular, I have supplied information on Mencken's reviews of books by the authors he cites. I have not included the names of well-known individuals except, in certain cases, to highlight Mencken's writings about them. In a few instances I have felt it more convenient to identify individuals in notes rather than in the glossary. In the preparation of the notes and the glossary of names, I have relied not only on many of the authoritative works about Mencken—including Fred Hobson's *Mencken: A Life* (1994), in some ways still the standard biography—but my own bibliography of Mencken (Scarecrow Press, 2009) as well as standard reference works and original research.

As with my previous Mencken work, I am grateful to Vincent Fitzpatrick (curator of the Mencken collection at the Enoch Pratt Free Library, Baltimore), Richard J. Schrader, Oleg Panczenko, and numerous others for assistance and support.

PROLOGUE

HENRY LOUIS MENCKEN (1905)

Henry Louis Mencken was born in Baltimore, September 12, 1880. He is the son of the late August Mencken and of Anna Abhau Mencken. His paternal grandfather, Burkhardt L. Mencken, came to Baltimore from Saxony in 1849. His paternal grandmother, Harriet McLellan, came to Baltimore from Kingston, Jamaica, in 1850. She was of Irish and English extraction. His maternal grandparents, Carl H. Abhau and Eva Gegner, were from Germany, the first was a Hessian and the latter a Bavarian. His mother and father were born in Baltimore.

Mencken was sent to F. Knapp's Institute when he was rather less than six years old and remained there until his twelfth year. Then he entered the Baltimore Polytechnic Institute and was graduated in 1896. He entered his father's office in July, 1896, but failed as a bookkeeper's helper and was sent to the cigar bench. There he served two and a half years, at the end of that time he was given a trial as a salesman. Here he failed again, and in 1899 left the cigar business to become a reporter on the staff of the late Baltimore *Morning Herald*. In 1901 he was made dramatic editor; in 1902, Sunday editor; and in 1903, city editor. January 1, 1905 he was given general editorial work. In 1903 he published a book of verses and in 1905 a book of dramatic criticism: "George Bernard Shaw: His Plays."

He has contributed short stories and special articles to the *Red Book, Short Stories, Leslie's Monthly*, the *Criterion* and other periodicals, and verses to *Leslie's Weekly, Life*, the *Bookman* and lesser weeklies and monthlies. He has done newspaper work for the New York *Evening Post*, the Chicago *Tribune*, the New York *Telegraph*, the Hongkong *Daily Press*, the Pittsburg *Dispatch*, the New Orleans *Picayune*, the Kobe (Japan) *Chronicle*, the Ceylon *Observer*, and the Nagasaki (Japan) *Press*, not to speak of fifty or sixty other daily papers.[1] He has never written a play or a novel. In all, his published writings, newspapers and other publications, have reached 5,500,000 words.[2]

Mencken weighs 172 pounds, is 5 feet 10¼ inches in height and is not beautiful. His chief amusement, after reading, is piano-playing, this he does very crudely. He takes no exercise except walking and is a moderate eater and drinker. He sometimes drinks as little as one bottle of beer a week, though this doesn't happen very often. He dislikes all forms of sport except prize-fighting, but likes music and the drama. He has tested all forms of dissipation except gambling. He is unmarried and glad of it.

Residence, 1524 Hollins Street.

MEMORIES OF A LONG LIFE

EARLY DAYS

My first recollection of beautiful letters has to do with "The Story of Simple Simon," published, in full color, by the old firm of McLoughlin Brothers in the early eighties.[1] My copy of it, still surviving though without the front cover, is elegantly inscribed "Harry Mencken, 1887¾." I was seven years old precisely in the year 1887¾, and could read for myself, but my mother had been reading it to me for several years before, and I recall very vividly sitting with her at an upstairs window in Hollins Street, looking down upon a snowstorm in Union Square, and hearing:

> Simple Simon went a-fishing
> For to catch a whale;
> All the water he had got
> Was in his mother's pail.

At seven—or more likely it was only five—this seemed to me to be a perfect comic situation, and it retains that character to this day. Indeed, I sometimes suspect that my lifelong view of the American yokel was generated by poor Simon, though he was, I believe, a British subject. I still know half of his saga by heart, and the rest comes back by merely glancing at it.

Most of my other primordial literary recollections also derive from the excellent books of McLoughlin Brothers. In the late eighties my brother and I (he was twenty months my junior) studied the imprint with fascination, and spent a great deal of time debating the pronunciation of the name. We finally settled on MacLawflin, and so it remains to me, though maybe something else is correct. One of the curious things I discover, thumbing through my shelf of McLoughlin incunabula, is that all of the books linger in memory only as fragments. There is, for example, "A Peep at Buffalo Bill's Wild West," published in 1887 and acquired instantly.[2] All the pictures save two strike me as new today, and all the stanzas of the text save this one about the cowboys' doxy, Madge:

And Buckskin Joe and Hurricane Dick
Regard her doings with pride,
For to them she owes whatever she knows;
They taught her to shoot and to ride.

Again there was a mysterious miscellany, apparently of English provenance, though part of it was American, which contributed a single distich:

No fiddle nebber played a jig
Wid de bow ten miles away.

I remember these lines as clearly as I remember "Now I lay me," and alongside them in my memory floats the excellent colored picture by L. Hopkins that faced them, and further on in the book I recall with equal clarity a drawing by Gustave Doré showing a clown and his wife coddling a child that has fallen in the arena and is spattered with blood, but beyond that the contents are as new to me today as a volume just off the press. By what power or process is it decided what we are to recall and what we are to forget? I have never heard an answer. If one ever comes it will tell us a great deal more than we now know about the way in which the likes and dislikes, the ideas and feelings of mankind are hatched.

OLD DAYS

Trust companies, when the passion to advertise seizes them, usually get out pamphlets full of Vision and the itch for Service—in brief, highfalutin garbage of the sort merchanted by Dr. Frank Crane and the windjammers who harangue Kiwanis. The eminent Mercantile Trust and Deposit Company of this city happily breaks the custom by printing a charming little book called "The Early Eighties": a description of the Baltimore of 40 years ago, when the company itself was a yearling. There are some excellent pictures, and there is mellow writing in the text, done by some anonymous one whose whistle in those days, you may be sure, was not wet with well water.[3]

It is a pity that the book is not ten times as large. The Baltimore of the 80's had a flavor that has long since vanished. The town is at least twice as big now as it was then, and twice as showy and glittering, but it is certainly not twice as pleasant, nor, indeed, half as pleasant. The more the boomers pump it up, the more it comes to resemble such dreadful places as Buffalo and Cleveland. I am not arguing here, of course, against the genuine improvements that the years have brought—the better streets, the sewerage system, the Guilford development, and so on. I am simply arguing against the doctrine that mere size is something—that bringing in scores of new and stinking factories and thousands of new morons has done us any good. The boomers seem to take a great delight in their own handiwork; they are forever giving one another banquets. Personally, I'd prefer to see them hanged.

Though I was born here in 1880, I first became aware of Baltimore in 1886, when I began going to school at F. Knapp's Institute, which stood on what is now the City Hall Plaza. The journey to and from school took me directly through the heart of the town twice a day, and I soon became familiar with all the old stores, many of them dating from long before the Civil War. I bought slate pencils and drawing books at Bond's, on Baltimore street just east of Holliday, and proved the durability of the end of my nose against the windows of Schwartz's toy store, on Baltimore street near Charles. Hamilton Easter's dry goods emporium still stood in the same block, and one block eastward was Sutro's music shop, where I remember buying a set of the Czerny exercises to replace one worn out by hard toil. At South street was the Sun Iron Building, still an object of interest, and greatly gaped at by visiting Eastern Shoremen.

Just when the Equitable Building, Baltimore's first office building, was built I don't know, but I clearly remember Barnum's Hotel, which used to stand on the site. Across the street, where the Courthouse now stands, was an earlier courthouse, and in the yard was an old-time hydrant. I doubt that any boy of those days ever passed the place without going into the yard and taking a drink. As the Equitable Building slowly arose it got as much attention as a two-headed boy. Crowds gathered to watch the steel beams hauled into place, and there was a great deal of talk to the effect that the elevators would be very dangerous, and that persons on the top floor would run grave risks in case of fire.

The old-time lawyers moved into it slowly, and, I believe, reluctantly. Many of them, indeed, held out against office buildings to the end, notably William Pinkney Whyte, Ferdinand C. Latrobe and, I believe, Bernard Carter. General Latrobe, to his last days, inhabited an office that had been unchanged since the 50's. It was, as I recall it, in St. Paul street, and consisted of a musty room heated in winter by an ancient stove. His office force was made up solely of an old colored man, who attended to this stove and ran errands. The General had no stenographer. He wrote all his letters by hand, seated at a walnut desk with a sloping top. His records were kept in battered tin and wooden boxes. He had no telephone, and one had to pass no barrage of secretaries to get to see him. One simply opened the door and walked in.

But it was not until years later that I knew him, or ever entered his office. While I was a schoolboy he was Mayor of Baltimore, and, for some reason that I don't know, a great hero to all boys. Perhaps it was because he was fond of attending school picnics, and always made a speech predicting that each and every boy present would end as Mayor, if not, indeed, as Governor or President. The General was a highly talented political goose-greaser of the old school. Whenever a German singing society had a picnic, which was at least twice a week in summer, he drove out to the scene in his celebrated buggy, and made a speech saying that his great-grandfather was a German, and crazy about music. If it was an Irish picnic, he addressed the multitude in a rich brogue, and said that his great-grandfather had been a Kerryman, murdered by the English.

Knapp's Institute had a picnic once a year, usually at Darley Park. The tickets, retailing at 25 cents apiece, were wholesaled to the pupils at five for a dollar. The boy who sold five to his father thus made a quarter profit. A quarter was a lot of money in those days. It would buy three enormous plates of ice-cream and a dozen rides on the flying-horses. The gaudy carousel of later days was still unknown. The flying-horses at Darley Park were six in number, all bare of paint, and they were operated by a bibulous German, laboriously turning a crank. Every half hour he would shut up shop, and go to the bar to refresh himself. There was always a bar. What innocent days, indeed! The fathers of the pupils inhabited it, buying many beers for the learned faculty of the school. At the close of the day it was not uncommon for Mr. Paul, the amiable teacher of penmanship, long division, English composition, freehand drawing, natural philosophy and part singing, to be so beery that the boys made bold to pull his coat-tails, or even to insert pepper into his snuff-box. Paul is dead and in hell these many years, but I remember him pleasantly still. He had a fine talent for drawing—in the *Gartenlaube* style of 1845[4]—and was suspected of subversive ideas. During the Knights of Labor uproar,[5] in which my father was enlisted on the side of what is now called the Interests, I remember that Mr. Paul greatly shocked me by delivering a harangue to his classroom advocating the eight-hour day. It seemed so anarchistic to me then that I was afraid to tell my father about it.

Baltimore in the eighties was very prosperous—more prosperous fundamentally, in truth, than it has ever been since. The South, having survived Reconstruction, was getting on its legs again, and sent up a great demand for goods. Having as yet developed no wholesale trade of its own, it had to come North, and Baltimore was the first big city on the way. That was the Golden Age of the local jobbing trade. It took but little capital to go into business and profits were almost certain. Until the panic of 1893 Baltimore was as busy as a bootlegger. Light street was jammed with trucks waiting to load the bay boats, and the wholesale district, once confined to the vicinity of the wharves, began to bulge northward and westward.

Good living kept pace with good *Geschäft*. Business men, I believe, worked harder than they do now, when their time is mainly taken up by golf, Rotary and sitting on committees, but they nevertheless found leisure enough to stretch their legs. There were at least a dozen celebrated restaurants in the downtown area—Mike Sheehan's, Kelley's, Ganzhorn's, Neale's, and so on. There were three or four in McClellan's alley, and others in similar backwaters. They put on royal feasts at inconceivably low prices. Most of them offered lunch at a quarter, with a nickel extra for coffee. The waiter got a nickel, and if the customer felt expansive the carver got another.

After the panic times were harder. The South, as it recovered, began to take over its own wholesaling and even its own manufacturing. A new swarm of ambitious Yankees crossed the Potomac, and soon Atlanta and Jacksonville were offering sharp competition to Baltimore. Many old firms quietly disappeared; others took in go-getters of a new school and changed their names. But a few of the oldest survived, and are, indeed, still in existence. Why doesn't some one write the history of them? The story of Samuel Kirk & Son, or Armstrong, Cator & Co., for example, would be almost the complete story of Baltimore.

SURDI AUDIUNT[6]

When I was a day scholar at F. Knapp's Institute in Baltimore, during the late eighties of the last century, a major part of the crime, melodrama and social gaiety of the place was provided by what the rest of us called the dummies. These dummies, in book English, were deaf-mutes, and they attended the school for the purpose of learning lip reading, which was taught to them, to the tune of loud roars and plenty of moral indignation, by Professor Friedrich

Knapp and his son and chancellor, Mr. Willie. The old Professor had picked up the teaching of lip reading in his native Swabia, some time before his immigration in 1848, and he had been practicing the art in Baltimore ever since, with considerable applause. At least once a year he could look for a writeup in one of the Baltimore Sunday papers, with a chalk-plate portrait of himself in all the glory of his pedagogical white tie and mutton chops and another of two prize pupils engaged in a frantic conversation suggesting the sidewalk acts of the Irish comedians of the time. And at other times Professor Knapp was visited ceremoniously by touring friends and harriers of the deaf in search of pointers, and the rest of us had a holiday while the poor dummies staged a show for them. One of these visitors in my time was the celebrated Edward Miner Gallaudet, the best friend the deaf and dumb of America ever had, and another was the even more celebrated Alexander Graham Bell,[7] whose mind, however, was already straying from dummies to the telephone business. The old Professor, who knew publicity when he saw it, received such rivals with the highest honors within the facilities of the school, beginning with a double round of Boonekamp bitters and ending with a substantial spread in the room where he kept what was then called philosophical apparatus; i.e., a static-electricity machine with a cracked glass wheel, a dozen large jars containing snakes dissolving in alcohol, a row of stuffed birds and a collection of minerals so dusty that they all seemed to be lumps of coal.

Unhappily, something usually went wrong with the performance of the dummies, and after the visiting dignitaries had departed it was common for a drumhead court-martial to follow, with a considerable fanning of pants bottoms. In theory, the Professor took both male and female pupils in his lip-reading seminary, but in my day, as it happened, there were none but males on the roll, and some of them were hearty louts who were kept in order only by a great many rough workouts. How the mystery they aspired to was taught I never found out, for the Professor and Mr. Willie carried on their arcanum in a room set apart for that exclusive purpose, and the general understanding was that their method was a valuable trade secret and that showing any curiosity about it was dangerous. Whatever the technique, it must have been exhausting to both pupil and teacher, for the dummies, when they came from a session, always looked played out and the Professor and Mr. Willie were in bad humor. With those candidates who were in the early stages of training we ordinary or dirt scholars could not communicate, for they could neither speak nor hear, but after they had been taught the elements of lip reading they were started on talking, and in a year or two the smarter ones began to jabber at a great rate, for jabbering was a novelty to them and they enjoyed it hugely. I so describe it for the reason that, at the start, it was pretty hard to fathom. One could gather that a dummy had something to say and was hellbent on saying it, but of its purport it was often possible to have more than one opinion. Both the Professor and Mr. Willie, however, could understand it even when it was still only a kind of gurgling, and high among the perennial shows of the school were the fracases between one of the professors and one of the dummies, with the former (if he were the old man) howling in German or (if he were Mr. Willie) in English and the latter sassing back in what sounded to us like Choctaw. Such uproars were almost everyday occurrences.

When a given dummy had made such progress that he could make out at least a fourth of what was said to him and had also learned to speak a little for himself, he was transferred to the main body of the school and sat through classes with the rest of us. Nine times out of ten, he was much older than his fellow-pupils, for his infirmity had naturally retarded him, and so the dummies in a given class were at least a head taller than the average pupil. Not only were they taller, they were also, in many cases, more sinful, for the lack of speech and hearing had not interfered with the development of their natural orneriness, whatever its degree. Thus it was usually a dummy who took the lead in the more contumacious and anti-social enterprises of the school, and that leadership was so well recognized that whenever there was any mass deviltry that baffled inquiry the larger and more wicked dummies were fanned first of all and with a clear conscience. More than once I have seen the corps fanned in a body, with loud revilings for their ingratitude to the Professor and Mr. Willie, to the parents who slaved away to keep them fed and in school, and to the Heavenly Father whose mercies had guided them to a scientific and effective way to cheat their affliction. The dummies, of course, could not take in these homilies, for their backs were turned, but even if they had been headed the other way they would have been very little impressed, for they were cynical fellows. The common opinion among them seemed to be that the Professor and Mr. Willie were a pair of fourflushers,[8] whose alleged teaching was what we would now call baloney. Whatever they learned, so the dummies professed to believe, was learned in spite of it, not because of it. In particular, they all complained of the Professor's marked Swabian accent, which made his remarks as hard to read by the lip, so they said, as their own first attempts at speech were hard for us to understand by the ear. They liked Mr. Willie much more than his pa, but that, I suspect, was only because he was a good deal less free with his rattan. Of the whole faculty of the school, once they entered the ordinary classes, they liked best Miss Bertha and Miss Elvina, the Professor's daughter and niece, for both confined their chastisements, which were very gentle, to girls and never touched a boy above the baby class.

The dummies all boarded at the Institute and were full of complaints about the food. One day, when my lunchbox happened to include a couple of dough-nuts, two of them told me that they had not tasted a doughnut for six months, and I handed over both. A week later they told me precisely the same thing and then again a week after that, and so on until suspicion began to dawn on my infant mind and I ate my subsequent doughnuts myself.

There were plenty of quite normal boarders in the school, but all the rows in the refectory were caused by the dummies. Once, the chief of them, a huge fel-low beginning to sprout fuzz on his cheeks, lifted a stuffed owl from the philo-sophical collection, sneaked it into the kitchen and dropped it into a caldron of vegetable soup. The inquiry that followed lasted a week, and in the course of it all the dummies were whaled daily, and along with them about forty per cent. of the non-dummy boarders. Another time a dummy sub-chief, a swarthy fellow from the West Indies, dumped half a pound of Glauber's salts into the coffee pot, with results that any druggist will be glad to tell you.

Being so much older than the rest of us, class for class, the dummies had a great influence for evil upon us and materially reduced the moral average of the whole school. At a time when the boys of my own class were at such an age that they thought of girls only as catlike creatures with pigtails to be pulled, the senior dummies viewed them with lubricious gloats and winks. It was a dummy, too, I believe, who introduced the device of filling the ink-wells in the old-fashioned school desks with powdered chalk, and another who put a handful of thumbtacks on the chair of Mr. Paul, the gloomy and inoffensive professor of drawing, elocution, calisthenics and arithmetic up to the multiplication tables. The dummies were always complaining that it was too hot or too cold in the classrooms. None of them ever had a lead pencil when he needed it or a sponge for cleaning his slate or the piece of chalk that Mr. Willie or Mr. Paul had issued to him only five minutes before. They were seldom permitted to leave the school premises; nevertheless, they often showed up in class with muddy shoes, and though the old Professor inspected the whole lot minutely every morning, they

managed somehow to get dirt behind their ears before roll call. When there
was singing they naturally made a shambles of it, for their lip reading could
not follow the Professor's violin or the reed organ of his daughter, Miss Bertha;
moreover, they could not hear their own vocalizing and thus squawked away in
an irrational and deafening manner.

Among the dummies, of course, there were various grades and degrees of
nefariousness, and some were actually more or less tame and respectable, at
least transiently. One such was a tall, cadaverous youth whose name I recall,
perhaps in error, as Smith. In 1889, having reached the age of fourteen or fifteen, he announced suddenly that he had resolved to study for the ministry.
This not only greatly impressed the rest of us but delighted the old Professor,
for it had been at least twenty years since any of his pupils, whether deaf and
dumb or normal, had shown any itch for the sacred sciences. The great majority of his boys were the sons of businessmen and their aspirations commonly
pointed toward running banks, breweries, hardware stores, bakeries, or stands
in Lexington Market. But this Smith not only declared for theology; he also
added some plausibility to his resolution by abstaining from all roughhouse,
washing carefully every morning, and giving voluble thanks to God, apparently
sincerely, for the food set before him in the refectory. The deaf and dumb, he
let it be known, needed and deserved much better spiritual servicing than they
were getting in Baltimore. All the Sunday schools provided for them were operated by ecclesiastical fossils who harangued them in the archaic sign language
and knew nothing of lip reading. And all the females who aided in this business were hyenas who also ran Bible classes for Chinese laundrymen. Smith
allowed that a really scientific church for the deaf and dumb, planned on the
most modern lines, would be a great benefaction to them and probably save
many of them from hell. He proposed to make himself the pastor of that church,
and in preparation for the office began to let the girls alone, adopted an aloof
and morose air and made very good progress in his studies, for he was a smart
fellow and had pushed so far ahead in lip reading that he could pick up ordinary
conversation at a distance of twenty feet.

This reformation pleased the old Professor so much that Smith was pro-
moted to the prime spot in our classroom, where no other dummy had sat for
years. This was not the first bench but the last, for the Professor had the idea
that idiots and anarchists had better be kept as close to the teacher as possible,
whereas the virtuous and diligent could be safely left to themselves. On a fine

spring day, near the end of the school year and with the windows up and a lazy balm in the air, Smith and I sat on the last bench together—he because of his general progress in grace and I as a reward for a composition on the Capitol at Washington, cribbed from a guidebook. The class, legally speaking, was in charge of a Mr. Fox, but he was off for the afternoon to help bury a fellow-Freemason and the old Professor was sitting as his locum tenens. I forget what subject we were struggling with, but I recall clearly that it was very dull and that the Professor, as was his wont after lunch, began to show signs of drowsiness. The boys and girls droned on, and finally he shoved his gold-framed spectacles up to his forehead, folded his fat hands across his corporation, and gave himself up to frank slumber. We knew by experience that it was now our cue to keep as silent as possible, for so long as we were silent the Professor would snore away. If, perchance, a wicked boy could not resist the temptation to pull a pigtail, the afflicted girl was social-minded enough not to yell. And if a wayward girl dropped a slate pencil down the neck of a boy, he scratched and wriggled without an outcry.

But dummies were dummies, even the reformed and admirable Smith. He heaved no blackboard rubber, he upset no inkwell, he started no volley of coughing, he blew no spitballs, but all the while his heavy share of Original Sin was laboring and fermenting in his system, and presently he began to show signs of agitation. His eyes wandered over the classroom, as if seeking whom he might devour; he writhed in his clothes and gritted his teeth; his usually gloomy and hopeless expression lighted into a sneer. Plainly enough, something was afoot, and I slid along the bench to get as far away from him as possible, for if he broke loose there would be a mass execution and all boys within his evil aura would be caned with him. Suddenly he gripped the desk in front of him, fixed his eyes on the snoring Professor, and whispered hoarsely, "I'd like to shoot the old son of a bitch!"

I say he whispered, but that is only a concession to his own notion of what he was doing. In point of fact, as I have already noted, dummies who had been taught to talk could not hear their own voices and so their dynamics were often aberrant. When their cue was to speak up in class they sometimes merely mumbled, and when they tried to whisper they often yelled. It was so in this case. Smith had sought only to relieve his feelings *sotto voce*, but what came out of his mouth was a blast like that of an auctioneer. All the girls in the class began to shriek, for "son of a bitch" was then still a wicked term in America and no female ever heard it without hysterics. The boys all fought their way to places as far away from Smith as they could get, for they rightly surmised that hell was in eruption.

It was indeed. The old Professor, roused from his dreams by that intolerable and unprecedented insult, was so thunderstruck that his face turned as white as his chalky hands. Letting his spectacles drop to his nose, he reached behind him with one arm for the battery of rattans that always stood against the wall, and then his other shot out and his forefinger beckoned. Not a word was uttered until Smith arrived at the place of execution beside the Professor's desk, and even then there was only the ominous count *"Eins! Zwei! Drei!"* At *"Eins"* Smith put up his hands like the victim of a bandit. At *"Zwei"* he dropped his arms until they stood out from his shoulders horizontally. At *"Drei"* he bent over until his fingertips touched his shoes, and simultaneously the Professor let go with the first of five mighty thwacks. Three clouts constituted the usual dose for even grave offenses, but Smith got five, and each came straight from the Professor's heart. The old boy was out of breath when the operation was over and quite forgot the usual good-measure fanning of bystanders. But there was still wind enough in him, when Smith began massaging feverishly the point of attack, for him to shout, "You can't rub it out!"

By the time Smith got back to the last bench, his lust to save the souls of other dummies had departed from him, never to return. He turned atheist on the spot, and on leaving the school got a job as second bookkeeper in the office of the Bismarck brewery. When he died, forty years later, he had, as the Baltimore *Sunpaper's* obituary reported, risen to the post of auditor and was a member of and officeholder in the Odd Fellows, Red Men, Knights of Pythias and Benevolent and Protective Order of Elks.

THE PASSING OF "THE HILL"

A Chronicle of Boyhood Days in the Perilous Wilds of the
Southwest Baltimore Steppes

It is but fifteen years since the last Comanche Indian lurked in homicidal ambush behind the hump of Stewart's Hill and a valiant band of rollicking daredevils went forth to slay him, and yet today the corner of Fulton avenue and Baltimore street is as quiet and safe and peaceful as the City Hall plaza. Where once the forefoot of the Hill stood out from the encircling cobbles like the prow of a great ship rows of staid dwellings now stretch their red and white fronts. Back along Lexington and Fayette streets there are more dwellings—red, buff and salmon pink. Behind the Greisenheim[9] there are still more, and further to the west and north there are more and more. The Calverton road is now an urban highway, and gone are the stockyards, the Ball-Grounds-Behind-the-Fence, the Canyon and—the Indians.

Once there were boys who went forth in bands to play ball behind the fence, and climb the dizzy walls of the Canyon, and prod the pigs in the stockyards and trail the murderous red men. But now, alas! the stockyards are one with Herculaneum, and the prim virtue of marble front steps and Venetian blinds hides their ancient wickedness. Gone is the Canyon's romance, with the rivulet of red blood that used to trickle down from the slaughter houses, and gone are the ball grounds and their shedding of youthful gore.

Gone, too, are the boys of those days, whose keen eyes kept watch for bandit and redskin. Most of them, it's true, are still atop the earth, but they are boys no longer. "Some have children, some have beards and some have political ambitions."

Every Baltimorean "raised" in West Baltimore has known in his time each nook and crevice of Stewarts (or is it Stuarts or Steuarts?) Hill. Beginning in a sharp bluff at Baltimore street and Fulton avenue, it became a rolling tableland half a block westward and stretched on, in undulating charm, clear to Calverton. The tin can was its adornment, with the dead cat and the melancholy half brick, and from its fertile bosom arose the assertive shoots of the nigger burr and the jimpson weed. Paths were in every direction—paths worn hard and leafless by the tramp of a youthful army corps—and here and there were mighty landmarks, each with its crown of legend and romance.

West by north of the Greisenheim, on Baltimore street, was (and is) the lime kiln. Here murderers had their resort in the old days, for what manslayer could resist the invitation of the red pits of fire? Assassinations of wealthy cattlemen, with pockets of bulging money and of blundering coppers, from Calverton were conducted each night at midnight, and the corpses of the victims, stark and bloody, were heaved into the fire and cremated with the oyster shells and the coal. On election nights there were bonfires nearby and big crowds watching them, and so it was safe to venture near. If you ventured you might see bones charring in the blaze and eyes rolling as they sizzled. Then, when you got home and were tucked into bed, you would dream of these things and awake suddenly and painfully.

During the day, of course, the lime kiln was harmless and legendless, and when the man wasn't looking it was great sport to climb its heights and make believe it was a fort. Sometimes, when the youthful flower of the aristocracy north of Baltimore street was thus embattled, the hardy young yeomanry of grim Mount Clare would come thundering down the plain. Then there would be a conflict more fierce than any Cæsar fought in Gaul, and shells would fill the air as they did at Vicksburg.

Romance teaches us that the boys in starched collars and luxuriant neckties should have overwhelmed the pikemen of the masses, but youth has its hard realities as well as age, and ordinarily the battle would be to the strongest muscles and toughest hides. Then there would be cut heads to bandage and pursuing policemen to elude, and the boss of the kiln would vow a solemn oath that the next boy who touched a single shell of its tempting store should be sent to the House of Refuge for the remainder of his natural life. But the cops were kind in those days, and, what is more to the purpose, of well nigh incredible girth, and so they did not chase their quarry far, nor did they endeavor to break records for speed.

Nevertheless, it was an exciting thing to have them bob up from the Canyon, and while the chase was on it seemed a very serious matter.

Only the smaller boys actually saw Indians on the Hill in the later days of its glory, but all boys, large and small, believed that they were there or that they had been there at some more or less recent time. In the matter of bandits there was general faith. Out on the banks of Gwynn's falls, as all knew, tramps had their camps, and along Calverton road, where the saloons elbowed the stockyards, there were hordes of red-shirted cattlemen from the land of the buffalo, who wore sombrero hats and chewed great twists of natural leaf and obviously carried arsenals beneath their coattails. It was a safe guess that some of these cattlemen were train robbers at home, and that they prowled the Hill at night and ensnared victims for the ever-busy murderers of the lime kiln.

Besides, there were beings akin to witches and Afro-American necromancers to fear. The former kidnaped boys and held them for ransom in a cave near the Edmondson avenue bridge and the latter carried them off to a retired spot in Hurley's woods and made medicine of them. All in all, there were many evil spirits on the Hill, and it had its terrors by day as well as by night.

Once the charm of the road agent's life fell with great force upon two boys of Gilmor street and they armed themselves with table knives filched from the maternal store and hid it in a cluster of tall weeds on the trail from Fulton avenue to the baseball grounds. Two scared youngsters of Hollins street fell into their clutches and surrendered without a struggle, and there, within the shadow of St. Martin's steeple and while a grunting hill-horse struggled with a Red line car not fifty yards away, a highway robbery of a most bold and desperate sort was committed.

"Throw up your hands!" commanded the first bandit, and up went four trembling hands. This seemed so tame that the second bandit's face showed the shadow of disgust, and he added: "Your money or your life!" in a tone intended to be sepulchral and impressive.

The two prisoners said that they wanted to go home, but the bandits searched them with loving thoroughness and spread upon the pathway the treasure of a dozen pockets—stray cogwheels, marbles, top cords, curious pebbles, shells, twisted nails, jackknives and stumps of slate pencils. Two grimy handkerchiefs they also found and four cents in current money. The junior bandit was for bundling up all of the swag and dashing for the Canyon and safety (for a big boy of unknown allegiance was seen upon the sky line to the northward), but the elder would not hear of it.

"To take the money," he said, meditatively, "would be stealing. We may be highwaymen, but we ain't no thieves."

And so the bandits retired with the handkerchiefs, the jackknives and the stray cogwheels, and the youngsters who had been robbed ran for home with their cash. Money was money, and they were glad to have it, but it would have pleased them vastly more had the disciples of Mr. James taken the coppers and left them the top cords and stumps of slate pencils.[10]

Calverton was a bustling town in the days of the stockyards, with saloons innumerable and a floating population of high-living, hard-drinking drovers. They would come in from no one knew where and while their porkine charges grunted in the acres of pens they would take their ease in the inns. The officious coppers would not permit small boys to loiter about these caravansaries, but there was no rule forbidding them gaze between the bars of the sties, albeit prodding the hogs or feeding them gravel, or casting nigger burrs upon them, or otherwise mauling or maltreating them was interdicted.

Down through the wilderness of pens, between moss-grown walls of stone, ran a stream that emptied a filthy burden into Gwynn's falls somewhere south of Baltimore and Potomac Railroad's bridge. Far away, in the direction of Lexington street, this noisome rivulet drained the studios of sundry German butchers, and on killing days it ran blood like the Place de la Revolution. This was before the ingenious Chicagoan devised means to market every vestige of the porker but his squeal, and hog blood, apparently, had no value.[11] So it ran down the stream, through the gorge called the Canyon and between the stone walls that traversed the pens.

A soft scent of singed hair, stale meat and neglected drainage arose from it, and an inoffensive youth from Snake Hollow way, who was credited with having once gone swimming in it, was an outcast and a pariah. Nevertheless, up in the Canyon the ruby stream had its air of romance, and it was pleasant to imagine that a gorgeous massacre was in progress a block away and that the water had been incarnadined by human gore.

The Canyon itself was not long and its walls, at a venture, were scarcely more than twenty feet at their highest point, but it made sharp jagged curves and, observing it from the level of the bloody stream at its bottom, it was a very fair imitation of the Grand Canyon of the Colorado. At its upstream end was a favorite resort for boys desiring to smoke cigarettes. Most West Baltimoreans puffed their first clouds of smoke there, and scores remember well the despairing, empty feeling that a sight of the Canyon's grim rocks inspired within them thereafter.

But that was its sinful, shameful side. As a bit of the real West, set down among the depressing cobblestones and horse cars of civilization, it had a more respectable standing. Unimaginative, indeed, was the boy who could not invest it with all the enchantments of the Bad Lands. Wasn't it a fact that the red clay of its walls hid gold and gems, and hadn't a boy from McHenry street once found a dead man on its brink at break of day? If there was any doubt remaining, one had but to observe the ruggedness of the gorge and its nearness to the lime kiln and the haunt of the midnight assassins. Once a fat copper, chasing two boys of Mount street, slipped on a banana peel and rolled down the unyielding face of its left wall. That was part of the humorous history of the Canyon. There were few legends of such levity. Most of them concerned horrible deaths and dreadful crimes. Nature planned such places for such dramas.

Civilization made its onslaught upon the Hill by a double flank movement and before the Hillmen quite realized it, the Hill was no more. First there arose blocks of brick houses at Fulton avenue, in the far southeastern corner, and then began a gradual advance of the building line along West Lexington street. Finally, news came one dreadful day that workmen were tearing down the hogpens. Some time before that the last hog had taken his departure (to depart from the earth, in turn, at the abattoir) and for a while the pens had been the resort of the bat and the owl and Calverton had fallen into decay. Now, with one fell swoop, it was to be wiped from the map forever, and so there was mourning and wailing and gnashing of teeth.

Soon after it became plain that the doom of the Hill was sealed. Trinity Lutheran Church arose upon Baltimore street and by and by a solid row of houses stretched from the car barn to Garrison lane. Then came carts and men and streets were cut through, east and west, and north and south. After that arose more rows of houses—red, yellow and pink. Cobblestones began to cover what were once trails through the wilderness, and a modern city, with its drugstore lights and lampposts and marble front steps and corner saloons—slowly and as if by magic such a little city encroached upon the Hill.

Then, one day, a boy grown long of leg fared forth to tread its well-remembered pathways once more. Alackaday, the Hill was gone!

WEST BALTIMORE

The other day, passing the corner of Baltimore and Paca streets, I was astounded to find J. J. Landragan's stationery store closed, and a realtor's card in the window. It was a shock almost equal to that of seeing workmen tearing down Winans' wall. How many years Mr. Landragan had been in business at the northeast corner of the two streets I don't know, but certainly it must have been a great many. His store was there when I was in short breeches, for I used to buy valentines of him in winter and firecrackers for the Fourth of July. He was (and is) one of these strange and fortunate men who never seem to age. His fierce, bushy mustache, true enough, picked up some gray hairs as year chased year, but otherwise it remained undaunted, and he himself seemed as active and hearty the last time I saw him as he was in 1886.

He and his store had seen some vast changes in West Baltimore. When he opened it the business district stopped at his door, and none of the warehouses which now line Paca street, and even Greene street, had been built. Diagonally opposite him, and in an ancient two-story house which still stands, was Little Joe Wiesenfeld's bicycle shop, and at the rear of it was a large yard, floored like a room. On that floor, coached by one of Little Joe's salesmen, I learned to ride a bicycle. It all seems remote and archaic today, like mastering the subtleties of mediæval equitation. But bicycling was a great and urgent matter in 1889, when the pneumatic tire came in.

At the southeast corner of Paca and Baltimore streets, for many years, was a saloon kept by a German named Ruth, the father of the eminent Babe Ruth of today.[12] The older Ruth seems to have worked at some trade or other before he embraced the immemorial art of the tavern-keeper, for his place was called the Union Bar, and was greatly frequented by the walking delegates who operated upon the rising industries of the vicinity. It had heavy competition in the saloon of another German named Ehoff, in Paca street between German and Lombard, next to Louis Coblens' romantic livery stable. Ehoff's place was patronized by the neighboring business men. Between the years 1886 and 1896 I consumed rather more than three tons of its pretzels.

Probably the oldest name upon the store signs of West Baltimore today is that of John C. Nicolai & Son, confectioners at 755 West Baltimore street. The house in which the business is still carried on was built by the original Nicolai in 1850. He had come to Baltimore from Hanover in 1834, and was one of the founders of the old Liederkrantz singing society, launched on December 30, 1836. For a number of years he operated a shoe store in Market street (now Baltimore street), near Holliday. But in 1850 he switched to the candy business and moved to Baltimore street near Fremont, and there his heirs and assigns have continued ever since. They have what is probably one of the oldest retail stores in all Baltimore.

Compared to such patriarchs as the Nicolais, even such ancients of West Baltimore as L. A. Speishouse, who has been selling lime, sand and brick at 1621 Frederick Avenue since just after the Civil War, seem relative newcomers. Mr. Speishouse's chief trade, when I was a boy, was in hay and feed, and I remember buying many a bag of oats from him. But there are no more stables in West Baltimore, and so he has devoted himself, in late years, to building materials. He is a builder himself and has put up hundreds of garages. I assume that he must be considerably beyond 35, but there are few signs of it in his face and frame. Like Mr. Landragan, he looks precisely the same to me today as he looked in 1886.

Most of his contemporaries of half a century ago are long gone and forgotten. Who remembers Thiernau's grocery-store, at Baltimore and Gilmor streets? Or Knoop's, on the corner opposite? Or the Dankmeyer confectionery? Or the Vienna bakery that used to be in Baltimore street near Stricker? Dr. Pue's drugstore next door is still there, but it has long borne another name. The Days are gone, and the Rolosons, and the Bitzes, and the Cooks, and the Knitzes (though they survive in the wholesale sugar business), and the Kunkels. Newton's stationery-store remains at Baltimore and Calhoun streets, but what has become of Henry Bingle, the tobacconist, and Carruthers, the plumber, and the old German—I forgot his name—who made harness and kept canary birds?

West Baltimore, in the 80's, was much further from downtown than it is today. Its main means of communication with the rest of the city was the old Red Line of horse-cars, which staggered out Baltimore street as far as Calverton road. For the long hill rising from Stricker street there were hill-horses, and the heroic boys rode them hitched on while the cars were in motion. It seemed a magnificent feat to the other boys of the neighborhood, and no doubt it was, for the horse-cars were probably more formidable than they look in retrospect. Once one of them, in Lombard street, killed three policemen. I forget the details, but I remember the blood on the cobblestones, and the crowds gaping at it.

That was the era of cobblestones, and in West Baltimore they sprouted luxuriant crops of grass and weeds. The more fastidious housekeepers, after seeing that their sidewalks were swept and their white marble steps scrubbed, sent their slaves and progeny into the streets to do battle with these weeds. The weapon most commonly employed against them was a decayed kitchen knife. Aspiring to merit, I volunteered for service with such a knife one day in 1888 or thereabout, but lasted only until I had half severed my thumb. Today such a war wound would cause an uproar, and the family doctor would come galloping with a squirt-gun full of tetanus vaccine. But in those days hemorrhages were stopped with cobwebs from the cellar or stable.

The heaviest crops of cobblestone grass—it often proceeded to the estate and dignity of hay—were in such quiet streets as Fayette, west of Gilmor. I have caught grasshoppers in that sedate thoroughfare, and even toads. Once my pony broke out of his stable and set out to lead his own life. Aided by a free corps of colored boys armed with clubs, I traced him to Mount street, above Lexington. There he was quietly grazing in the middle of what is now a main-traveled motor highway. I rode him home bareback, with the colored boys leaping and yelling behind. He protested bitterly all the way. He needed grass, and knew it.

The noblest shop in West Baltimore, in the days before the Y.M.C.A. ruined me, was kept by Old Man Kunkel in Baltimore street, near Calhoun. His specialty was grab-bags. One paid a cent and reached into a huge basket filled with small paper bags. Every bag, at worst, contained a large knob of tough taffy; at best it might contain half a dozen caramels or a top, or even a ring set with a piece of red glass. Old Man Kunkel prospered in this traffic, with its overtones of gambling, and died rich—that is, as wealth was reckoned in those far-off days. As a side-line he did a thriving business in paper kites, also at a cent apiece.

It was unusual then for the young of *Homo baltimoriensis* to employ any medium of exchange save copper. It was not until the hoky-poky wagons appeared on the streets that nickels were in common use. Across the street from every schoolhouse there was a shop that did nine-tenths of its business in pennies. A slate pencil was a cent, and so was a pickle, and so was an all-day sucker, and so was a stick of horehound candy. I suppose that $20 would have bought the entire stock of such a shop, and yet, the shopkeepers—mainly widows—appeared to dodge the sheriff. But that was before paying assessments and tax "reduction."

Maybe they still exist, doing business in silver instead of in copper. If so, their proprietors have probably changed, and more than once. For shopkeepers, as a class, do not seem to last. The names on the signs are constantly changing. Now and then one encounters an old one—but the next day, perhaps, it is gone. The name of Schaub was on a shoe store in West Baltimore street for years; lately it suddenly vanished. Who, in all that region, remembers Fuller Waters? Or Lemkuhl the jeweler? Or Loechel the shoemaker? Or Nordlinger the notions man? Or Baer? Albert Smith died a year or so ago, and that was the end of Asa Smith & Son, paperhangers since the Civil War. The Nicolai sign begins to take on the dignity of a public monument. It becomes almost fabulous.

MR. KIPLING

A Belated Memorial to an Obscure But Honest Man

What his actual name was I don't recall, and probably, indeed, never knew. It was the custom in our house to identify neighborhood worthies by clapping nicknames upon them, and very often these nicknames were suggested by their chance resemblance (sometimes very remote) to eminent men of the time. Thus there was an old fellow down the street, bushy with whiskers, who passed among us as Mr. Darwin, and another, with an elegant goatee, who was always Admiral Schley.[13]

Mr. Kipling got his name because of his short, stocky figure, his disorderly mustache and his large, glittering spectacles. He followed the trade of an expressman, and had a wagon that was not only patched but actually bandaged, and a horse that must have been foaled soon after the Civil War. At first glance there was something vaguely bellicose about him, but on acquaintance he turned out to be a very mild and even violet-like man. In all those years he was never seen to touch his horse with a whip, or heard to use a swear-word upon a boy who "hooked on behind"; and never, to my knowledge, did he charge more than thirty-five cents for hauling any package, however heavy.

His chief quality, if so colorless a person may be said to have qualities, was his unearthly imperturbability. Nothing ever upset him or hurried him. One morning, coming through our back-gate with a trunk on his back, he was attacked with a horrible roar by a new and saucy family dog. But he kept on up to the house without so much as a glance at the animal. Arrived at the kitchen door, he eased down his burden, took off his spectacles, mopped his face quietly, and contemplated the dog for the first time. "When I come in," he said calmly, "it didn't hardly seem like he knowed me." He mopped some more, and then added the serene corollary: "But he won't not know me no more." That was all. The dog, baffled and out of breath, retired idiotically to the side-yard.

The only time I ever saw Mr. Kipling even mildly disturbed was on a day when his Paleozoic horse made incredible history by balking—or maybe it was only by falling asleep. It was in the alley behind our house, and Mr. Kipling had just loaded the trousseau and house furnishings of a maid leaving to be married. Mounting his creaky seat, he took up the reins and made the clucking sound that was his "Giddap." The horse didn't budge. Mr. Kipling then clucked again, and shook the reins, but still the horse was immovable. Three times more he did it, and then he climbed down, went ahead, grabbed the two sides of the bridle and gazed earnestly into the animal's eyes. "Say there," he said very politely, "what's eatin' you?" I heard no reply from the horse, but apparently it said something, for Mr. Kipling gave it a pat, climbed back to his seat and clucked again—and at once the prehistoric contraption rumbled off over the cobblestones. His only comment was flung over his shoulder: "God knows *what* it was!"

Mr. Kipling seldom showed any interest in the visible universe. He slept all through the first night of the great Baltimore fire of 1904—and thereby missed, I suppose, some first-rate hauling jobs. When, in the course of his jolting journeys he encountered any impediment, he simply drove around it. When spoken to he answered, but he seldom addressed a word to anyone. If he had any politics no one ever discovered what they were. If he practiced any religious rite it must have been in the strictest confidence. He had a family, but its measles and skinned shins, if it had any, never interfered with his professional preoccupations.

Only once did I ever hear him ask a question. That was on a morning when he noticed for the first time, though he had passed and repassed it for years, a sun-dial in our backyard. He stopped, stared at it for a moment as if expecting it to move, and then said: "What's that?" The nature and uses of the instrument were explained to him briefly, and he apparently understood. But his only comment was: "Good God! What won't they be gittin' up next!"

MAN OF MEANS

An Obscure Chapter in the History of Capitalism

As I grew into an awareness of the visible world, back there in the middle 80's of the last century, old Jim the carriage-washer was one of the first creatures to emerge from the void. He was a gigantic black man, and he pursued his art and mystery in the spooky depths of Gorton's livery stable in Baltimore, under a skylight so caked with dirt that it was impervious to anything short of lightning. A couple of fan-shaped gas lights gave him such meager illumination as he had, and a frayed hose, full of crude patches, supplied him with water.

I remember him always in rubber boots and a heavy rubber apron, coal-black from head to foot. The badge of his office, a mangy sponge, he carried with him all the time, even when he rushed out of the stable to see the fire-engines go by, or the cops fighting a drunk.

To my brother and me, in those remote days, Gorton's stable was the very heart, gizzard and umbilicus of Christendom. Where else could one see a mule having its tooth pulled, or four prancing horses being harnessed to a red trap, or a buggy-whip set with what were said to be diamonds!

We had a legal excuse for hanging about, for our father kept a horse there, and later on we had a pony to join it. But all the other boys of the neighborhood hung about too, and all of them knew and admired Jim. It was said that he could wash a Dayton-wagon[14] in three minutes flat—in fact, the druggist at the corner said that he could do it in two.

Especially, we were all struck by the way he drank from the end of his hose—in one great gulp, and without spilling a drop. We all tried it and all of us choked.

Jim's great time came when his son, a youth of fifteen or so, was blown to smithereens in the explosion of a one-horse soda-water plant in a nearby alley. The cops came to tell him on a Saturday morning, the busiest time of his week, but he applied instantly for half a day off, and went clomping down the street after them without taking off his apron and boots.

That afternoon a locum tenens went to work in his place—a short, spotty, brown fellow from the rear reaches of the stable. Inasmuch as the explosion had been so complete that there was no *corpus delicti*, my brother and I assumed that Jim would be back at work on Monday, so we dropped in after school to offer our condolences. But he was not present and the spotty fellow could give us no news of him.

Toward the end of the week it began to filter in. Jim, it appeared, had been visited by a lawyer and the lawyer had urged him to sign a paper. Jim refused flatly. The only papers he knew anything about were warrants and they boded no good to the darker races.

The lawyer, mistaking this uneasiness for avarice, began to talk money, and, as Jim still hung back, gradually raised the ante. The result was that Jim presently found himself seized and possessed of the enormous sum of $300 in cash.

No such amount had ever been in black hands in West Baltimore before. It made history—and it came near killing Jim. The cops took charge of him on Friday, and used up a quart of ammonia trying to revive him. When he got to his legs at last he found that $250 of his money was gone. In place of it he had burial-society policies for $3,000, a new morganatic wife with a gold tooth, a plug hat, a guitar and three suits of clothes, all too small.

He was sick a week, and in hiding. Emerging, he took a dram to steady his nerves—and awoke three days later to find his wife fled, his burial policies lost, his plug hat smashed, his guitar stolen and his wardrobe reduced to a pair of overalls. In cash money he had ten cents.

He was back at his post the next day and thereafter he washed carriages faithfully for twenty-seven years, and then quietly departed this life. He became, in his later days, a metaphysician and, like Socrates, specialized in the evils of wealth. "Ef I hadda stayed rich," he used to stay, "I'd wouldn't a-been worth hell-room. Money ain't no good when you has it. Et's only good when you ain't got none. Listen to me tell you! No darkie evah heerd of was es rich es ah was, an' no darkie since them old Bible days evah had so much troubles."

TALE OF A TRAVELLER

In the West Baltimore of my youth, now buried beneath the dust and lava of the years, there was a street cleaner named Jock who astonished everyone by saving enough out of his wages of two dollars a day to take a trip abroad every summer. This singular achievement was not only astonishing to the burghers but downright incredible, yet the briefest resort to statistical analysis would have shown them that there was really nothing incredible about it. In the first place, Jock was the meanest man in the whole Sanitary Corps of the city, and never blew in more than ten cents at a time on anything save travel and victuals. And in the second place, he always went steerage, which was almost the same, in those days of ocean rate wars, as going deadhead. I doubt, indeed, whether one of his eastward voyages ever cost him more than twenty-two dollars or any westward voyage more than twenty-seven fifty, and there was a memorable summer when the North German Lloyd, then at gory grips with the English lines, seems to have hauled him eleven days to Bremen and twelve back to Locust Point, Baltimore, at the record-breaking return rate of $33.33 1/3, or say, in round figures, $33.34.

Thus I must deflate him as a prodigy almost at the moment of introducing him, which is after all no great loss, for he was much more interesting for his day-in-and-day-out way of life than for his annual indulgence of his wanderlust. His age in those days ·I do not know, since all laboring men look ancient to boys, but I suppose he must have been in his later middle years, for the oldest indigenes of West Baltimore said that he had been pushing a city broom as long as they could remember. He was tall and skinny and showed the occupational stoop of his craft, and he had lost every other tooth in the upper register. This gave him a look of quiet ferocity when he smiled, which was very seldom. In repose, his face indicated imbecility rather than bellicosity, but his extremely thrifty shaving habits sometimes caused babies to squall at the sight of him. When he reported for work on Monday morning, his beard already suggested the stubble of a hayfield, and by Saturday night it was long overripe for the harvest. He then dropped into Charlie Weisman's five-cent barbershop on Gilmor Street, waited in silent patience his turn at the *Police Gazette* and after that at the chair of Julius, the apprentice boy, and presently emerged with his hollow cheeks showing the clammy pallor of a dead man. This pallor was sicklied o'er with shadows by Sunday noon, and by Monday morning, as I have noted, it was wholly overcast.

His professional costume was that of any other contemporary poor man doing dirty work, for he lived and had his being before the *dies infaustus* when some poet thought of putting street cleaners into duck uniforms and calling them white wings. He wore brogans with such thick soles that as he hoofed over the Baltimore cobblestones in his gloomy pursuit of cigar stumps and horse apples, they made a noise like banging shutters. Above them arose the two barrels of a pair of pants that must have been of corduroy and of a greenish-yellow color in their infancy but were now worn to mangy patches, predominantly black. Above the pants, which were held up by a leather rigging then called policemen's suspenders, appeared an undershirt of red flannel, which, despite an occasional soak in caustics, maintained something of its color for months and even years. Such florid undershirts, in those days, were believed to be sanitary, and Jock subscribed to the theory. When he condescended to speak, which was only when he was somewhat in his cups, he pointed out that wearing them had enabled him to escape, through hard years of mulelike labor, the rheumatism that was the curse of outdoor work, and also countless waves of smallpox, typhoid fever, malaria and cholera morbus, all of them then endemic in Baltimore. It was his boast that he was even immune to catarrh, dyspepsia, kidney weakness, liver complaint and that tired feeling, the principal themes of the patent-medicine advertising of the era. The only medicament he ever resorted to, save his sanitary undershirt, was sulphur and molasses, which he took in the spring to thinnen his blood, and a mush made with buttermilk, which he took in the fall to restore its viscosity.

Jock was either a bachelor or a widower; no one knew which. Whatever his legal status, he was plainly without a wife, so he had to do his own housework, including cooking, washing, and ironing. The last, on the rare occasions when he tackled it at all, occupied him no more than an hour or two a year, and the first two he reduced to such simplicity that an hour a week sufficed for them. After his weekly shave on Saturday night, he would proceed to Hollins Market, stand around dumbly until the stalls were about to close, and then, as all prices went tumbling, do his marketing for the ensuing seven days. His diet was healthfully varied, but only from week to week, not from day to day. On a given Saturday, he would buy, say, a smoked shoulder of pork and a cabbage or two, along with a peck of potatoes, a quart of apple butter, and a long loaf of dense, durable rye bread of the sort known as a sour John. Returning to his room, he would boil the shoulder, the potatoes, and the cabbage in the pot that began and ended his kitchen gear, and proceed to wolf a hearty meal. This repast, however hearty, made only a small dent in the shoulder, and no greater one in the cabbage and potatoes. The rest he would store in a cupboard equipped with a lock large enough for a pawnshop or a poorbox, and out of it would come his evening meals for the rest of the week. His midday eating he got free with the stupendous beers which then sold at five cents in all the fifty thousand saloons, more or less, of West Baltimore. There was a saloon at every corner of every alley, and there was an alley between every pair of streets. Jock knew them all, and had friendly words for the cuisines of all, though he freely admitted that some were better than others.

He told everyone who got his rare confidences that it was madness to switch victuals every day, and not only madness but also ruin. If shoulder and cabbage were good on Saturday then why should they not be equally good on Sunday, Monday, Tuesday, Wednesday, Thursday and Friday? Beyond that, however, he did not go; instead, he laid in something new every Saturday—one week, a large slab of soup meat, with enough vegetables to compose a seven-day *pot-au-feu;* the next week, a small keg of herring, with potatoes to be boiled in their jackets; the third, a length of veal neck, with the appropriate greens; the fourth, a double stand of pigs' feet, with a bucket of sauerkraut; and so on. He drank neither coffee nor tea, and regarded sweets as poisonous. Such auxiliary carbohydrates as his system craved he derived from the malt liquor of the time, which he got by day as aforesaid and of an evening by rushing the can to Otto Frackmeyer's saloon, across the street from his residence. His can was a very roomy one, and he enlarged its tonnage by greasing it inside every time he set out. This device, according to all the recognized physicists of West Baltimore, whether white or black, kept down the foam and so raised the net content of beer.

Jock had an upstairs back room in the house of a colleague, Willie by name, on St. Christopher Street, which was a small and mean thoroughfare. Willie had a wife and seven children and was a man of cruel and incessant misfortunes. There was never a time when one or another of his children was not down with measles, chicken pox or whooping cough, and there was seldom a time when all of them were present and voting. Usually, at least one was missing, with Mrs. Willie yowling that child stealers had made off with it, and Willie rushing to the watchhouse on Calhoun Street, demanding that the cops recover it, dead or alive. The cops, taught by long experience, had come to regard such demands lightly. Instead of bestirring their lazy bones, they would suggest oafishly that the missing brat had run away with Buffalo Bill's Wild West or shipped on a Chesapeake Bay oyster boat or gone on a drunk. When Willie returned home, he would usually find his darling restored by neighbors and Mrs. Willie in process of whaling it with a lath.

But such troubles, of course, were only the normal afflictions of a man of family, and nearly all the other fathers of St. Christopher Street shared them.

If his wife had only pulled her weight in the domestic boat, Willie might have borne them with resignation and even with a certain quiet pride, for he often remarked that a man who had sired seven head of potential (and even probable) candidates for the gallows had done a hell of a lot for his country and deserved a better city job than that of street cleaner. But Mrs. Willie, unhappily, was a despairist, and, like most despairists, a shirker. When things got a bit too thick for her in the house, she would rush across the street to Otto's, get half a pint of gin on credit, gulp it down on her brief way home, heave the empty bottle through a neighbor's window, and then develop all the antisocial symptoms of a crying jag.

Her malfeasances not only greatly irked Willie; they also forced him to take on a lot of drudgery that was properly wifely and to neglect his own work, to the damage of his pay envelope. This was long before the emancipated proletarians of America were running up installment bills of billions of dollars, but he nevertheless got into the red, and it was gossip on St. Christopher Street that his debts, if amalgamated, would amount to more than fifty dollars. The grocer at the corner was pressing him, Otto Frackmeyer was pressing him, and he was nearly two years behind with his dues to the Improved Order of Red Men.

Jock viewed all these miseries of his colleague sardonically and even with a certain satisfaction. He had said goodbye to women and all their hellish works many years before, and had no truck with them now. Many a time, so the tale ran, some predatory widow woman or some maiden in trouble had fixed her basiliscine eye on him and undertaken to drag him to the altar of God, but he had always brushed her off. Mrs. Willie he regarded as no better and no worse than the rest of her sex. If she was more fecund than most and more devoted to the jug, she had at least managed to keep her weight within human limits and was thus not unsightly at a distance, though far from appetizing at point-blank range. When she cut loose below stairs and Willie began trying to jaw her down, Jock would see to the lock on his door, stretch himself out voluptuously and give himself over to his one vice, which was reading. His profession made him free of the West Baltimore trash, and in it he found plenty of literature. Now and then he came home with a dog-eared copy of a book, but more often his trove ran to periodicals. He could read anything and had few if any preferences. Thus he took the *Atlantic Monthly* and *Puck,* the *Century* and Bonner's *Ledger* in his stride, and when back numbers of *Godey's Lady's Book* and *Bow Bells*[15] began to disappear from the trash cans, he turned with complacency to the rising star of the *Ladies' Home Journal.*

Jock was not surprised when news filtered to his ivory tower that Mrs. Willie, following the classical female road to ruin, was proceeding from booze and slatternliness to monkeying with her marriage vows. I say the news filtered to him, but in reality it came in blasts, for Willie roared the accusation in a voice of brass. Jock chuckled when he first heard it, but not for long. A few days later there were horrible screams and calls for help from below, and when he rushed downstairs to find out what was up, he found Willie hanging by the neck from a door lintel and Mrs. Willie frantically dancing about him. It took only a moment to cut Willie down, and a minute more to unharness and revive him, and he was presently lying out on two chairs, rubbing his neck and saying his say. Life with a loose woman, he said, had become intolerable to a man of honor, and he preferred his chances in hell. He would consent to live only on condition that Mrs. Willie take oath on the Sacred Scriptures that she would never again give him cause for complaint, or even for suspicion. She agreed, in tears, but a search failed to discover a Bible in the house, so Jock, resorting to his shelf of salvaged books, swore her on a foxed and ragged copy of "Ben Hur."[16]

In those days, unhappily, it was extremely difficult for a reformed and repentant wife to keep to the narrow path, for accessible females were by no means as numerous as they have become since January 16, 1920, and when news got about that a new one had appeared in society, all the roués for miles round began trailing her. The second time Mrs. Willie was caught *in flagrante,* Willie threw a chair at her and then swallowed a horse doctor's dose of roach, ant and termite powder. It warmed him painfully and he bellowed all the way to the University of Maryland Hospital, whence he was conveyed in a passing delivery wagon, but the young doctors there detoxified him with such dispatch that in a couple of days he was back behind his broom. The third time he tried the rope again, but was again cut down by Jock. The fourth time he leaped out of a second-story window of his house, but landed on a basket of wash and suffered no injury save a barking of the shins. The fifth time he tried to cut his throat with a table knife, but it was too dull to achieve even a scratch. The sixth time he took aim at his right temple with a .22-caliber revolver found in an ash barrel, but the revolver refused to go off. The seventh time he returned to the rope, and was once more cut down by Jock.

And so it went, from early Spring to Michaelmas, with hanging gradually prevailing as what the surgeons call the operation of choice. Poor Willie used up, first and last, almost the whole of his wife's clothesline, even though the same length was often employed more than once. Jock, whose cynicism extended to husbands as well as to wives, presently discerned a certain circumspection, not to say a kind of craft, in these shenanigans. He noted that Willie, before taking one of his headers into eternity, made sure that Mrs. Willie was within hearing and Jock himself in the house. As the months passed, Jock got more and more tired of his rôle of heroic rescuer, especially after Mrs. Willie took to hugging and kissing him in her deliriums of gratitude. He began to suspect that this gratitude of hers was largely bogus, and he found himself wondering, ever and anon, whether it would not be a sound idea to let Willie go the whole route. One evening, when the usual yells reached him, he pretended at first that he did not hear them, and then came downstairs very deliberately. When he had performed his now boresome office with his jackknife, he found that Willie was limp and indeed unconscious. There were no ambulances in Baltimore in those mediæval days, and the unconscious patient was hauled to the hospital in a fish wagon. The young doctors there, glad to see an old customer presenting a harder problem than usual, fell upon him in a body, and after they had pumped his arms, jabbed pins into him and filled him with all the latest drugs of the time, he revived and was put to bed.

It was four or five weeks before Willie tried to bump himself off again, and Jock had begun to hope that he had given up the practice. Husband and wife quarrelled regularly and the seven children kept going through their usual routine of catastrophe and alarm, but the ominous scream for help was not heard. And then, on an otherwise quiet evening, it suddenly sounded again, and with a piercing shrillness that brought Jock up with a start. He had taken off his pants and got into bed, and was just preparing to relax and go to sleep. Leaping up, he reached for a match, but could not find one, and then began groping for his pants. A really humane man, I suppose, would have rushed downstairs without them, but Jock's humanity by this time had been definitely staled by custom. He made up his mind to find the pants though the heavens fell, and find them he did, eventually, but when he had got them on and lumbered down to the first floor, Mrs. Willie herself had cut Willie down and was dousing him with cold water as he lay on the floor. Alas, it was too late. The pitcher had gone to the well once too often. By the time Jock, still without shoes, had rushed out for help and returned with a doctor from the neighborhood, Mrs. Willie was a widow. So informed, she staged a faint, and then set up a caterwauling that brought all St. Christopher Street to the door. When the cops arrived, they insisted on hauling Willie to hospital in their hurry wagon, but the doctors there could only confirm the verdict of the local practitioner. Willie was really dead at last, and three days later the Red Men gave him a funeral fit for a great incohonee.[17]

The rest of the story oozed out only slowly, and perhaps it was somewhat embellished in transmission, but the substance of it was unanimously believed in West Baltimore. Mrs. Willie, it appeared, had had her eye upon Jock all the while, and once she was in her weeds, with seven children to care for, she proposed, without any maidenly fumbling, that he lead her to a pastor and swear himself into Willie's place. The idea was so shocking to him that he fled to his room and locked himself in. But the widow women of those days were not to be stayed by bolts and bars, and Mrs. Willie followed him to the door and had at him with an argument so powerful as to be downright appalling. If he continued to spurn her, she said, she would go to the cops and tell them that he had deliberately let Willie hang; more, that he had revealed his diabolic intent to her in advance and carried it out despite her prayerful protest. Jock was so staggered by this threat that he trembled like a man with ague, and to get rid of her promised to meet her at the parsonage of the nearest Presbyterian church at eight-thirty the next morning. Then, stealthily and silently, he packed his lean wardrobe. By dawn he was in hiding in the railroad yards at Locust Point, and by noon he was bound down the Patapsco on the first leg of his last ocean voyage from Baltimore. He was never seen in the town again.

AN EVENING ON THE HOUSE

In the days of trolley parks, now gone forever, there was almost as much spread between park and park, culturally speaking, as you will now find between night clubs. Some, catering to what was then called the Moral Element, showed all the hallmarks of Chautauqua, Asbury Park and Lake Mohonk, with nothing stronger on tap than ginger ale, soda pop and sarsaparilla, and no divertisement more provocative to the hormones than quoit-pitching and the flying horses. But in others there was a frank appeal to the baser nature of mankind, and at the bottom of the scale were some that, by the somewhat prissy standards of those days, were veritable sewers of wickedness. One of the latter sort was operated, in the Baltimore I adorned as a young newspaper reporter, by a cashiered police sergeant named Julius Olsen—a man who believed, as he would often say, in living and letting live. His place lay at the terminus of a Class D trolley line that meandered down the harbor side to the shore of one of the affluents of the Patapsco River. Most of his customers, however, did not patronize this trolley line, which was outfitted with senile cars that often jumped the track, and shook the bones out of their passengers when they didn't. Indeed, it was rare to encounter an actual Baltimorean in the place, which had the name of Sunset Park. Nearly all the males who frequented it were sailors from ships berthed along or anchored in the river, and nine-tenths of the females were adventuresses from either the Norfolk, Virginia, region, then famous throughout the Eastern seaboard for its levantine barbarities, or the lower tier of Pennsylvania counties, where the Vice Trust, backed by Wall Street, maintained agents in every hamlet.

If there was any among the lady visitors to Sunset who had not lost her honest name long before she ever saw it, the fault was not Julius Olsen's, for he had a ground rule rigidly excluding all others. Every evening at eight o'clock he would take his place at the garish entrance to his pleasure ground, and give his eye to each female who presented herself, whether alone or with an escort. If there was anything in her aspect that raised a suspicion of chastity he would challenge her at once, and hold her up at the gate until she convinced him that her looks were false to her inner nature. Once, as I stood there with him—for I greatly admired his insight into such things and was eager to learn its secrets—a young couple got off the trolley car and made as if to enter. To my unpracticed eye they looked to be the run-of-the-mine yahoos and nothing more: I could detect no stigmata of chemical purity in the lady. But Julius saw deeper than I did, and as the couple came abreast of his sentry post his heavy paw fell upon the shoulder of the young man, and his eyebrows drew together in a fearful frown. "What in hell do you mean," he roared, "to bring a nice young girl to such a goddam dump as this? Ain't you got no goddam sense at *all?*" The young fellow, amazed and abashed, stood speechless, and Julius bellowed on. "Don't you know," he demanded, "where you are at? Ain't you ever heerd tell of Sunset Park? Goddam if I ever seen the like of it in all my born days! Do you want a gang of sailors to bash in your head and make off with your girl? What would you have to say to her mama if that happened? How would you square yourself with her pa? Goddam if I ain't got a mind to bust you one myself. Now you take her home and don't let me see you around here no more. As for *you*"—turning to the silent and trembling girl—"all I got to say is you better get yourself a better beau. Such damn fools as this one is poison to a religious young lady, and don't you go telling me that ain't what you are. *I know, I do.* Now, scat, the goddam bothen of you!"

Whereupon he half bowed and half heaved them onto the waiting trolley car, and stood by muttering until it started back to the city.

From all this the maker of snap judgments may conclude that Julius was a Puritan at heart—perhaps even that there was a Y.M.C.A. secretary hidden in him. Nothing could be more untrue. He simply did not want to clutter up his conscience, such as it was, with gratuitous and unnecessary burdens. Otherwise he was the complete antinomian, and of all the tough and abandoned trolley parks around the periphery of Baltimore, his Sunset was undoubtedly the worst. Every sort of infamy that the vice-crusaders of the time denounced, from crap shooting to hoochie-koochie dancing, and from the smoking of cigarettes by females—then still *contra bonos mores*—to riotous boozing by both sexes, went on within its gates, and there was no dilution of these carnalities by anything of an even remotely respectable nature. If a customer had called for a lemonade the waiters would have fanned him with the billies they carried up their sleeves, and if either of the two comedians in the so-called burlesque show that went on in a big shed had ventured upon a really clean joke, Julius himself would have given him the bum's rush. The striptease had not been invented in that remote era, but everything that the fancy of ribald men had yet concocted was offered. The stock company, like most other such organizations, played a loutish version of *Krausmeyer's Alley* [18] every night, but it was given with variations suggested by the conceits of whiskey drummers and medical students. The taste of the time being for large and billowy women, there was no girl in the chorus who weighed less than 170 pounds, and the rear elevation of each and every one of them was covered with bruises from head to foot, all made by the slapsticks of the comedians. In the intervals of the performance on the stage, these ladies were expected to fraternize with the customers. This fraternizing consisted mainly in getting them as drunk as possible, and then turning them over to scamps who dragged them out to a dark spot behind the shed and there went through their pockets. When a customer resisted—which happened sometimes in the case of sailors—the scamps gave him a drubbing, and it was not at all unheard of for the harbor cops to find the clay of a jolly jack tar in the adjacent river, especially of a Sunday morning, for Saturday night was the big night at Sunset Park, as it was at all such places.

The land cops, who knew Julius when he was a poor flatfoot like themselves and now took a certain amount of fraternal pride in his success in life, made occasional raids upon him, but only under pressure from reformers, and never with any hope or intent of bringing him to heel. Once I was present when a party of reformers undertook a raid in person, with a squad of cops trailing along, theoretically to protect them. Julius, who was on watch as usual at his front gate, let them enter unmolested, but they had hardly snooped their first snoop before his whole company of goons, male and female, fell upon them, and in two minutes they were in full retreat, with the cops following after to clout them as they ran. The next day he swore out a warrant for their leader, charging him with lifting a diamond sunburst worth 18,000 dollars from one of the chorus girls, and under cover of the ensuing uproar their counter-charges were forgotten. Julius had a dozen witnesses willing to swear that they had seen the reformer throttle the girl with one hand and grab the sunburst with the other, and another dozen schooled to testify that they had recovered it only by *force majeure* and in the face of wild slashings with a razor by the accused. The sunburst itself was brought into court, along with five cut-rate jewelers hired to certify to its value, and for a while things looked dark for the poor reformer, for he was a Sunday-school superintendent, and Maryland juries, in those days, always said "Guilty" to Sunday-school superintendents; but his lawyer filed a demurrer on some obscure ground or other.

Rather curiously, there was seldom any serious disorder at Sunset Park—that is, within Julius's definition of the term. Now and then, to be sure, a sailor ran amuck and attempted to stage an imitation of some massacre he had seen in Shanghai or Port Said, but he seldom got beyond teeing off, for all of Julius's waiters, as I have said, were armed with billies, and his head bartender, Jack Jamieson, was a retired heavyweight, and worth a thousand men. Even the comedians in his show lent a hand when necessary, and so did the four musicians who constituted the orchestra—the leader, Professor Kleinschmidt, who doubled in piano and violin and fed the comedians; the cornet player, George Mullally; the trombonist, Billy Wilson; and the drummer, Bing-Bing Thompson, himself a reformed sailor. Julius himself never entered these hurly-burlies, but stood on the sidelines to boss his lieges. Even when a customer insulted one of the lady help, say by pasting her in the nose or biting off an ear, the head of the establishment restrained his natural indignation, and let the *lex situs* prevailing at Sunset Park take its course. Only once, indeed, did I ever hear of him forgetting himself, and on that occasion I happened to be present as his guest, for he was always very polite to newspaper reporters, as he was to detectives, precinct leaders, coroners and other such civic functionaries.

It was the opening night of his 1901 season, and I made the uncomfortable trolley trip to the park in the company of Leopold Bortsch, *Totsäufer* of the Scharnhorst Brewery, who had to attend *ex officio,* for Julius had Scharnhorst beer on tap. Unfortunately, there had been complaints about it of late, as there had been in Baltimore proper, for it was then, and had been for years, the worst malt liquor ever seen in the town. Leopold himself, who had to drink it day in and day out on his tours of customers' saloons, and at the innumerable funerals, weddings, wedding anniversaries, christenings and confirmations that went on in their families, was constrained to admit, in candid moments, that it was certainly doing his kidneys no good. But when a Class A customer had an opening, he had to get it down willy-nilly, and at the same time he had to foment its consumption by all the assembled bibuli. For the first night of Sunset Park, which in a normal week consumed two hundred half barrels, he was expected to stage a really royal show, and to that end the brewery allowed him 100 dollars to spend over the bar. He did not know, as he marched up radiating his best promotional manner, that there was trouble ahead. Specifically, he did not know that Julius, succumbing at last to the endless complaints about Scharnhorst beer (which had by now become so bad that even the Scotch engineers from British ships sometimes gagged at it), had resolved to give a look-in to seven other Baltimore breweries. Nor did he know that all of their seven brews were already on tap at the bar, and that he would find the *Totsäufer* of each and every one lined up before it, to fight him to the death.

It was a shock, indeed, but Leopold was not one to be easily flabbergasted, and his reply was characteristically prompt and bold. The immemorial custom was for a *Totsäufer* to begin proceedings, on such an occasion, by slapping down a five-dollar bill and inviting all comers to have a beer. Leopold slapped down a *ten*-spot. The seven other *Totsäufer,* thus challenged, had to respond in kind, and they did so with panicky dispatch, each, of course, calling for his own beer. Jack Jamieson, for the opening night, had put in two extra bartenders, which, with his regular aides and himself, made five in all, but how could five men, within the space of five minutes, draw 1,600 five-cent glasses of beer? It seemed beyond human power, but I saw them do it, and while they were still shoving over the last couple of hundred—by now at least 80 per cent. foam—Leopold threw down *two* ten-spots, and commanded a double ration of Scharnhorst for all hands. What would the other *Totsäufer* do now? What they would do was instantly apparent. Six of the seven saw him with crisp *twenties,* and simultaneously bellowed orders for wholesale rounds of their own beers. The seventh, Hugo Blauvogel of the Peerless Brewery, raised by peeling off *three* tens.

The situation, as the war correspondents say, now began to develop rapidly. Jack Jamieson relieved it somewhat by palming one of the twenties and one of the tens, and his chief assistant helped a little more by collaring another of the tens, but there remained the sum of 130 dollars for the cash-register, and a simple calculation will show that it called for 2,600 beers. Half of them had been drawn—God knows how!—before Jack thought of raising the price to ten cents, but by that time the bar was packed as tightly as a bus-load of war workers, and great gangs of reinforcements were swarming in from all parts of the park. When the news reached the hoochie-koochie show, where a hundred or more sailors from the Battleship *(censored)*, then on a good-will tour of the Atlantic ports, were spoofing the performers, they arose as one man, and began a lumbering sprint for the bar. Passing the show-shed on their way, they gave the word to its patrons, and in ten seconds the girls and comedians were mauling and jawing one another to empty tables. Not a waiter was left on the floor, and in half a minute more not a girl or comedian was left on the stage, or a musician in the orchestra pit. By the time these artists arrived at the bar the crowd in front of it was twenty men deep, and all semblance of decorum had vanished. The boozers close up were so dreadfully squeezed and shoved that they could hardly get down the beers in front of them, and the later-comers on the outskirts fought in despair for better places. The sailors from the battleship, forgetting chivalry, tried to climb in over the heads of the ladies of the ensemble, and the comedians, musicians and special policemen slugged it out with the waiters. Only the eight *Totsäufer* kept their heads. They went on throwing money into the whirlpool of suds that covered the bar.

Up to this time Julius himself had been at his usual post at the park gate, searching the faces of inpouring fair ones for vestiges of innocence. But he had ears as well as eyes, and though it was a good city block from where he stood to the bar, he eventually picked up the roar that was mounting there, and made off to investigate. The crowd, by now, bulged outside the entrance like a swarm of flies around the bung of a molasses barrel, and hundreds of newcomers were arriving at a gallop and trying to horn and worm their way into it. Julius accordingly ducked to the rear, and entered behind the bar. He was just in time to hear Leopold Bortsch give the signal for the final catastrophe. It consisted of the one word "Wine!" uttered in a kind of scream. "Wine! Wine! Wine!" echoed the massed and macerated boozers. "He's opening wine! He's setting up wine! Hooray! Hooray! Hooray!"

There were, in fact, but five bottles of wine in the whole of Sunset Park, and they had been lying in Jack's cooler for three or four years, awaiting the remote chance that John W. Gates, Stanford White or Charlie Schwab might drop around some evening. The first two were duds, but the remaining three popped with magnificent effect, and as the so-called champagne seethed out of them, the last restraints of civilized society blew off, and the whole company yielded to its *libido boozalis*. In half a minute not a single sailor from the battleship was on the floor: they were all climbing over the merchant mariners and other civilians, and in dozens of cases a sailor thus climbing had another sailor climbing over *him*. Julius, with his long experience as cop and *Wirt*, saw a riot was in the making. "No more!" he roared. "Not another goddam drink! The bar is closed!"

Alas, it was a bad idea, and even if it had been a good one it would have come too late to work. As well challenge Behemoth with a spit-blower or Vesuvius with a squirt. Jack and his colleagues, in obedience to the boss's command, downed their tools instantly, but there were plenty of sailors present, both of the Navy and the Merchant Marine, who knew very well which end of a bottle had the cork, and they were over the bar in no time at all. Nor were they bound and hobbled, once they got into action, by the stiff, professional technique of Jack and company. When an outcry for gin came from the far reaches of the crowd they sent a whole bottle of it sailing through the air, and then another. Nor did they hesitate to use bottles on Julius's own head when he plunged into the thick of them, and essayed to lay them out. Of the details of this phase I can give you only hearsay, for I had been working my way out since the beginning of the action, and had by now taken a rather unfavorable post of observation some distance away, behind a large oak tree. But I went to the trouble during the weeks and months following to run down the full story, and these were its principal elements:

1. The rioters emptied not only every container of lawful goods in the park, from beer kegs to sprinklers of Angostura bitters; they also got down a barrel of cologne spirits that Julius used to sophisticate his five-cent whiskey, the contents of forty seltzer siphons, and a bottle of Mickey Finns.

2. Julius's first act, on recovering his faculties, was to get a revolver from his

office and go gunning for the eight *Totsäufer*. All had disappeared save Hugo Blauvogel. At him Julius fired six times, missing him every time. The next day he served notice on the Baltimore breweries that any *Totsäufer* sent to the place thereafter would be shot like a dog.

3. The sailors from the Battleship *(censored)*, returning aboard at dawn, took with them five of the ladies of the Sunset Park ensemble and both comedians. The officer of the deck refused admission to the ladies, but apparently swore in the comedians as mess attendants, yeomen, chaplain's mates or something of the sort, for a couple of weeks later the men of the whole North Atlantic Fleet staged a show at the Guantanamo base that is still remembered in the Navy as the damnedest ever seen. Its stars were two comics of unprecedented virtuosity. From the first glimpse of their red noses to the last reverberation of their slapsticks, they had the assemblage rolling in the aisles.

BALTIMORIANA

Why there is not a good history of Baltimore I don't know, and often wonder. Certainly the town is old and romantic enough to deserve one. It goes back nearly 200 years, and it was of importance from the start. So recently as 1860 it was the third American city in population; from the earliest times it has been among the leaders in trade, foreign and domestic. Every American has heard of the Baltimore clipper ship and the Baltimore oyster, to say nothing of Baltimore rye. The city has character, and is regarded amiably. But its own citizens seem to take little interest in it, and it has bred few bards to sing its glories.

If I had the time I'd certainly undertake a history of it myself, despite the fact that I lack the historiographer's gift. For my memories of it, now that I slip into senility, are almost all pleasant, and I am heartily glad that I was born here. The great fire of 1904 did Baltimore a vast damage, not by burning down houses, but by turning loose the Babbitts who still rage. They converted a charming, dignified and amusing old town, well-to-do and contented, into a den of absurd go-getters. They invented the art of enthusing, and so drove all self-respecting Baltimoreans into the sewers. The social structure has never recovered. Baltimore is run today by second-raters.

I am glad I was born long enough ago to remember, now, the days when the town had genuine color, and life here was worth living. I remember Guy's Hotel. I remember the Concordia Opera House. I remember the old Courthouse. Better still, I remember Mike Sheehan's old saloon in Light street—then a mediæval and lovely alley; now a horror borrowed from the boom towns of the Middle West. Was there ever a better saloon in this world? Don't argue: I refuse to listen! The decay of Baltimore, I believe, may be very accurately measured by the distance separating Mike's incomparable bar from the soda-fountains which now pollute the neighborhood—above all, by the distance separating its noble customers (with their gold watch-chains and their elegant boiled shirts) from the poor fish who now lap up Coca-Cola.

In my later teens I was already an aged man, and hence had a job as a political wiseacre. My field was the City Hall, and the reigning behemoth there was the peppery Thomas Gordon Hayes. Why has no one ever printed a memoir of him? (His old secretary, William P. Ryan, could do it capitally.) He was not only an immensely picturesque fellow, full of almost fabulous quirks and inconsistencies; he was also a man of very solid ability, and hard, indeed, to catch napping. No man, I believe, ever served Baltimore more faithfully, or to better effect. He completely reorganized its government, and he did the job so well that his work is visible yet.

Hayes was a short, spare fellow with a small, round head and an enormous waterfall moustache—the very image, in almost every detail, of Friedrich Wilhelm Nietzsche. He was a bachelor, and lived with his sister, an elderly schoolma'm. The good lady, I suspect, had a hard time of it policing him. When at his ease at home he arrayed himself in a frayed boiled shirt with no collar, a pair of sloppy old pantaloons, and slippers that seemed to have come out of Harrison street. Thus he would sit in his library, reading for hours on end—never, so far as I could make out, anything entertaining, but always law, newspapers and municipal reports. A large spittoon flanked him: he was a practitioner of the ancient American art. Now and then he permitted himself a free-smoking spotted cigar.

Hayes had a weakness for the cup, and shortly before (or was it after?) his inauguration as Mayor he got boiled at a public banquet and made a dreadful spectacle of himself. Cardinal Gibbons and President Gilman of the Johns Hopkins were present: it was a far worse scandal in those days than it would be today, with Prohibition debauching us all. Worse, he insisted upon wobbling home alone, and when he got there fell down a stairway and broke his leg. For weeks thereafter he was in bed. But he kept on mayoring just the same. Persons who had business with the city had to see him in his bedroom. What they saw there was certainly not inspiring, for Hayes was a most untidy man, and wore frightful nightshirts. He shaved once or twice a week, and had his Niagara of a moustache mowed once a year.

As a part of the art and mystery I then practised I had to call upon him at his house every Sunday night. There was little news stirring on Sundays in that remote era, for it was before Prohibition and the motor car, and so I was expected to stir up something. I had a formula that never failed to work. All I had to do was to tell his Honor that Major Richard M. Venable had said this or that—and he was off with a refutation of it, hell-bent and belching smoke. For he hated Venable magnificently, and Venable hated him. The very name of the one was poison to the other. Each, discussing his enemy, rose to such profanity that brimstone filled the air.

What their original quarrel was about I have forgotten, if, indeed, I ever knew. They had both been Confederate soldiers: perhaps it ran back to some difference over military strategy. Again, both were bellicose bachelors: perhaps one had tried to unload a girl on the other. Yet again, both were lawyers: ground enough for enmity. It was as lawyers that they came to their supreme combat. The issue was the interpretation of the new City Charter. Venable, as boss of the City Council, challenged Hayes as Mayor, and they went to the Court of Appeals on nine points of law. The case dragged through weary months. Every day Venable let it be known that Hayes was a jackass and would come to grief, and Hayes told all who would listen that Venable knew no more law than a cockroach and would be exposed when the learned judges reached their decision.

Certainly Venable knew a great deal more law than a cockroach; nevertheless, he lost, and on all nine points. The rejoicing of Hayes was appalling to witness. He was so delighted that he almost jumped out of his skin. For days he walked upon air, and was unfit for all ordinary business. Characteristically, he hated Venable the more for losing. Nothing that Venable ever said, after all, had any sense at all. As depicted by Hayes, the old Major was simply a doddering idiot, crazed by atheism.

Hayes himself was a Methodist, and in his last years devoted himself furiously to theology and good works. He became, indeed, a very pattern of piety, and put the jug behind him. On Sunday mornings he taught a Baraca class in a Methodist church opposite Harlem Square, and so greatly improved the moral tone of that neighborhood. His class was so well patronized that one of the local papers asked him to favor it with a weekly exposition of the Sunday-school lesson, that seekers after the truth all over the city might profit by his exegesis.

He accepted with alacrity, for he loved to write, but what he produced was only drivel—in fact, a pathetic exposure of the poor old fellow.

In his closing years, indeed, he became very silly. He appeared in court now and then, but his main interest was religion—and religion, as he understood it, was a fantastic Fundamentalism that would have made even Judge Raulston cough behind his hand. All truth was in the Bible. What could not be found there was of the devil. So his old friends and admirers dropped off, and his last years, I suspect, were very lonely. When he died he was almost forgotten. Few remembered the convivial Tom Hayes of so many wet evenings, or the shrewd, competent, immensely energetic Hayes of the City Hall.

Venable wore better, and remained in full eruption until the end. He, too, was greatly interested in religion, but his conclusions were almost exactly opposite to those of his old enemy. I remember him chiefly for two things. One day I asked him how he, a bachelor, managed to keep such good servants. He told me that he did it by making them a standing offer of double the wages they could get from anyone else. The other memory has to do with his days as czar of the City Council. It was the custom then, and had been so for years, for the Council to give $100 a year to each of the newspaper reporters who reported its proceedings. The money was simply a tip, and it was shameful to see certain of the reporters lobbying for it. When the ordinance came up that year Venable arose in the Second Branch, and gave notice that, if it were passed, he would start a taxpayer's suit for an injunction restraining the City Comptroller from paying the money. That was the first blow ever struck in Baltimore for self-respecting journalism. No such tip has been offered to reporters since.

OBSEQUIES IN THE GRAND MANNER

When I was a young newspaper reporter in Baltimore, in days now romantically remote, there were a dozen Class A and Class B breweries in the town, and each and every one of them maintained a functionary who was known in the trade as a *Totsäufer*. This revolting NHG word, when clawed into the language of liberty and democracy, was commonly toned down to *collector*, but its literal meaning was *dead-drinker*, and that is precisely what a *Totsäufer* was. His business was to register grief. When there was a funeral in the family of a saloonkeeper, he attended it in mourning garb and wept with the bereaved. If the deceased happened to be the saloonkeeper himself, he not only wept but moaned and beat his breast; and if the saloonkeeper happened to be a man of mark—which is to say, a man who worked off anything above twenty-five half-barrels of beer a week—, then the *Totsäufer* had to put on a show of consternation, horror and despair which made the hullabaloo of the widow, however frantic, seem pale and phony. He was charged also, to be sure, with other duties. He was present *ex officio* at all weddings in saloonkeepers' families, and at all wedding anniversaries, birthday parties, christenings and confirmations, and in the intervals between them he even did some actual collecting, especially of sticker and absconding accounts. But his principal duty, year in and year out, was to go to funerals.

The expectation that he would carry out his office in a striking and even staggering manner was never disappointed, so far as I am aware, in all the years before Prohibition. The paper I worked for did not give much space to the obituary orgies of saloonkeepers, though it covered those of police captains, baseball players and the more *distinguée* sort of fancy woman; but I often went to them in my private capacity, if only to bathe myself in the voluptuous delight of seeing a real virtuoso of mental anguish perform. There were among *Totsäufer*, as in the other crafts, practitioners who were good and others who were not so good; and among the former there was a small moiety of what may be almost described as geniuses. One such was Leopold Bortsch, of the Scharnhorst Brewery.

There was nothing in his aspect to reveal his incomparable mastery of his art and mystery. He looked, indeed, like any other *Totsäufer*. He had the same professional paunch, the same venous complexion, the same closely-clipped head, the same vestigial neck, and the same somewhat protruding eyes; he even wore the same fraternal-order emblems along his N 10 parallel of latitude, and the same balloon diamond on the ring finger of his left hand. But all that was only the outer shell of the man. Inside he was a furnace of talent beyond compare, and no colleague could touch him, or even approach him. When, standing beside the abyss of a saloonkeeper's grave, he rolled his eyes heavenward and began to throw off desolation, the effect was that of a great tragic actor saying farewell to the leading woman before being beheaded. When he moaned it was a rumble from the unfathomable sewers of Acheron. When he gasped and clutched his breast he seemed to be suffocating. And when his tears began to flow they came, not in drops, but in jets.

Inasmuch as Baltimore, in those remote days, was devoured by incessant murrains of typhoid fever, smallpox, cirrhosis of the liver and *mania à potu*, each with a high death rate, Leopold had to give such a show at least once a week, and sometimes as often as twice a day. It was thus easy to scoff at him as a mere ham, and at his heavings and gurglings as artificialities. Indeed, I am not one to deny (though my admiration for him as man and artist was unbounded) that there must have been occasions when his private emotions were only defectively engaged by the job in hand, and he had to depend, at least to some extent, upon his bald professional technique and momentum. But I am sure that there were plenty of other times when his secret heart responded fully to every plunge and tremor of his midriff, and he was scalded in sad reality by every tear that rolled down his nose. One such occasion I recall with great clarity over all these years. It was the funeral of a saloonkeeper by the name of Gustav Haubenschmidt, and it roared on in Loudon Park Cemetery for nearly the whole of a lovely October afternoon in 1901.

No one who knew both men, as I did, could doubt for an instant that Leopold's grief for Haubenschmidt was perfectly sincere. They were not only business associates of long standing, each with a high respect for the other; they were also intimate friends. Both were natives of the Lüneburger Heide; both had started up the road to worldly success as drivers for the Scharnhorst Brewery; both sang bass with the Rosenkranz Singing Society; both had substantial involvement in the Carl Schurz Permanent Building and Loan Association; both were members of the Freemasons, the Odd Fellows, the Knights of Pythias and the Red Men; above all, both were conscientious freethinkers, and enemies of the clergy of whatever denomination. This last bond was the tightest of all, if only because the ideology under it isolated them in their otherwise happy family circles, for Mesdames Bortsch and Haubenschmidt were not only faithful Lutherans, but also more or less active in church work. If there had been sons in either household there might have been serious trouble in both, since the husbands and fathers would have made a natural effort to indoctrinate them with their own views; but Haubenschmidt had only five daughters and Bortsch had no children at all, so the question never became acute, for both put the mentality of women below rational scientific speculation.

Haubenschmidt died, one might almost say, in Bortsch's arms, for at the moment he collapsed behind his bar Bortsch was standing directly in front of it. There was no warning whatever; the poor fellow simply gasped and went down, carrying with him a shell of Scharnhorst beer that was in his hand. He was a large man and made a considerable clatter in falling, but he said nothing, not even "Ouch!" or "Help!" Was he actually dead? Bortsch dispatched a dozen loafers for all the doctors in the neighborhood, but every doctor was out looking at tongues, so he decided to rush his friend to the University of Maryland Hospital, only half a dozen blocks away. Unhappily, there were no ambulances in the Baltimore of that day, and all such work had to be done by patrol wagons. Three objections to calling one presented themselves. First, there was, as usual, no cop in sight, and only cops had keys to the call boxes. Second, there was something revolting about being hauled in a patrol wagon, even though the man was unconscious; for if he recovered, his friends would kid him and if he died, his family would be afflicted by a more or less blushful memory. Third, it was notorious that whenever the cops took charge of a man unable to protest, they galloped him to the morgue straightway, and proceeded to a hospital only after the morgue-keeper had turned back his eyelids, stuck pins into him, and declared him still alive. A happy chance solved the problem. One of the magnificent beer-wagons of the Scharnhorst Brewery, drawn by two Percheron horses, dashed up to the front of Haubenschmidt's place only a few seconds after he fell. Bortsch and the driver threw off kegs enough to make room for him, and the run to the hospital was made at dizzy speed, with Bortsch holding the patient's head. Alas, it was all in vain. The young doctors found that heartbeat and respiration eluded their most delicate instruments. In brief, life was extinct.

It fell to Bortsch, I suppose, to notify the widow, but of that I know nothing. What I recall is the funeral three days afterward—an immense outpouring on a gorgeous autumn day, with La Haubenschmidt and her five daughters so swathed in crepe that they seemed hardly human, and delegations present from at least a dozen organizations of one sort or another. The widow, with her husband screwed down safely in a 450 dollar casket, had insisted on her dower right to call in her pastor, the Rev. Dr. Liebmann, for the last rites, and he took his place, not without a certain unction, at one end of the grave, with the family running down the two sides and the delegations fanned out behind them. At the other end stood Leopold Bortsch, calm, serene and confident—a fine figure of a man in his black cutaway coat, his striped gray trousers, his plug hat with its six-inch crepe band, his white Masonic apron and his brilliant blazoning of Shriner, Knights Templar, Odd Fellow, Red Men, Knights of Pythias and other badges and watch-charms.

He and the pastor eyed each other coldly, for there had been constant belligerency between them, as there had been between the pastor and the deceased. The pastor, a true ecclesiastic, was not unaware of the advantages lying in his sacred immunities and the piety of the widow; he was free, he knew, to give poor Haubsenschmidt (and Bortsch likewise) the works, and this he proceeded to do in a painfully slow *tempo* and with every mark of sacerdotal gloating. But

Bortsch was not to be upset by any such boorish challenge. The Lutheran Book of Common Prayer was no mystery to him; he knew it, in fact, backward and forward, just as he knew every other such textbook of the enemy, and he was well aware that there was no way for any pastor using it, however anti-social, to drag out the office for the dead to more than twenty minutes. He could bide his time, for the whole afternoon was ahead of him. He not only bided it with a fine show of tolerance and even cordiality; he astounded and disconcerted the pastor by making correct responses whenever there were cues for them in the service.

At long last this painful mummery was over, and the members of the Rosenkranz Singing Society stepped up to pay their last honors to their dead colleague. They were prepared to sing two compositions—"Morgenrot" and "Ich hatt' einen Kameraden"—both written originally for fallen soldiers, but also more or less appropriate for an heroic civilian, dead at the post of duty. Bortsch, as a bass, was supposed to confine himself to the lowest reaches of the harmony, but before the first stanza of "Morgenrot" was done he reached out for the melody, and thereafter he led with all the power of his triple-expansion lungs. The effect was very striking, and when, in the last stanza of the second song, he introduced a dramatic tremolo and then proceeded to a series of unmistakable sobs, first *sforzando* but quickly diminishing to *pianissimo*, thus:

the whole company, including even Pastor Liebmann, burst into a stealthy "Ah-h-h-h" that could not be altogether shushed down. The leader of the Rosenkranz, Professor Windhorst, thereupon glanced at Bortsch, Bortsch gave a flicker of his eye, and the brethren burst into "Es hat nicht sollen sein" as an encore. This was the toughest of the pieces that they commonly attempted, and Professor Windhorst had to do some deft herd-riding to get them off in consonance, but again Borscht saved the day, for at the first occurrence of the words "Behut' dich Gott" he staged another sob, this time *crescendo*, and when the last words were reached every eye in the assembly was dripping wet and the widow was launched upon the first of the classical series of six bouts of hysterics.

Once she was quieted the Freemasons took over, and Bortsch's robust bass led every "So mout it be" of their poetical graveyard ritual, which was done in English. The Odd Fellows, Knights of Pythias and Red Men followed with their more prosaic lamentations, and Bortsch led again. There followed a slight stage wait, and some anxious glances, for everyone knew that both the deceased and the officiating *Totsäufer* had been professed freethinkers, and everyone wondered if Bortsch would speak in that character, and if so, what he would say. He did not keep them waiting long. Raising the right hand for attention, he launched without ceremony into a discourse upon the nature, pains, costs, social effects and philosophical significances of somatic death which soon had the whole gathering in a lather of mingled horror and delight. As it began Pastor Liebmann took a firm stance and gritted his teeth, for he naturally expected a bitter denunciation of the Christian view; but in this he was disappointed, for Bortsch avoided everything even remotely approaching the controversial. There was, in fact, not a word in his speech that could have offended the most pious Lutheran, or even Calvinist, or Hard-Shell Baptist, or Buddhist, or spiritualist. Not once did he raise the delicate question whether Haubenschmidt, lying there in his Sunday black suit, was simultaneously roving, in gaseous form, the fields of asphodel. He put all that to one side and confined himself to quoting the safely neutral sages and poets—Socrates, Confucius, Goethe, Schiller, Heine, Jean Paul Richter, Victor von Scheffel, Longfellow, Eugene Field, Ella Wheeler Wilcox. Some of his extracts from them were of considerable length, but no one showed any impatience, no one got an overdose. In the midst of a scene from *Faust,* done in the original German, the widow came down with her second fit of hysterics; at the second shot of Heine she had her third.

And so, at last, he came to his peroration—in form, a solemn farewell to the dead Haubenschmidt. "Good-bye, Gustav!" he intoned. "The time has come to shake hands forever. Take care of yourself, dear friend, and don't let anybody tell you we will ever forget you. You were a faithful husband, father, brother, brother-in-law, nephew and cousin. *(Sobs from the family reservation.)* You were an honored member of the Masons, Odd Fellows, Red Men and Knights of Pythias. *(Murmurs of approval.)* Many a poor widow, left with a mortgage on her humble home, had reason to be thankful that you were chairman of the loan committee of the Carl Schurz Permanent Building and Loan Association. *(A burst of wailing from far back in the crowd.)* You were a business man who discounted his bills and kept a respectable family place. No one ever dared to speak a word against you, not even the Prohibitionists. *(Faint hisses.)* And now we part, as all friends must. You have our good wishes as we know we always had yours. Good-bye, Gustav! Farewell, old friend! We are here today and gone tomorrow. May we all learn by your example how—"

But what they were to learn the assembled mourners and fans never heard, for at that moment Bortsch began to stage his Class A exhibition of woe. His voice broke and was silent, tears gushed out of his eyes, his chin fell upon his breast, and his whole frame heaved and shook. At his first audible moan the widow gave an unearthly shriek, sank into her weeds, and launched into her fourth attack of hysterics. Pastor Liebmann rushed to her aid, but was so affected himself that he could do no more than pat her on the shoulder. In a few seconds dozens of Freemasons, Red Men, Odd Fellows and so on were sobbing, and even Professor Windhorst, though it was now nearly an hour and a half since he had had a drink, was mopping his eyes with his red bandana handkerchief. I was myself no novice to such scenes of mass melancholy. I had attended some of the historic performances of the greatest *Totsäufer* of Baltimore, Washington, Philadelphia and Norristown, Pa. Once I had seen three of them do their stuff simultaneously, while the widow of the deceased fought it out at the graveside with his lady friend and a blood-sweating pastor of the German Reformed Church hurled anathemas at both. But never had I been present at a more genuinely dramatic spectacle—not even at a hanging in the yard of the Baltimore city jail. The widow had barely recovered her legs after her fourth paroxysm of hysterics when a rapid series of piercing sobs by Bortsch plunged her into her fifth, and in this one all five of her daughters, hitherto silent, joined with sepulchral yells.

The end was now on us. Resuming articulate speech, Bortsch issued his solemn command to the undertaker, Hugo Eisenmenger, "It's all over! Do your duty, Eisenmenger! Let the clóds fall!" Down they went with a dismal rumble, and simultaneously the widow leaped from her corner and made as if to jump into the grave. It was the traditional climax expected of her, and Pastor Liebmann was not unprepared. One of his hands grasped her left arm and the other gripped her veil, and with all five of her daughters helping, it was an easy matter to haul her back. But what of Borscht? Who would have expected *him* to attempt anything of the same wild, desperate sort? Where did it stand in any book that the *Totsäufer* too should demand the consolation of suttee? No wonder there was a gasp when he took a little run to the very brink of the grave and made as if to dive in! How many hands were laid upon him I did not know, but there must have been dozens, for the whole delegation of Freemasons rushed up to drag him ashore, and on their heels came the Odd Fellows, the Knights of Pythias, the Red Men and the members of the Rosenkranz. Bortsch not only amazed them; he also fought them, and by the time he was safely collared and Eisenmenger's goons began hurrying in the rest of the sand and gravel, his cutaway coat was a sad mess, his fraternal-order jewels were all awry, and his plug hat was squashed flat. "Let me go with him!" he sobbed piteously as they led him away. "My best friend is gone! Take me with you, Gustav! What is life without you?"

By this time we had all been standing for more than two hours, and it was a relief when the Freemasons loaded Bortsch into one of their hacks, and made off at a gallop for Adam Dietrich's beer-garden, just outside the cityward walls of Loudon Park. All Baltimore hack horses turned into Adam's drive automatically on their way home from funerals, for they knew that pallbearers accumulated raging thirsts, especially when the obsequies were prolonged. I followed on foot, and when I reached the place found that Bortsch was already virtually recovered. Anchored at the bar, with swarms of Freemasons, Red Men, Odd Fellows and Knights of Pythias milling about him, he was getting down a large mug of Scharnhorst beer and apparently enjoying it, though it was the worst in Baltimore. Presently, a group of four or five men armed with rifles pushed their way through the crowd and began to upbraid him. They were members, it appeared, of the Moltke Schützenverein, a club of riflemen to which Haubenschmidt had also belonged, and they had gone to the funeral on the understanding that they were to be permitted to fire a salvo over his grave. They were now indignant, because Bortsch, in his capacity of stage manager, had forgotten them. But he refused to listen to their complaint.

"You got enough for your money," he said, "as it was. You don't see such a funeral every day."

"So say we all of us," piped up Eisenmenger, the undertaker, and without another word the riflemen slunk away.

LOVE STORY

The secrets of the female heart have engaged authors both sacred and profane since the 3 A.M. of history, but the result of all their labor seems to be indistinguishable from nil. I have no theory about the story that follows. It will suffice to state the bald and baffling facts, which have to do with an ex-policeman named Charlie and his wife Irene—a sweet and juicy name, and one so ancient that it was borne by a Byzantine empress who died in the year 803. But the Irene I speak of was very far from an empress; her trade, in truth, was the humble one of chorister and hoofer in a Class D honky-tonk that flourished in Gay Street, Baltimore, at the turn of the century.

The place was patronized mainly by third mates, fourth engineers and other such obscure and lonely strangers from the ships tied up at the nearby docks, and when they came ashore they liked entertainment of a rather unbuttoned type. Thus Irene and her colleagues flung themselves about their little stage in a violent and even abandoned manner, and in the intervals of their cavorting they came down on the floor and drank with the trade. The standard price for a straight whiskey in such places at the time was ten cents, but when a girl asked for one her customer was billed fifteen, and the bartender gave her ginger ale. This was good *Geschäft,* and the waiter always slipped her a brass check with her drink, redeemable at the bar for five cents cash.

Charlie met Irene in the course of his official duties. He came in one night looking for a ship's cook wanted for homicide in Cartagena, and lingered long enough for a couple of drinks. It could not have been the whiskey that fetched him, for the policemen of those days often drank much worse, and it is hard to believe that it was Irene's beauty, for she was squatty in figure, and her hair and complexion fell a good deal short of the fetching. But whatever the psychology of it, Charlie fell for her in the manner of an ox hit with an axe, and the next night he returned and began begging her to marry him.

Irene held him off for a week or so, for she had a couple of brothers who were wayward and apparently feared that taking a cop into the family might produce some uncomfortable crossing of wires. But she consented at last, and the proprietor of the honky-tonk staged a betrothal party after 1 A.M., when such places had to close. The party rapidly became febrile, and by the time two o'clock was struck by the City Hall bell, a block away, all hands were far gone in gaiety, and especially Charlie. When his sergeant burst in at two-thirty and announced a raid, Charlie's old-style helmet was on Irene's head, his badge adorned her bosom and his belt, espantoon, chewing tobacco, handcuffs and other equipment were being bandied about by the other revellers. Next morning the Police Board broke him, and he and Irene, after they left the trial room, went to a sailors' bethel near the honky-tonk and were married by a former lush-roller who had got salvation and taken holy orders.

Before the end of the day, Charlie had a job as bouncer in another honky-tonk, but Irene, having seen him fall once, was fearful that he might fall again, so she soon persuaded him to abandon bouncing for a more sanitary post in a feed warehouse. They rented one of the little houses that then abounded in Baltimore, paying nine dollars a month, and it was presently reported by the cops that they were ecstatically happy—in fact, a pair of lovebirds. Irene turned out to be an excellent plain cook, and despite Charlie's heavy work in the feed warehouse he put on weight. Soon he bought her a phonograph, then a novelty in the world, and thereafter he spent almost every evening at his own fireside, sitting by the latrobe stove in his stocking feet and listening to "A Hot Time in the Old Town," "Break the News to Mother," "Two Little Girls in Blue" and the other semi-classics of the time.

So month chased month and there came winter. One sleety morning, Charlie awoke with a pain in his chest and by noon he had a chill. Irene plied him with all the home remedies then in esteem, including mustard plasters fore and aft, but he grew steadily worse and next day she sent for a neighborhood doctor. The doctor's diagnosis was pneumonia in its most venomous form, and after a two-day hit-or-miss tour through the pharmacopeia, he threw up his hands and ordered Charlie to the Johns Hopkins Hospital. For three months following, the young internes there had a circus with him, for he developed every complication known to pathology. Finally, he came so close to Heaven that they asked Irene for permission for an autopsy. Concluding in alarm that they were about to give him *quant. suff.* from the black bottle, she dragged him home at once, and there, under her soft ministrations, he gradually recovered.

But he was too weak to resume his job in the feed warehouse, and the need of money soon became pressing, for Irene, at the time of their marriage, had saved up but a hundred and seventy-five dollars, and all their current revenues above living expenses had gone for furniture, carpets, objects of art, etc. Charlie's five brothers were called into consultation, along with a couple of his more prosperous buddies on the police force, and it was resolved to set him up in a small saloon in a proletarian neighborhood. The cops induced the Scharnhorst brewery to get him a license and supply his fixtures, and before long the brewery's *Totsäufer*, Leopold Bortsch, staged a magnificent grand opening with at least fifty head of local boozers milling in the little bar, and free beer, whiskey and even cigars for all comers.

Charlie recovered his strength only slowly, but his new work turned out to be within his powers, and his place soon brought him a neat income. To be sure, most of its trade was in growlers,[19] on which the profit was small, but on hot evenings he sometimes sold two or three hundred of them, and in the early mornings he did a brisk trade with wage slaves on their way to work. No bricklayer in those days would touch a brick until he had got down at least two drams, and there were plasterers, moving men and other such laborious fellows who needed three or four. Charlie opened the place at six o'clock every morning and remained on duty until 3 P.M., when Irene relieved him for the afternoon lull. At 6 P.M., he returned to stay until midnight, when the law forced him to close. From three to six, he took a nap.

Irene was the perfect wife and helpmeet, full of the most delighted lovey-dovey. She prepared all the free lunch with her own hands, working at it from 9 A.M. to eleven, when it was unveiled. She also washed the windows, scrubbed the floor and polished the glassware. During the afternoon, as I have said, she relieved Charlie for three hours, and on busy evenings she often lent him a hand. Also she did all the housework in their living quarters upstairs. Their domestic life continued rapturous to a superlative degree. Though their affection precipitated no offspring, they kept on the tenderest terms, and never passed each other, even with a crowd in the bar, without a love tap, a pinch, the pulling of an ear, or the gentle slapping of an arm or backside. Some of Charlie's old colleagues among the cops had predicted gloomily that their marriage would not last, for they believed that Irene would pine for the merriment and glamour of her former public life, but they knew better now, and on their nights off they often went to the little place—it was called Charlie's Cafe, pronounced "kaif"—to do their routine guzzling and admire and envy so affectionate a couple.

Irene, in fact, never showed the slightest itch for her old art and mystery. On the contrary, she pointedly avoided mentioning it, and when the honky-tonk she had adorned was the scene of two murders in three days, and the cops padlocked and effaced it, she professed to approve. Thus matters went for a year, and then Charlie fell ill again. It began this time not suddenly, as before, but with insidious symptoms that mounted only gradually. First there were pains in the legs, then there were spots before the eyes, and finally Charlie began to talk wildly in his sleep and to leap out of bed in a semi-maniacal manner.

When he reached the Johns Hopkins, the young doctors, knowing his profession, naturally diagnosed *mania à potu*, which is to say jimjams, but it soon appeared that there was much more to his illness than that. In the end, the celebrated Dr. William Osler, then at the height of his fame, was persuaded to take a hand, and it was established that there were evidences not only of the aforesaid malady but also of typhoid fever (then epidemic in Baltimore), malaria (also epidemic), gallstones, two or three different kidney diseases and pleurisy. After Osler thus launched them, the young doctors had at their patient in eight-hour shifts, and more than one of them got enough exercise out of him to shine as a high-toned consultant in the years to come. But Charlie neither died nor got well, and when he was brought home at last he was hobbling on two sticks and fit only for loafing.

This threw a cruel burden of work on poor Irene. While Charlie was in hospital, she had got in a part-time bartender, but he was a psychopath who had to be watched constantly, and what with this watching, her free-lunch activities, her relief bartending and the nursing of her lord, she now put in a day that ran from 5 A.M. to midnight. Though there was a Sunday-closing law in Baltimore in those days, most saloons in quiet neighborhoods kept their side doors open of an afternoon, but Irene was so exhausted when she rolled into bed at one o'clock on Sunday morning that she turned the key and slept until 6 P.M., with only half a dozen or more interruptions to give Charlie his medicine, stroke his hair and hold his hands. This cost her some revenue, for Sunday drinkers are immemorially assiduous, but it at least saved her from worrying about the psychopath.

Charlie, unhappily, got no better. Instead, he developed several new malaises, none of them fatal but all of them disabling. The young doctors came in from the Johns Hopkins to see him now and then, fascinated by the pathological kaleidoscope that he presented. Whenever a new drug or treatment was announced in the medical journals, they tried it on him, and usually gave him double doses, but he resisted their science in a way that seemed almost stubborn. Finally, one of them, a smart fellow who later built up a practice worth fifty thousand dollars a year, took him on for intensive study and soon declared that the problem was solved at last: what really ailed him, underneath and mingled with all his other ailments, was tuberculosis.

Irene gave a squawk when she heard this news, and even threatened to pass into hysterics, for tuberculosis in those days was still regarded as incurable. The young doctors, however, told her that such was no longer the case: it had been found that mountain air and plenty of fresh milk and eggs would arrest it. There was no mountain air in Baltimore, and the milk and eggs on sale there, especially in proletarian neighborhoods, were both dubious. But the alternative that presented itself was yet worse. Who would take care of the bar if Charlie were shipped to the Himalayas of western Maryland and Irene went along to nurse him and cook for him? And if the bar had to be closed, who would pay the freight?

All these problems were solved by the financial ingenuity and humanitarian libido of Leopold Bortsch, *Totsäufer* for the Scharnhorst brewery. First, he found a locum tenens for Charlie's Cafe, and induced him to pay four dollars a week for the franchise, with the reversion of it in case Charlie were not restored within three years. Second, he rounded up Charlie's five brothers—they were all poor men—and dragooned three of them into forking up a dollar a week apiece. Third, he tackled two rich police sergeants who knew and esteemed Charlie, and nicked them for a dollar-fifty a week apiece.

This counted up to ten dollars—just enough, by Leopold's calculations, to keep the bodies and souls of Charlie and Irene assembled. Nor was this all that he did. Through the agent of the Scharnhorst brewery in Hagerstown, Maryland, he found a two-room house at five dollars a month in the mountains near Pen Mar, and through the same agent he found a Dunkard farmer willing to supply it with milk, eggs and other provender at least twice a week. Yet more, he arranged for the transportation of Charlie and Irene by rail and farm wagon to their new home, and for the conveyance of enough house furnishings to make them comfortable. Finally, he slipped a twenty-dollar bill into Irene's hand and bade her cherish it as an umbrella for a rainy day.

What life came to on that bleak mountaintop during their first winter must be referred to the imagination, for Charlie and Irene had no visitors from town, and neither of them was a letter writer. There were snows and sleet storms that penned them in for weeks, though the Dunkard somehow got to them with his milk, eggs, corn meal and hog meat. This, remember, was before the day of radios, and the exiles both eschewed reading, on the ground that it hurt their eyes. They took the phonograph along, but the first explorers who visited them in the spring reported that every record save those of "Massa's in de Cold, Cold Groun'" and "Break the News to Mother" had cracked or worn out after the first six weeks.

Over all these years I think of the long, long days and the long, long nights, with Charlie—he had acquired the invalid complex by now—groaning and complaining on his couch, and Irene busy with her lowly offices. She not only had to feed him, nurse him and keep him clean; she also had to entertain him, for all the nearby yokels regarded tuberculosis as a sort of demoniacal possession and never came into the house if they could help it. Today there are sanatoria in the Blue Ridge Mountains approaching in luxury the hideaways of movie actors, with huge staffs of doctors, nurses, masseurs, cooks, maids, psychologists, social workers and so on, but in 1900 they were unknown. In good weather, a homeopathic doctor from Waynesboro, Pennsylvania, dropped in about once a month, but at all other times Irene managed the whole treatment herself.

Charlie made good progress the first year, and the only one of his brothers who ever visited him reported that he would be restored to normalcy by its end, but then he had the usual setback, and for months he was pretty ill. Irene, however, never despaired, nor did she ever abate her assiduities. Even on that desolate alp, where all the hill women were drudges, she became noted for her unremitting diligence. She was not only cook and nurse but also seamstress, and in summer she worked a small garden, and grew tomatoes, cabbages, onions and the like. She and Charlie were not facile conversationalists, and in the course of time she and he often talked each other out, but until they recovered speech she sat in stolid silence, sewing, humming tunes and anticipating his every wish and whim.

I never knew her very well, and so I can't tell you whether she was romantic devotee or mere slave, masochist or saint. One could not determine anything from her face, which bore the neutral expression of a pumpkin or toy balloon. But whatever the inward springs of her incomparably benign behavior, she certainly qualified as the champion wife of the whole region south of Harrisburg, Pennsylvania. One of the rich police sergeants, who visited her and Charlie during their second year on the mountain, told me that her total expenditure on her own dress from end to end of that year amounted to six dollars and seventy cents and that her only luxury was a fifty-cent box of mail-order chocolates. But out of her lean savings she yet managed to keep Charlie in chewing tobacco, and on his second birthday in the mountains she got him a bottle of blackberry wine.

The other sergeant, hearing this moving tale and having run into some good luck in speculation, sent Irene ten dollars and sweated Charlie's brothers into raising their joint ante to five dollars a week, so Irene's income leaped to twelve dollars. With the surplus, she bought more milk and eggs from the Dunkard, and presently Charlie began to recover in earnest. During the third year he put on weight, took to his legs and prepared to come home. He and Irene got back just in time to oust the locum tenens, but it soon turned out that Charlie was still a far from well man. Moreover, as I have said, he had acquired an invalid complex, and a couple of days after his grand reopening, arranged by Leopold Bortsch, he took to his room upstairs and left the whole burden of the establishment on Irene.

The psychopath had been fired by the locum tenens, and the best substitute Irene could find at the wages she could pay was an old and boozy fellow who had started at the top of his profession at the Rennert Hotel and then come rapidly downhill to jail and helping-up missions. He was still competent enough, despite his disintegration, but he ate more free lunch every day than a dozen customers. Also, he sometimes failed to show up in the morning, or got drunk in the evening and had to be thrown out. But Irene was never heard to complain, even to the booze-sisters who ducked in and out of the bar's family entrance, and neither did she complain when Charlie himself began to tipple, and now and then fell out of his chair or out of bed. Always and invariably, she was the faithful and consecrated wife. When she had to lift him up from the floor, sometimes with the aid of a customer, she dealt with him gently, addressed him as "honey," and usually straightened his clothes and combed his hair.

One day, alas, Charlie undertook to come downstairs when he was severely in his cups and suffered a header down the dark and narrow steps. When the cops got him to the Johns Hopkins in a patrol wagon—there were then no ambulances in Baltimore—the young doctors found that he had broken his right wrist, his collarbone, and both ankles. They kept him a couple of weeks, and then sent him home in a series of heavy casts, with huge swathes of bandages running this way and that all over him. He had some pain and swore a good deal, but never at Irene. They remained on their old loving terms, and she petted and gentled him whenever she could get away from the bar. This went on for four or five months, and then one of the young doctors dropped in one morning and knocked off the casts. Charlie would be as good as new, he said, in a few more weeks. Moreover, his lungs were as clear as bells.

Irene no more exulted than she had complained, but it was plain to see that she was filled with bubbles of quiet rejoicing. She cooked special dishes for Charlie, she made him four new shirts, and she bought him a rocking chair. At long last his dreadful illnesses were all over, from pneumonia and *mania à potu* to typhoid and broken bones. The day before he was to resume service in the bar— the last young doctor had knocked out his invalid complex by denouncing him as a lazy hound—Irene hugged him so violently that he was almost suffocated, and they kissed something on the order of two hundred times. This, of course, was *in camera*, but the customers downstairs could plainly hear the smacks.

That night, toward morning, Charlie awoke with violent sneezing, and all the next day he snuffled and panted. Toward evening, Irene sent for a neighborhood doctor, and the doctor made the astonishing diagnosis of measles, which was raging among the children of the vicinity. He said that with good nursing it would not amount to anything and ought to pass off in a week or ten days. "Have you ever had it yourself?" he asked Irene. She replied that she had, in childhood. "Then you can nurse him," said the doctor. He thereupon gave Charlie an opium pill to make him sleep, and left three or four prescriptions for medicines.

Charlie slept soundly, and when he awoke in the morning he felt somewhat better, though he still had an itchy rash. Not seeing Irene, he called for her. Getting no answer, he called again. He heard no rumble of talk below, and concluded that she had not opened the bar. He began to be uneasy. Then he sighted a piece of paper on a chair by the bed. When he unfolded it, this is what he read:

> dere Charlie. I cant stand it No More. It has got to be 2 Much. You will never see me Agen.
>> Your loving Wife.
>> Irene.

And he never *did* see her again, though he lived ten years—a widower unconsoled, even by the prehensile widow women who fought for him.

Why did the loving and faithful Irene, after holding fast so long, desert him at last? Why, after withstanding pneumonia, malaria, pleurisy, tuberculosis, typhoid and jimjams, did she succumb in the end to so trivial an affliction as measles?

I started off by telling you that I had no theory, and I now say the same thing again. You will have to work out this mystery of the female heart for yourself.

THE LIFE OF AN ARTIST

Down to World War I, the late Theodore Dreiser, the novelist, lived a strictly bourgeois life in the horse latitudes of upper Broadway, a region then chiefly inhabited by white-collar workers who were slightly but not much above the rank of slaves. His modest quarters were in an apartment house with bumpy ornaments of terra cotta outside and a friendly smell of home cooking within. The somewhat grand entrance was flanked by a delicatessen to one side and an up-and-coming drugstore to the other. It was a place almost as remote to me, a chronic stranger in New York, as the Jersey Meadows, but I made the trip to it often, for Dreiser, in those days, was being strafed unmercifully by the Comstocks,[20] and I was eager to give him some aid. Besides, I liked him very much and greatly enjoyed hearing him discourse in his ponderous, indignant way, suggesting both the sermons of a Lutheran pastor and the complaints of a stegosaurus with a broken leg.

His remarks, to be sure, sometimes set my teeth on edge, for I was a born earthworm and he had an itch for such transcendental arcana as spiritualism, crystal gazing, numerology and the Freudian rumble-bumble, then a scandalous novelty in the world. Once landing in his den on a rainy night, I found him nose to nose with an elderly female who undertook to penetrate the future by scanning the leaves in a teacup. She predicted in my presence that he was about to be railroaded to jail by the Comstocks, and added that he'd be lucky if he got off with less than five years in Sing Sing. Inasmuch as he was then sweating away at two books and eager to finish the manuscripts and collect advances, this threw him into a considerable dither, and it took me an hour to restore him to normalcy after I had shooed the sorceress out.

But in realms less unearthly we got on quite well. He believed, and argued with some heat, that the human race was the damnedest collection of vermin in the sidereal universe, and against this I could think of nothing to say. If we differed on the point, it was only because he excepted all ruined farm girls and the majority of murderers, whereas my own bill of exceptions was confined to the classical composers, Joseph Conrad, and a bartender in Baltimore named Monahan. Dreiser believed that every politician alive, including especially the reformers, should be hanged forthwith, and I went along without cavil. The same for social workers, with stress on the so-called trained ones. The same for all persons having any sort of connection with Wall Street. The same for pedagogues of all ranks. The same for the rev. clergy of every known persuasion. The same for hundred-per-cent. Americans. When it came to authors, we again differed slightly, for there were then, besides Conrad, half a dozen whom I admired more or less—as artists, if not as men. But Dreiser, in my hearing, never praised any save Frank Norris, who had whooped up Dreiser's own first novel, "Sister Carrie," [21] and Harris Merton Lyon, a young short-story writer, now forgotten. He also had some respect for Balzac, but not much; I recall that he once declared that all Frenchmen were too ornery for so humane a mortuary tool as the guillotine. He read the Russians but denounced them unanimously as psychopaths of marked homosexual and homicidal tendencies. Dickens he consigned to the bilge deck of his private Gehenna, along with Howells, Henry James and H. G. Wells. Even when it came to Arnold Bennett, who, on landing in New York, had told the gaping reporters that "Sister Carrie" was one of the greatest novels of all time, the most he would concede was that Bennett was probably tight or full of dope at the time, and hence not up to the customary viciousness of an Englishman.

What caused this highly orthodox citizen, almost between days, to throw off the shroud of correctness and precipitate himself into Greenwich Village is more than I can tell you, though I knew him well and pondered the question at length. The Village in that era had a very dubious reputation, and deserved it. Nine-tenths of the alleged writers and artists who infested it lived on women, chiefly from the small towns of the Middle West, and I never heard of one who produced anything worth a hoot. Whenever, in the pursuit of my duties as a literary critic, I denounced the whole population as fraudulent and nefarious, the elders of the community always threw up Eugene O'Neill and (later) Dreiser himself as shining disproofs, but O'Neill had actually made off at sight of the first refugee from Elwood, Indiana, and Dreiser was a famous man before he moved to Tenth Street. The typical Village ménage was made up of a Cubist painter who aspired to do covers for pulp magazines and a corn-fed gal who labored at an erotic novel and paid the bills. This gal, in the standard case, was the daughter of a rural usurer who had died leaving her three thousand dollars a year in seven-per-cent. farm mortgages. Until her father's executors cabbaged the money, she was a rich woman, and a rich woman, in Schmidtsville, was a target of intolerable scandal and contumely. If her I.Q. was above 7 or 8, it inevitably occurred to her, soon or late, that her dreadful experiences would make a powerful novel, so she entrained for New York and sought the encouragement of æsthetic society. She got it without delay, for the resident bucks heard of her the moment she crossed Fourteenth Street, and fought for her ferociously. If she was above the average in guile, she made the winner marry her, but this was seldom necessary, and when it happened, the marriage did not outlast her money.

Dreiser, moving to Tenth Street, found himself in a dense mass of such Little Red Riding Hoods and their attendant wolves. They swarmed in all the adjacent courts and alleys, and spilled out into the main streets and even into Washington Square. He had no more than unpacked his quills and inkhorn and hung up his other suit when they began to besiege him, for the gals all believed that his word was law with magazine editors, and their parasites were well aware that he knew every art director in New York. They barged in on him at all hours, but chiefly between 10 P.M. and 3 A.M., and the gals all brought manuscripts for him to read. I once found him with his desk surrounded by a breastwork of such scripts at least three feet high, and in a corner was a stack of canvases showing women with purple hair, mouths like the jaws of hell, gem-set umbilici, and three or four vermilion and strabismic eyes. He was then virtually a teetotaler, but soon he had to lay in booze for the entertainment of his guests. Their tastes, it appeared, ran to liqueurs of the more exotic kinds, and they were not slow to ask for them. He then made his first acquaintance with such fancy goods as mescal, arrack, Danziger Goldwasser and slivovitz, and had to take to massive nightcaps of bicarbonate of soda. Once, a lady poet induced him to try a few whiffs of marijuana, and his sensations were so alarming that he preached a crusade against it for years afterward.

All this cost him more money than he could afford, for the Comstockian assault had cut off his book royalties, and his magazine market was much depleted. Moreover, his working hours were invaded by his visitors, many of whom stayed a long while, and there were days when he couldn't write a line. He was a very kindly man, and the memory of his own early difficulties made him push tolerance of neophytes to the edge of folly. One night, a bulky pythoness from the Western Reserve of Ohio broke into his studio, helped herself to half a bottle of *crème de violette* and proceeded to read to him the manuscript of a historical novel running to four hundred and fifty thousand words. He got rid of her only by what the insurance policies call an act of God. That is to say, a fire broke out in one of the art-and-love warrens across the street, and when the firemen came roaring up and began fetching æsthetes down their ladders, the pythoness took fright and ran off. The next day, he had an extra lock put on his door, which opened directly into the street, but it worked so badly that it often locked him in without locking the Village literati out. After that, he shoved an armchair against the door, but they soon learned how to climb over it.

Toward the end of 1916, the Comstocks closed in on Dreiser with psalteries sounding and torn-toms rolling, and many of his fellow-authors began to take alarm, for if he could be suppressed for a few banal episodes of calf love in his latest book, "The 'Genius,'" then the whole fraternity might find itself facing an idiotic and ruinous censorship. Accordingly, a manifesto was circulated protesting against the attack on him, and a number of bigwigs signed it. William Dean Howells, Hamlin Garland and a few lesser old fellows of the prissier sort refused to do so, but most of the other authors of any consequence stepped up eagerly, and in a little while the paper had a hundred or more important signatures. But then Dreiser himself took a hand in gathering them, and the first list he turned in threw the committee into a panic. For all the quacks of the Village, hearing what was afoot, rushed up to get some publicity out of signing, and their new neighbor was far too amiable to refuse them. This list and those that followed day by day were really quite extraordinary documents, for a good half of the signers had never had anything printed in magazines above the level of the pulps, and the rest had never seen print at all. The nascent Communists of the time—they were then thought of as harmless cranks—were all there, and so were the poetical advocates of free love, the professional atheists and the great rabble of yearning females from the Cow States. The Harlem poets signed unanimously. Not a few of the hand-painted-oil-painter signatories were being pursued by the indignant mothers of runaway daughters, and several of the etchers were under police scrutiny for filling the Village art shoppes with aphrodisiacal steals from Anders Zorn.

When Dreiser began sending in the signatures of psychoanalysts—they were then called sexologists, and their books had a great undercover sale—the committee howled in earnest, and there ensued an unseemly wrangle between the beneficiary of the manifesto and its promoters. The latter had common sense on their side, but Dreiser was too adamantine a man to be moved by any such consideration. All his fellow-Villagers, of course, leaped up to defend him and themselves, and one night when I waited on him in Tenth Street I found him palavering with a delegation that insisted that he insist on retaining the signature of a Buddhist writer from Altoona, Pennsylvania, who had been collared that very day for contributing to the delinquency of a minor; to wit, a psychopathic free-verse poetess from the Upper Peninsula of Michigan. It made me dizzy to see how easily they fetched him. They had not got out a hundred words before he was pledging his life, his fortune and his sacred honor to the Buddhist, who had got out on bail and was present in person, in a mail-order suit of clothes, with a towel wrapped around his head. I slunk out much depressed, determined to advise the committee to disband at once and tear up its manifesto, but that, happily, was never necessary, for soon afterward the Comstocks began to flush other game, and Dreiser was forgotten.

As I have said, his flat was on the ground floor of the old house he lived in, and its door opened directly upon the street. It was comfortable enough during the first six months of his occupancy, but then excavations began for the Seventh Avenue subway, and the eastern edge thereof ran along his wall. The tearing down of the house next door did not bother him much, for in the throes of literary endeavor he had a high power of concentration, but when the gangs of workmen got down to the rocks underlying Manhattan Island and began rending them with great blasts of explosives, he sometimes made heavy weather of it. More than once, his whole collection of avant-garde art came tumbling from his walls, and on several occasions he was bounced out of bed in the middle of the night. Such adventures gave him nightmares, and even when no dynamite was going off, he dreamed of being pursued by hyenas, lawyers, social workers and other authropophagi. But the most curious of his experiences in those days did not have to do with detonations but with a quiet neighbor who occupied the basement under his apartment. In the New York fashion, Dreiser had had no truck with this neighbor, and, in fact, didn't know his name, but now and then the man could be seen ducking in or out of the areaway at the front of the house. He operated some sort of machine downstairs, faintly audible between blasts in the larval subway, and Dreiser assumed that he was a tailor, and so gave him no thought.

One day, there was a ring at the front door, and when Dreiser opened it, three men wearing derby hats brushed past him into his apartment. An ordinary author might have been alarmed, but Dreiser was an old newspaper reporter, and hence recognized them at sight as police detectives. Keeping their hats on, they got down to business at once. Who was the man who lived below? What was his name? What sort of trade did he carry on? Did he ever have any visitors? If so, who were they, and at what time of day did they visit him? Dreiser replied that he knew nothing about the fellow and couldn't answer. He had seen and heard no visitors, though the place might be swarming with them without his knowledge. Well, then what sound *did* he hear? Dreiser mentioned an occasional subdued thumping, as of a sewing machine. Was that in the morning, in the afternoon, or in the evening? Dreiser, urging his memory, replied that he had heard it at all hours. After midnight? Probably not after midnight. After eleven o'clock? Perhaps. After ten o'clock? Yes. Was it loud or soft? Soft. How long did it go on at a stretch? Sometimes half an hour; sometimes less; sometimes more. Did he hear any heavy weights being thrown about? No. Any clank or clink of metal? He couldn't recall any. Did the neighbor look suspicious when he used the areaway? Did he peer up and down the street? Did anyone ever meet him? What sort of clothes did he wear? Did he ever carry packages?

By this time, Dreiser was growing tired of his callers, and invited them to go to hell. They showed no resentment but did not move. Instead, they became confidential. The man below, they revealed in whispers, was a counterfeiter— one of the leaders of the profession. He made half dollars out of solder melted from old tin cans, and what seemed to be his sewing machine was a contraption for casting them. The dicks said that they were preparing even now to raid and jug him. Half a block down the street, two federal agents waited with a truck, and he would be taken with all his paraphernalia. Of the three cops now in attendance, one would guard the areaway and the two others would climb down through the subway excavation and rush him from the rear. As for Dreiser, he was instructed on pain of prosecution to keep his mouth shut and maintain complete immobility. If he so much as walked into his rear bedroom, it might scare the culprit off. Meanwhile, a few last questions. Had the counterfeiter ever tried to work off any bogus half dollars on him, or proposed that he help work them off on others? Had Dreiser ever smelled burning lead? Had he ever noticed any glare of flame at night? Had there been any excessive heat, as from a furnace? Had he heard any banging, bumping, booping or bubbling?

Dreiser now renewed his invitation to his visitors to go to hell, and this time they departed. He waited a few minutes and then peeped out of the bedroom window that gave onto the yard in the rear. The two cops of the storming party were having a hard time crawling and stumbling through the subway crater, but eventually they made it and began thumping on the basement's rear door. When they got no answer, they borrowed a scantling from a subway foreman and proceeded to batter the door down. Once they were inside, Dreiser began to see copy for one of his novels in the affair and took to the excavation himself. By the time he got to the door, muddy and bruised, the dicks were preparing to depart. While they had been sweating him upstairs, the counterfeiter had made tracks, and not only had made tracks but had taken his machine with him, and not only his machine but also his spare clothes (if any) and all his secret documents. There was nothing left save half a dozen defective counterfeit coins on the floor and a note on the table. It was written in a good, round hand and read:

Please notify the Gas Company to shut off the gas.

JAMES HUNEKER

[I]

I think of him, in these days of his recent passing, not primarily as artist, but as man. There was a stimulating aliveness about him always, an air of living eagerly and a bit recklessly, a sort of brittle resiliency, if you can imagine it. In his very appearance something provocative and challenging showed itself, a sort of insolent singularity, obvious to even the most careless glance. That Roman profile of his was more than simply unusual in a free republic consecrated to good works; to a respectable American, encountering it in the lobby of the Metropolitan or in the smoke-room of a *Doppleschraubenschnellpostdampfer*, it must have suggested inevitably the dark enterprises and illicit metaphysics of a Heliogabalus.[22] More, there was always something rakish and defiant about his hat—it was too white, or it curled in the wrong way, or a feather peeped from the band—and a hint of antinomianism in his necktie. Yet more; he ran to exotic tastes in eating and drinking, preferring occult goulashes and *risibisi* to honest cuts from the joint, and great floods of Pilsner to the plain beverages of God-fearing men. Finally, there was his talk, that cataract of sublime trivialities, gossip lifted to the plane of the gods, the unmentionable bedizened with an astounding importance and even profundity.

In his early days I was at nurse and too young to have any traffic with him. When I encountered him at last he was in the high flush of the middle years and already eminent in the little world that critics inhabit. We sat down to luncheon at one o'clock; I think it must have been at Lüchow's, his favorite refuge and rostrum to the end. At six, when I had to go, he was bringing to a close *prestissimo* the most amazing monologue that, up to that time, these ears had ever funneled into this consciousness. What a stew, indeed! Berlioz and the question of the clang-tint of the viola; the inner causes of the suicide of Tschaikovsky; why Nietzsche left Sils Maria between days in 1887; the echoes of Flaubert in Joseph Conrad, then but newly dawned; the precise topography of the warts of Liszt; George Bernard Shaw's heroic, but vain, struggles to throw off Presbyterianism; how Frau Cosima saved Wagner from the Swedish baroness; what to drink when playing Chopin; what Cézanne thought of his disciples; the defects in the structure of "Sister Carrie"; Anton Seidl and the musical union; the complex and moony love affairs of Gounod; the early days of David Belasco; whether a girl educated at Vassar could ever really learn to love; the exact composition of chicken paprika; the correct tempo of the Vienna waltz; the style of William Dean Howells; the abstruse international scandals at Bayreuth in 1886; what George Moore said about German bath-rooms; the true inwardness of the affair between D'Annunzio and Duse; the origin of the theory that all oboe-players are crazy; why Löwenbräu survived exportation better than Hofbräu; Ibsen's dislike of Norwegians; the best remedy for *Katzenjammer*; how to play Brahms; the degeneration of the Bal Bullier; the sheer physical impossibility of getting Dvořák drunk; the last words of Walt Whitman.

I left in a sort of fever, almost a delirium, and it was two days later before

I began to sort out my impressions and formulate a coherent image. Was the man allusive in his books—so allusive that popular report credited him with the actual manufacture of authorities? Then he was ten times as allusive in his discourse—a veritable geyser of unfamiliar names, shocking epigrams in strange tongues, unearthly philosophies out of the back-waters of Scandinavia, Transylvania, Bulgaria, the Basque country, the Ukraine. And did he, in his criticism, pass facilely from the author to the man, from the man to his wife, and to the wives of his friends? Then at the *Biertisch* he began long beyond the point where the last honest wife gives up the ghost, and so, full tilt, ran into such complexities of elective affinity that a plain sinner, content to go to hell placidly under Rule VII, could scarcely follow him. I try to give you, ineptly and grotesquely, some notion of the talk of this man, but I must fail inevitably. It was, in brief, chaos, and chaos cannot be described. But it was chaos made to gleam and coruscate with every device of the seven arts; chaos drenched in all the colors imaginable, chaos scored for an orchestra that made the great band of Berlioz seem like a fife-and-drum corps. One night a few months before the war I sat in the Paris opera-house listening to the first performance of Richard Strauss's "Josefs Legend," with Strauss himself conducting. On the stage there was a riot of hues that swung the eyes round and round in a crazy mazurka; in the orchestra there were such volleys and explosions of tone that the ears (I fall into a Hunekeran trope) began to go pale and clammy with surgical shock. Suddenly, above all the uproar, a piccolo launched into a new and saucy tune, in an unrelated key! Instantly and quite naturally, I thought of the incomparable James. When he gave a show at Lüchow's he never forgot that anarchistic passage for the piccolo.

[II]

I observe a tendency to estimate him in terms of the content of his books. Even Frank Harris, who certainly should know better, goes there for the facts about him. Nothing could do him greater injustice. In those books, of course, there is a great mass of perfectly sound stuff; the wonder is, in truth, that so much of it holds up so well today: for example, the essays on Strauss, on Brahms, and on Nietzsche, and the whole volume on Chopin.[23] Now and then one strikes a false note and even a falsetto note; for example, in the treatise on Ibsen's "symbolism," that phantasm of the primordial drama-leaguers of twenty years ago, and in the too facile nonsense about Maeterlinck:[24] but that is not often. The real Huneker, however, never got into these books, if one forgets "Old Fogy." They were made up, in the main, of articles written for the more intellectual magazines of their era, and they represented a conscious striving to qualify for respectable company. So born, they came to their growth under the shadow of a publishing tradition that was even further from the Hunekeran instinct; it was hospitable and intelligent, but it surely did not foster *héliogabalisme* for its own sweet sake. Under the same tradition there had to be room also for the gospel of art for the soul's sake. Not, to be sure, that Huneker ever put on robes that were not his own. Nowhere in all his books will you find him doing the things that all right-thinking critics are supposed to do: essays on Coleridge and Addison, of the relative merits of Booth and Macready, solemn disquisitions upon the relations of Goethe to the romantic movement, dull scratchings of exhausted and sterile fields. Nay, such enterprises were not for James; he kept himself out of that black coat. But I am convinced that he always had his own raiment pressed carefully before he left Lüchow's for the temple of Athene, and maybe changed neckties, and put on a boiled shirt, and took the feather out of his hat. The simon-pure Huneker, the Huneker who was the true essence and prime motor of the more courtly Huneker, remained behind. This real Huneker survives in conversations that still haunt the rafters of the beer-halls of two continents, and in a vast mass of newspaper impromptus, thrown off too hastily to be reduced to complete decorum, and in two books that stand outside the official canon, and yet contain the man himself as not even "Iconoclasts" or the Chopin book contains him; to wit, the "Old Fogy" aforesaid and the "Painted Veils" of his last year. Both were published, so to speak, out of the back door, the former by a music publisher in Philadelphia, and the latter in a small and expensive edition for the admittedly damned. There is a chapter in "Painted Veils" that is Huneker to every last hitch of the shoulders and twinkle of the eye—the chapter in which the hero soliloquizes on art, life, immortality and women. And there are half a dozen chapters in "Old Fogy," superficially buffoonery, but how penetrating! how gorgeously flavored! how learned! that come completely up to the same high specification. If I had to choose one Huneker book and give up all the others, I'd choose "Old Fogy" instantly. In it Huneker is utterly himself. In it the last trace of the pedagogue vanishes. Art is no longer, even by implication, a device for improving the mind. It is wholly a magnificent adventure.

This notion of it is what Huneker brought into American criticism, and it is for that bringing that he will be remembered. No other critic of his generation had a tenth of his influence. Almost single-handed he overthrew the æsthetic theory that had flourished in the United States since the death of Poe, and set up an utterly contrary æsthetic theory in its place. If the younger men of today have emancipated themselves from the puerilities of the Puritan æsthetic, if the schoolmaster is now palpably on the defensive, and no longer the unchallenged assassin of the fine arts that he once was, if he has already begun to compromise somewhat absurdly with new and sounder ideas, and even to lift his voice in artificial hosannas, then Huneker certainly deserves all the credit for the change. What he brought back from Paris was precisely the thing that was most suspect in the America of those days; to wit, the capacity for gusto. Huneker had that capacity in a degree unmatched by any other critic. When his soul went adventuring among masterpieces, it did not go in Sunday black; it went with vine-leaves in its hair. The rest of the appraisers and criers-up—even Howells, with all his humor; nay, even such fellows as Meltzer—could never quite rid themselves of the professorial manner. When they praised, it was always with some hint of ethical, or, at all events, of cultural purpose; when they condemned, that purpose was even plainer. The arts, to them, constituted a sort of school for the psyche; their aim was to discipline and mellow the spirit. But to Huneker their one aim was always to make the spirit glad—to set it, in Nietzsche's phrase, to dancing. He had absolutely no feeling for extra-æsthetic valuations. If a work of art that stood before him was honest, if it was original, if it was beautiful and thoroughly alive, then he was for it to his last corpuscle. What if it violated all the accepted canons? Then let the accepted canons go hang. What if it lacked all purpose to improve and lift up? Then so much the better. What if it shocked all right-thinking men and made them to blush and tremble? Then damn all right-thinking men forevermore.

The theory had its defects. It was a bit too simple and often very much too hospitable. Huneker, clinging to it, did his share of whooping for the sort of revolutionist who is here today and gone tomorrow; he was fugleman, in his day, for more than one cause that was lost almost as soon as it was started. More, it made him somewhat anæsthetic at times to the new men who were not brilliant in color, but respectably drab and who tried to do their work within the law. Particularly in his later years, when the old gusto began to die out, and all that remained of it was habit, he was apt to go chasing after strange birds, and so miss seeing the elephants go by. I could put together a very pretty list of frauds that he praised. I could concoct another list of genuine *arrivés* that he overlooked. But all that is merely saying that there were human limits to him;

the professors, on their side, certainly sinned far worse and in both directions. Looking back over the whole of his work, one must needs be amazed by the general soundness of his judgments. He discerned the new and the important long before most of his contemporaries discerned it, and he described it habitually in terms that were never bettered afterward. His successive heroes, always under fire when he first championed them, almost invariably moved to secure ground and became solid men, challenged by no one save fools: Ibsen, Nietzsche, Brahms, Strauss, Cézanne, Stirner, Synge, the Russian composers, the Russian novelists. He did for this Western world what George Brandes was doing for Europe, sorting out the new-comers with sharp eyes, and giving mighty lifts to those who deserved it. Brandes did it in terms of the old academic bombast; he was never more the professor than when he was arguing for some hobgoblin of the professors. But Huneker did it with Gallic verve and grace; he made it not schoolmastering, but a glorious deliverance from schoolmastering.

As I say, his influence was enormous. The fine arts, at his touch, shed all their American lugubriousness, and became provocative and joyous. The spirit of senility got out of them, and the spirit of youth got into them. His criticism, for all its French basis, was thoroughly American, vastly more American, in fact, than the New England ponderosity that it displaced. Though he was an Easterner and a cockney of the cockneys, he picked up some of the Western spaciousness that showed itself in Mark Twain. And all the young men followed him.

[III]

A good many of them, I dare say, followed him so ardently that they got a good distance ahead of him, and often, perhaps, embarrassed him by name in vain. For all his enterprise and daring, indeed, there was not much of the fighter in him, and though he was the greatest of all the enemies that the guardians of tradition had to face, it was seldom that he tackled them directly. Something of Mark Twain's timorousness hung about him; he was always loath to set himself directly against a concrete champion of orthodoxy; he could never get quite rid of the feeling that he was no more than an amateur among such gaudy doctors, and that it would be unseemly for him to flout them too openly. I have a notion that this timorousness was born in the days when he stood almost alone, with the whole faculty grouped in a pained circle around him, and that modesty prevented his throwing it off after all logical support for it had vanished. He was always, as I have said, somewhat book-shy. Often I have heard him talk of his first book and of the glow that warmed him when he got news that an old and eminent publishing house was to print it. There was no vanity in this, but a sort of grotesque awe. He could never quite understand the view that this publishing house had done honor to itself by printing him; to the end he was a bit amazed that no catastrophe had followed its temerity and that it remained eager to do his successive volumes. Perhaps this fear of wading out beyond his depth, of exposing himself too recklessly to the attack of the orthodox *intelligentsia*, explains his fidelity to the newspapers, and the strange joy that he always took in his forgotten work for the *Musical Courier*.[25] In such waters he felt at ease. There he could disport without thought of the dignity of publishers and the eagle eyes of campus reviewers. Some of the connections that he formed were full of an ironical inappropriateness. His discomforts in his *Puck* days showed themselves in the feebleness of his work; when he served the *Times* he was as well placed as a Cabell at a colored ball. Perhaps the *Sun*, in the years before it was munseyized,[26] offered him the best berth that he ever had, save it be his old one on *Mlle. New York*.[27] But whatever the flag, he served it loyally, and got a lot of fun out of the business. He liked the pressure of newspaper work; he liked the associations that it involved, the gabble in the press-room of the opera-house, the exchanges of news and gossip; above all, he liked the relative ease of the intellectual harness. In a newspaper article he could say whatever happened to pop into his mind, and if it looked thin the next day, then there was, after all, no harm done. But when he sat down to write a book—or, rather, to compile it, for all of his volumes were reworked magazine, and sometimes newspaper, articles—he became self-conscious, and so knew uneasiness. The tightness of his style, its one salient defect, was probably the result of this weakness.

The fact is that the growth of Huneker's celebrity in his later years filled him with wonder and never quite convinced him. He was certainly wholly free from any desire to gather disciples about him and found a school. There was, of course, some pride of authorship in him, and he liked to know that his books were read and admired; in particular, he was pleased by their translation into German and Czech. But it seemed to me that he shrank from the bellicosity that usually got into praise of them, that he disliked being set up as the opponent and superior of the professors whom he always vaguely respected and the rival newspaper critics whose friendship he esteemed far above their professional admiration or even respect. I could never draw him into a discussion of these rivals, save, perhaps, a discussion of their historic feats at the beer-table. He wrote vastly better than any of them and knew far more about the arts than most of them, and he was undoubtedly well aware of it; but it embarrassed him to hear this superiority put into plain terms. His intense gregariousness probably explained part of this reluctance to pit himself against them; he could not imagine a world without a great deal of easy comradeship in it, and much casual slapping of backs. But under it all was the chronic underestimation of himself that I have mentioned—his fear that he had spread himself over too many arts, and that his equipment was thus defective in every one of them. "Steeplejack" is full of this apologetic timidity. In it he constantly takes refuge in triviality from the harsh challenges of critical parties. It is the biography of a man who came to the end of his life harboring doubts of his own chief accomplishments, and a bit intimidated by his own fame.

More than once, indeed, the book sinks to downright banality; for instance, in the Roosevelt episodes. Certainly no one who knew Huneker in life will ever argue seriously that he was deceived by the Roosevelt buncombe, or that his view of life was at all comparable to that of the great demagogue. He stood, in fact, at the opposite pole. He saw the world not as a moral show, but as a sort of glorified Follies. He was absolutely devoid of that obsession with the problem of conduct which was Roosevelt's main virtue in the eyes of a Puritan and unimaginative people. Nevertheless, the sheer notoriety of Roosevelt, the general acceptance of his tosh as immortal wisdom, had its effect on Huneker, and so he was flattered when Roosevelt took notice of him, and accepted gravely the pious nonsense that was poured into his ear, and even repeated it without a cackle in his book.[28] To say that he actually believed in it would be to libel him and the human intelligence with him. It was precisely such hollow pieties that he stood against in his rôle of critic of art and life; it was by exposing their hollowness that he lifted himself above the general. The same timorousness induced him to accept the accolade of the National Institute of Arts and Letters. The offer of it to a man of his age and attainments, after he had been passed over year after year in favor of all sorts of cheap-jack novelists and tenth-rate compilers of college text-books, was intrinsically insulting; it was almost as if the Musical Union had offered to admit a Brahms. But with the insult went a certain gage of respectability, a certain formal forgiveness for old frivolities, a certain abatement of old doubts and questionings; and so Huneker accepted. In later years, reviewing the episode in his own mind, he found it the spring of doubts that were even more uncomfortable. His very last letter to me was devoted to the matter. He was by then eager to maintain that he had got in by a process only partly under his control, and that, being in, he could discover no decorous way of getting out.

[IV]

But I devote too much space to the elements in the man that worked against his own free development. They were, after all, grounded upon qualities that are certainly not to be deprecated—modesty, good-will to his fellow-men, a fine sense of team work, a distaste for acrimonious and useless strife. These qualities gave him great charm as a man. He was not only humorous; he was also good-humored; even when the crushing discomforts of his last illness were upon him his amiability never faltered. And in addition to humor there was wit, a far rarer thing. His most casual talk was full of this wit, and it bathed everything that he discussed in new and brilliant lights. I have never encountered a man who was further removed from dullness; it seemed a literal impossibility for him to open his mouth without discharging some word or phrase that arrested the attention and stuck in the memory. And under it all, giving an extraordinary quality to the verbal fireworks, there was a solid and apparently illimitable learning. The man knew as much as forty average men, and his knowledge was well ordered and instantly available. In his books the display disconcerted many a reader, and so it was not uncommon to hear the doctrine that his tremendous allusiveness was largely affectation—that he invented authorities to adorn his tale. But there was, as I said earlier, precisely the same allusiveness in his conversation. He had read everything and seen everything and heard everything, and nothing that he had ever read or seen or heard quite passed out of his mind.

Here was the main virtue of his criticism—its gigantic richness. It had the dazzling charm of an ornate and intricate design, a blazing fabric of fine silks. It was no mere pontifical statement of one man's reactions to a set of ideas; it was a sort of essence of the reactions of many men—of all the men, in fact, worth hearing. Huneker discarded their scaffolding, their ifs and whereases, and presented only what was important and arresting in their conclusions. It was never a mere *pastiche*; the selection was made delicately, discreetly, with almost unerring taste and judgment. And in the summing up there was always the clearest possible statement of the whole matter. What finally emerged was a body of doctrine that came, I believe, very close to the truth. Into an assembly of national critics who had long wallowed in dogmatic puerilities, Huneker entered with a taste far surer and more civilized, a learning vastly greater, and an address vastly more engaging. No man was less the reformer by inclination, and yet he became a reformer beyond compare. He emancipated criticism in America from its old slavery to stupidity, and with it he emancipated all the arts.

THE LIFE OF TONE

Next to journalists, doctors, liberals and waiters, I have probably spent more of my time since 1900 with musicians than with any other class of men, and on the whole, despite some harrowing experiences, I do not regret it. Not, of course, that I subscribe to the common delusion that music in some mysterious way is elevating to the psyche and makes for nobility of character. I have known some musicians who were plausibly describable as noble, at least to the extent that our democratic institutions permit, but I have also known some who were unmistakable congeners of the hyena, the crocodile and the polecat. Once, early in my newspaper days, I actually had the pleasure of attending an accordion-player to the gallows, and of all the men I saw hanged in that era he deserved it the most, for he was guilty of killing a Chesapeake Bay oyster-boat captain who had only lately bailed him out of jail, bought him a suit of clothes and a hat, and lent him three dollars.

But such inordinate scoundrels are naturally scarce among musicians, just as they are scarce among other men, and the great majority of tone artists I have known have been nothing of the sort. On the contrary, they have run pretty close to the human norm in behavior, if one overlooks, for the moment, alcoholism and polygamy. What keeps them out of trouble, when they happen to be actual musicians and not merely union workmen hired to play so many notes for so much money, is the fact that music is a full-time job. Even when it is pursued only as an avocation, not a trade, it keeps its votary so busy that he has no time and energy left for any deviltry save maybe the two that I have mentioned. When he is not engaged in turmoils of tone himself he is commonly listening to those of other musicians, and it is this incessant engrossment that constrains him to be relatively quiet and decent, not any transcendental effect of sharps and flats upon the personality. There is plenty of music that in itself is very far from uplifting. The waltzes of Johann Strauss, properly played, fill even a virtuous mind with wayward thoughts, and I am inclined to believe that the first movement of the "Eroica" symphony of Ludwig van Beethoven has launched more heresy upon the world than all the speculations of Nietzsche.

The tendency of music to engulf and consume a man was well exemplified by the case of John Girschner, an amateur flute-player who adorned my native Baltimore forty years ago. John was a bachelor of easy means who, with his military figure and flowing mustaches, might reasonably have been described as handsome, and in consequence he was under heavy pressure from the antisocial people who, in those days as in these, gave parties. He might have dined out five nights a week if he had been so inclined and on the off nights he might have gone to an endless succession of balls, after-the-theatre suppers, Masonic pep meetings (for he was a Freemason) and miscellaneous booze fights. For every Sunday in winter he had invitations to at least half a dozen oyster roasts and for every Sunday in summer he had as many to crab feasts. But it was rare indeed for him to go to any of these affairs and when he did so it was only after long and frantic propaganda by his family and friends, including his five sisters-in-law. Instead, he devoted nearly all the leisure that business left him to the single enterprise of blowing the flute. Every evening each week save one, after a sparing dinner at home, he would tuck under his arm the black case which housed his two flutes, one silver and the other gold, and proceed to some place where music was on tap and that of the flute was esteemed.

On Monday nights he played with a woodwind ensemble which met year in and year out at the home of Anton Benning, an amateur clarinetist who in secular life ran a veneer factory. On Tuesdays he sat in with two other flute-players and they devoted two hours to performing flute trios. On Wednesdays and Sundays he played with amateur orchestras, on Fridays he assisted a string quartet which had a large library of compositions with added flutes, clarinets, oboes and so on, and on Saturdays he joined in the uproars of the Saturday Night Club, of which I was also a member. This left only the Thursdays vacant, and the Thursdays he gave over to the weekly meetings of the Mozart Permanent Building & Loan Association, which he served as president and treasurer and in which he was the majority stockholder. As if to make up for this treason to music on one evening of the week, he usually dropped in on Sunday mornings at the home of Rudolph Emmelmann, a rich agnostic who had been entertaining a motley posse of musicians at his house every Sabbath, beginning at the customary hour for opening divine service in the Baltimore churches, since 1874.

I wish I could tell you that John's devotion to the flute made him a master of it, but that unhappily was not the case. The more he played the worse he played, and inasmuch as he played much more than most, he eventually became much worse than most. In the course of time, in fact, the tones that he projected from the instrument took on such unpleasantness that he could not stand them himself and he accordingly abandoned the flute for the oboe. For a year or more he was neither seen nor heard by any of his old colleagues in the tone art, for he kept to his house and practiced in secret. Everyone, of course, speculated about the outcome and the prevailing opinion was that he would quickly land in a lunatic asylum, for it was well known that playing the oboe had deteriorating effects upon the mind. But one evening John showed up at a session of the Saturday Night Club with his oboe under his arm, showing no sign whatever of mental decay, and when he called for the oboe part to the "Poet and Peasant" overture[29] and proceeded to play it, we were all astonished to discover that he played very well; indeed, considering his short schooling, extraordinarily well. Thereafter he was our oboist, and soon he had resumed membership in some of his other clubs and was playing four or five nights a week. More, he began to accept an occasional professional engagement, though he didn't need the money, for in those days oboists were very scarce in Baltimore and whenever two or more operetta companies came to town the same week there was a downright famine.

John died years ago, but he is still remembered by the local musicians not only as the worst flute-player since Apostolic times but also as the hero, or maybe it would be better to say victim, of a curious musical contretemps. This mishap befell him in his early oboe days. He had been engaged to assist the orchestra of a traveling operetta company headed by a decayed star of the Metropolitan, and had got through the Monday-morning rehearsal without difficulty, though one of the numbers in the operetta was a sort of duet between the star and the oboist. First she would sing a coloratura passage lifted from Mozart and then the oboe would echo it. Unhappily, she began to feel bad after the rehearsal, and just before the opening performance, in the evening, she decided that it would be imprudent for her to attempt her highest note, which was E natural above the staff. After several trials she found that she could still reach the tone below it—to wit, D—so she asked the leader of the orchestra to play the number transposed a tone lower. All his colleagues in the pit were equal to this operation, but John was dubious, for he was still a bit strange to his instrument. He therefore decided to lower it a tone by lengthening the tube, and this he did with some difficulty, for the various sections, though made of wood, had sort of rusted together. Then he squared himself off to echo and assist the madam, who presently bounced upon the stage and began her song.

The first echo went well enough, though John was trembling, but when he came to the second he blew a little too hard, with the result that he blew the bottom section off his oboe and made an explosive, unearthly sound that startled the audience and set the orchestra to laughing. But the madam did no laughing. She was a woman of intensely artistic temperament and any interruption while she was performing made her virtually crazy. This time her insanity took the form of bellowing, "What goddam idiot done that?" Such language was shocking in those innocent days, even in an opera singer, and the stage manager rang down the curtain at once. When it lifted again, ten minutes later, the performance was resumed with the number which followed the madam's solo and she was represented by an understudy, for she had become hysterical on returning to her dressing room and it was not until she had heard two or three hearty rounds of applause for the understudy and had got down four or five shots of gin that she was sufficiently restored to resume.

John had to stand a lot of kidding after this episode, but it did not dissuade him from the oboe, which he continued to blow until his lamented decease. He once told me, in his old age, that he figured he had played no less than three hundred and fifty billion notes in his time and did not regret a solitary one. His pertinacity was typical of musicians; indeed, I often think that if music has any actual effect upon human character, it is in the direction of fostering patience and endurance. So thinking, I always recall a stout and hearty fellow named Mac,[30] who spent six weeks rehearsing a part which consisted of but two notes, and then missed them. This Mac was not, strictly speaking, a musician at all but simply a music-lover, and his ordinary functions in our club were confined to listening while the rest of us played and then checking up the bar bill at the beer party which always followed. He came from the hill country of Virginia and had never heard any music save that of country fiddles and bazookas until he went to Charlottesville to study law. But at Charlottesville he became aware of many other instruments and also of a repertoire reaching far beyond "Old Black Joe" and "I Got a Gal at the Head o' the Holler," and by the time he migrated to Baltimore he was one of the most fervent music-lovers ever heard of. His taste was catholic and omnivorous. He not only rolled and wallowed in the music of such tony composers as Bach, Beethoven and Brahms, he also retained his early love of more primitive stuff, and whenever he encountered a colored band on the streets of Baltimore he fell into line behind it and sometimes marched along for miles. Thus he got a great kick out of our Saturday Night Club, though he did not play himself, for its average program ran all the way from Schubert's Unfinished Symphony and the "Emperor" concerto to the waltzes of Gung'l,

Ziehrer, Komchak[31] and the whole Strauss family (including Richard) and "Funiculì-Funiculà."

We had in the club in those days a member who was a very competent composer and now and then he wrote something for us that displayed our several talents and foibles. The second piano part, written for me, was commonly marked *fortissimo* throughout, with instructions to tie down the loud pedal, and the first violoncello part, written for a 'cellist with Doric shoulders and hairy arms, was made up largely of electrifying *glissandi* on the A string. This composer was very fond of Mac and lamented the fact that he could not take a hand in our proceedings. On second thought, why not? To be sure, he could not read music and could not play any instrument that we used, but the fact remained that he was a university graduate and a man of proved sagacity at poker and amour, so the composer, an optimist, concluded that, given sufficient time and patience, he might be taught. The more subtle and difficult instruments, of course, would probably be too much for him, but what of one of the simpler ones? What, for example, of the *grosse Trommel, gran cassa,* or bass drum? What, again, of the *Becken, cinelli,* or cymbals? What, above all, of the triangle?

The triangle certainly was simple enough. It needed no tuning or fingering and could not get out of order. It sounded but one tone, and that tone had a dynamic range no wider than the squeal of a mouse. If men of such low mentality that they were hardly more than idiots could yet attain so much virtuosity on the violin and piano that thousands paid money to hear them, then why shouldn't a *legum baccalaureus* of the University of Virginia, under proper tutelage, learn the triangle? The composer could think of no reason, so he spit on his hands forthwith and wrote a triangle part into a composition that he had under way for the club. This composition, like the many others that he did for us, was adroitly adapted to our needs and interests. There was a gorgeous nine-inch cadenza for our first violin, a whole page of *glissandi* for the violoncellist, a bold paraphrase of the horn motive in "Don Juan"[32] for our horn-player, and a long series of *fortissimo* chords for me. Also, there were some artful suggestions of the beer parties that always followed our hours of music—the rattle of the pewter lids of our mugs, our brisk commands to the waiter, and the shrill chromatic laugh of Otto Stiefelmeyer, the saloonkeeper we then patronized. Above all, there was a swell part for the Confederate jurisconsult—a solo passage for triangle, running to four measures.

I wish I could tell you that the result was a masterly and memorable performance, recalling that of Brahms' Requiem in the Bremen Cathedral on Good

Friday, 1868. Unhappily, history is history, and the truth must be served. Mac not only showed no natural talent for the instrument, he appeared to be completely incapable of fathoming even the elements of its technique. Worse, he could not be taught to clout it at the proper place in the score; either he was a hundred measures ahead of time or a hundred behind. The composer, a most patient fellow, took him on for private lessons and rehearsed him daily for weeks on end, but to no appreciable effect. He was as bad after his twentieth lesson as he had been at his first. The composer thereupon rewrote his part, thinking that maybe it was too long, but when it was brought down to three measures Mac boggled it just as sadly as he had boggled it when it ran to four, and so again when it was reduced to two, and finally to one. By this time the composer was beginning to lose hope, but it occurred to him that if one whole measure was still too much, then perhaps Mac could play two notes, and the score was accordingly revised. The idea turned out to be a good one, for Mac struck the two notes accurately and even neatly. But he struck them ten measures too soon, and so the desired effect was again spoiled. The composer then wrote in a cue for him that seemed to be bulletproof. Two measures before his entrance, the whole hand brought up in a powerful *sforzando,* and it was followed by a grand pause. "Count eight," he said, "and then lay on." But Mac was so addled by the melodramatic contrast between the *sforzando* and the pause that he counted only seven, and the next time nine, and the next time six, and so on.

This stumped the composer, and he retired to the *Kaisersaal* behind Otto Stiefelmeyer's bar to meditate. He emerged a week or so later with a scheme that really seemed sure to work, and at the next meeting of the club it was given a trial and went off magnificently. In its fundamentals it was very simple. Thirty or forty measures before Mac's entrance the composer laid down his baton and took a stance behind his pupil. As the critical moment approached he took Mac's trembling right paw into his own right hand and got a firm grip upon Mac's neck with his left. Simultaneously, he dug his right knee into Mac's back. So standing upon his left leg, like a stork, he brought down Mac's right hand at the precisely right instant, then lifted it and made the second and last stroke of the solo. The effect was so excellent that at the end of the movement the whole club arose to applaud the soloist, the fiddlers all drummed upon their fiddles with their bows, and the piano and wind struck up the felicitatory tonic chord of G major.

So far so good. We were all glad to see Mac master the triangle at last, but alas and alack, success had the same deleterious influence upon him that it has always had upon artists, time out of mind. Within a week he was negotiating with a Baltimore goldsmith for a fourteen-carat gold triangle, to cost four hundred dollars, and within two weeks he was criticizing the performance of the rest of us very tartly and advising us to get a hump on. By the end of that winter he was speaking of himself as the best triangle player in the Western Hemisphere and sending challenges by post card to his rivals in the Boston, Philadelphia, and Philharmonia Orchestras. During the summer, after insuring his gold triangle for ten thousand dollars, he sailed for Europe and let it be known that he had been called to the Gewandhaus at Leipzig. But if they gave him a trial there something must have slipped, for when he returned in the autumn his gold triangle was missing, he was considerably subdued and all his sneers had disappeared.

AUTHOR AND JOURNALIST

A FOOTNOTE ON JOURNALISM

From the View-Point of a Worker in the Ranks

Much has been written about the newspaper business as a career for the American young man and many units of brain power have been wasted in the endeavor to work out a system of philosophy to fit its requirements and limitations. Some optimistic sages have pictured it as a thing of golden opportunities, and others—of the pessimistic breed—have gone to great pains to show that the city room is paved with moral and mental quicksands. Acres of paper and tons of ink have been spent in discussing the craft which brings them together; wells of vituperation have been emptied in declaiming against it; mountains of approval and praise have been used in covering its imperfections.

But with all of these attempts to make its dark places luminous, journalism remains a trackless waste to the young man who would enter its gates. Ahead of him he can see no guide posts; when he forces his entrance he must hew out his own way gropingly and blindly. Until he has, in a measure, platted the newspaper field for himself, he may have no hope of becoming acquainted with its characteristics. As he stands at the boundary and looks across he sees nothing plainly. In his hand there is no book of directions. In his memory there are no words of counsel intelligible enough to be useful.

The reason for this lack of information regarding the journalistic domain lies in the fact that the men who write of the newspaper business are men whose point of view is diametrically opposite to that of the worker in the ranks. Glance through an index of magazine articles on journalism and note the names of the writers. Immediately you will observe that they may be divided into two classes. The first of these consists of old newspaper men—editors of thirty years standing, editor-publishers and pen wielders who have forsaken the craft for the higher rungs of the literary ladder. The second is made up of people whose knowledge of the city room is as purely theoretical as their knowledge of the Silurian period; college professors, dabblers in the field of letters and professional philosophers.

Now, I submit that no one of these self-constituted authorities has a practical acquaintance with the subject he presumes to discuss. Those in the first named class, to the layman, may seem to be experts. But as a matter of fact, they are the least competent of all to write with full knowledge and impartial judgment. The managing editor of today was the reporter or copy reader of thirty years ago—when the newspaper business was a far less complex thing than it is at present. When he yet marched in the rank and file, the interview was in its swaddling clothes, the newspaper illustration—I set aside the wood cut—was unborn, and the tremendous enterprise of today was undreamed of. The "yellow journal" had not yet appeared to create havoc among the old line papers, the colored supplement was unknown, the "double column," the "stud head," and the "every minute extra" were absolutely non-existent. Consequently the reporter of 1870, when he sets out to write about "The Opportunities of Journalism" or "The Newspaper Business as a Career," either wastes valuable space in telling how he found things a generation ago or wisely confines himself to a discussion of those subjects which concern the city room not at all.

Therefore it happens that when the average reporter alights upon an article by the editor-in-chief of a metropolitan journal he smiles sarcastically. When he wades through the opening paragraphs and comes to a statement that "in journalism, as in other things, plain, honest merit is more to be desired than spectacular effect" he laughs aloud. When he encounters a page of philosophizing regarding the "reporter's duty to his paper" he stuffs the offending screed into the fire.

And no wonder! Is it not evident to him, in every line, that the editor writes from the point of view of a man to whom the depths below have become dim and half forgotten? Does not the entire article bristle with fallacies and shop-worn articles of faith and exploded theories? Is it not more of an irritating sermon than a practical exposition of the subject? The editor's imagings are of no interest to the reporter and of little more than no interest to the general public. What he says is valueless to the aspirant waiting at the city room door and worse than disheartening to the struggling, and perhaps unsuccessful, young men who labor in the glare of the city editor's eye. Nine times out of ten he begins his preachment by saying, "My advice to all would-be newspaper men is, Don't!" And yet he declaims against the lack of energy among the men under him and declares that the good workers of his day are no longer to be found.

Of the other wise men in the first class of journalistic advisors it is almost useless to speak. The editor-publisher, in his make-up, is 99 per cent. publisher and 1 per cent. editor. As the former he is the natural enemy of the men at the city room desks. What he says of them is usually ridiculous; what they say of him is often more sweeping than just. In no way is he fitted to undertake a sensible discussion of their work.

The literary ex-journalist, similarly, labors under many disadvantages. As a rule the average reporter does not like him. This may be due to jealousy, and it may be due to his patronizing air. Its cause, however, is immaterial. When he sets out to tell the story of the men who write news he devotes all of his time and space to those features of their work which appeal to him. He forgets that the hewers of wood and drawers of water who provide the paper with its daily columns of "local briefs" are every bit as important as the man who does the "special" work or the sad-faced cynic who grinds out the diurnal column of jokes. He sees or remembers the police reporter as the romantic hero who solves murder mysteries and brings bank robbers to justice and forgets all about his hours of tiresome loafing about lockups and police offices in search of smaller grain for his never-satiated mill. He gives no attention to the salary question and fails to touch upon the vagaries of city editors. In a word, he presents the newspaper business in the light in which the great reading public loves to look upon it, for it is his trade to give the public what it wants. To him, more than to any one else, is due the blame for the avalanche of manuscripts which come to the busy editor's desk from Brownstown and Jones' Corner.

In the second class of journalistic advisors are to be found the most industrious and disgusting workers in the entire army. These are the cheerful wiseacres who blacken good paper and waste valuable ink in giving the public information about "The Mission of the Press" and "The Future of Journalism." They address themselves, very often, to "the young journalist," and with solemnity and many wise maxims, tell him that his work is as important as the labors of a member of Congress. When he comes to the end of their batch of theories he goes to the cashier's window in the business office of his paper and draws his week's salary—$15. What, in the name of all that is true and beautiful, does he care for the mission of the press ? He is but human, like the rest of us, and his own individual future is of more interest to him than the future of such a great, unwieldly, clumsy abstraction as that represented by the word journalism. He knows that newspapers will continue to appear every morning until the end of the world. It requires no philosopher to tell him this. Axioms need not be repeated. He also knows that, in the ordinary course of events, publishers will continue to make profits until long after he is dead and forgotten. The problem with which he is doomed to wrestle is the problem as to whether or not the great engine which moves the world will give him, in the years to come, enough money and glory to compensate him for his services as tender of its fires.

From the theories of the philosophers he obtains no enlightenment. From the cashier in the business office he obtains—$15. From the written opinions of the managing editors he absorbs nothing but discouragement. From the writings of other ready penmen who tell the world his troubles he gets naught but excuse to swear. Consequently he laughs at all of them, from the top of the list to the bottom, and with one eye on his official head—to see that the city editor allows it to remain upon his shoulders—he sets out with a valiant heart to fight his way to the upper rung. Sometimes he comes within hailing distance of his goal and sometimes—or rather oftentimes—he makes a misstep and falls. Then he lands upon the ground with a crash which breaks every bone of ambition within him.

But if he is made of the real stuff he will grasp the lower rung of the ladder and start anew up the ascent. It is one of the advantages of the newspaper business that a man may never fall so low into its depths as to have no chance to make a re-beginning. When he learns that the average salary of reporters in a city like Chicago is only $21 a week he may lose heart. But if he remembers that the average yearly earnings of the generality of American physicians are only $1000 a year he should be more content. It is usually six years after a physician matriculates at his college that he begins to make money enough to pay his board. The reporter who has given three years to his trade is considered experienced. The physician, while his six years of preparation have been passing over him, has had need of outside financial assistance in order that he might eat and drink. The reporter, during his three years of apprenticeship, has been paid enough, at least, to settle the bills of his landlady. On the whole he has no cause for complaint.

Some day one of his brethren or an observant city editor will take his pen in hand to tell him all about it. Then, whether he be an aspirant at the city room door, or a patient slave writing business office "puffs," or one of the thousands in whose hearts ambition and despair are fighting a mighty battle, he will be helped as the lucubrations of the theorists can never help him. Particularly will it benefit the hopeful young man from college to thus see the battle from afar. One glimpse of it, as it is, may send him from the field with his coattails standing out behind him. But on the other hand it may only whet his appetite for a place in the ranks. If he runs away, the goddess of journalism—if there is such a divinity—may say, with truth, "Good riddance." And if he stays to fight it out, he will at least have the advantage of knowing something of the ground. This, said a man of battles many years ago, is nine parts of the victory.

REMINISCENCES OF THE *HERALD*

Looking back over a dull life, mainly devoted to futilities, I can discern three gaudy and gorgeous years. They were my first three years as a newspaper reporter in Baltimore, and when they closed I was still short of twenty-two. I recall them more and more brightly as I grow older, and take greater delight in the recalling. Perhaps the imagination of a decaying man has begun to gild them. But gilded or not, they remain superb, and it is inconceivable that I'll ever see their like again. It is the fate of man, I believe, to be wholly happy only once in his life. Well, I had my turn while I was still fully alive, and could enjoy every moment.

It seems to me that the newspaper reporters of today know very little of the high adventure that bathed the reporters of my time, now nearly thirty years ago. The journalism of that era was still somewhat wild-cattish: all sorts of mushroom papers sprang up; any man with a second-hand press and a few thousand dollars could start one. Thus there was a steady shifting of men from paper to paper, and even the most sober journals got infected with the general antinomianism of the craft. Salaries were low, but nobody seemed to care. A reporter who showed any sign of opulence was a sort of marvel, and got under suspicion. The theory was that journalism was an art, and that to artists money was somehow offensive.

Now all that is past. A good reporter used to make as much as a bartender or a police sergeant; he now makes as much as the average doctor or lawyer, and probably a great deal more. His view of the world he lives in has thus changed. He is no longer a free lance in human society, thumbing his nose at its dignitaries; he has got a secure lodgment in a definite stratum, and his wife, if he has one, maybe has social ambitions. The highest sordid aspiration that any reporter had, in my time, was to own two complete suits of clothes. Today they have dinner coats, and some of them even own plug hats.

This general poverty, I suspect, bore down harshly upon some of my contemporaries, especially the older ones, but as for me, I never felt it as oppressive, for no one was dependent on me, and I could always make extra money by writing bad fiction and worse verse. I had enough in Summer to take a holiday. In Winter, concerts and the theaters were free to me. Did I dine in a restaurant? Then I knew very well that opinion in the craft frowned upon any bill beyond 50 cents. I remember clearly, and with a shudder still, how Frank Kent once proposed to me that we debauch ourselves at a place where the dinner was $1. I succumbed, but with an evil conscience. And Frank, too, looked over his shoulder when we sneaked in.

The charm of the life, in those remote days, lay in the reporter's freedom. Today he is at the end of a telephone wire, and his city editor can reach him and annoy him in ten minutes. There were very few telephones in 1899, and it was seldom that even the few were used. When a reporter was sent out on a story, the whole operation was in his hand. He was expected to get it without waiting for further orders. If he did so, he was rewarded with what, in newspaper offices, passed for applause. If he failed, he stood convicted of incompetence or worse. There was no passing of the buck. Every man faced a clear and undivided responsibility.

That responsibility was not oppressive to an active young man; it was flattering to him. He felt himself a part of important events, with no string tied to him. Through his eyes thousands of people would see what was happening in this most surprising and fascinating of worlds. If he made a good job of it, the fact would be noticed by the elders he respected. If he fell down, then those same elders would not hesitate to mark the fact profanely. In either case, he was almost completely his own man. There was no rewrite-man at the other end of a telephone wire to corrupt his facts and spoil his fine ideas. Until he got back with his story there was no city editor's roar in his ear, and even after he had got back that roar tended to be discreetly faint until he had got his noble observations on paper. There was, of course, such a thing then as rattling a reporter, but it was viewed as evil. Today the problem is to derattle him.

I believe that a young journalist, turned loose in a large city, had more fun a quarter of a century ago than any other man. The Mauve Decade was just ending, and the new era of standardization and efficiency had not come in. Here in Baltimore life was unutterably charming. The town was still a series of detached neighborhoods, many of them ancient and with lives all their own. Marsh Market was as distinct an entity as Cairo or Samarkand. The water-front was immensely romantic. The whole downtown region was full of sinister alleys, and in every alley there were mysterious saloons. One went out with the cops to fires, murders and burglaries, riding in their clumsy wagon. Any reporter under twenty-five, if not too far gone in liquor, could overtake the fire-horses.

I do not recall that crime was common in Baltimore in those days, but certainly the town was not as mercilessly policed as it is today. Now the cops are instantly alert to every departure, however slight, from the Y.M.C.A.'s principles of decorum, but in that era they were very tolerant to eccentricity. The dance-halls that then flourished in the regions along the harbor would shock them to death today, and they'd be horrified by some of the old-time saloons. In such places rough-houses were common, and where a rough-house began the cops flocked, and where the cops flocked young reporters followed. It was, to any youngster with humor in him, a constant picnic. Odd fish were washed up by the hundred. Strange marvels unrolled continuously. And out of marvels copy was made, for the newspapers were not yet crowded with comic strips and sporting pages. What was on the police blotter was only the half of it. The energetic young reporter was supposed to go out and see for himself. In particular, he was supposed to see what the older and duller men failed to see. If it was news, well and good. But if it was not news, then it was better than news.

The charm of journalism, to many of its practitioners, lies in the contacts it gives them with the powerful and eminent. They enjoy communion with men of wealth, high officers of state, and other such magnificoes. The delights of that privilege are surely not to be cried down, but it seems to me that I got a great deal more fun, in my days on the street, out of the lesser personages who made up the gaudy life of the city. A mayor was thrilling once or twice, but after that he tended to become a stuffed shirt, speaking platitudes out of a tin throat. But a bartender was different every day, and so was a police sergeant, and so were the young doctors at the hospital, and so were the catchpolls in the courts, and so were the poor wretches who passed before the brass rail in the police station.

There was no affectation about these lesser players in the endless melodrama. They were not out to make impressions, even upon newspaper reporters; their aim, in the phrase of Greenwich Village, was to lead their own lives. I recall some astounding manifestations of that yearning. There was the lady who celebrated her one hundredth arrest for drunkenness by stripping off all her clothes and throwing them at the police lieutenant booking her. There was the policeman who, on a bet, ate fifty fried hard crabs. There was the morgue-keeper who locked himself in his morgue, drunk and howling, and had to be clawed out by firemen. There was the detective who spent his Sundays exhorting in Methodist churches. There was the Irish lad who lived by smuggling bottles of beer to prisoners in the old Central Police Station. There was the saloonkeeper who so greatly venerated journalists that he set them a favored rate of three drinks for the price of two. Above all, there was the pervasive rowdiness and bawdiness of the town—the general air of devil-may-care freedom—the infinite oddity and extravagance of its daily, and especially nightly life.

It passed with the fire of 1904. I was a city editor by that time and the show had begun to lose its savor. But I was still sufficiently interested in it to mourn the change. The old Baltimore had a saucy and picturesque personality; it was unlike any other American city. The new Baltimore that emerged from the ashes was simply a virtuoso piece of Babbitts. It put in all the modern improvements, especially the bad ones. It acquired civic consciousness. Its cops climbed out of the alleys behind the old gin-mills and began harassing decent people on the main streets. I began to lose interest in active journalism in 1905. Since 1906, save as an occasional sentimental luxury, I have never written a news story or a headline.

ON BREAKING INTO TYPE

According to Vincent Starrett, who should know, my "Ventures into Verse," Baltimore, 1903, is one of the rarest of modern American books. Every now and then I hear of a sale at a fantastic price: the last one, as I recall it, was beyond $150. Such news naturally caresses an author's gills; nevertheless, I find myself somewhat disquieted, for the book, in the main, is dreadful stuff, and any buyer who happens to be a man of taste must needs conclude that he has been rooked, and lay some of the blame for the swindle upon me. In my defense I can only say that I was young when the thing was published and even younger when most of it was written, and that the wisdom which now radiates from me was late in developing. In 1903 I was not a metaphysician, but a newspaper reporter, and in 1895 I was a schoolboy.

Some of the verse in the book goes back to the latter year, and one or two pieces were probably written, at least in first draft, in 1894. I was then torn between two aspirations: one to be a chemist and the other to be a poet. Neither seemed possible of realization, for my father had his heart set upon taking me into his tobacco business, and there was no apparent way of escape. But I kept on playing in my laboratory and writing verse, putting one hope against the other. In 1894, when I was fourteen, I invented a platinum toning solution for photographs, and at once put it into a solemn article. Whether or not I submitted it to the photographic magazines I can't remember: at all events it was not printed. At the same time I began a furious verse-writing, and for a while, like many another ambitious young poet, tried to produce at least one poem a day.

They fell into two classes. Half were experiments in the old French forms that were then so popular, and the rest were imitations of Kipling, then the god of all literate youngsters. I made no effort to sell this stuff, but put it in a drawer, and there most of it still remains. In 1896 the tobacco business gobbled me, and thereafter, for three years, I wrote next to nothing. Chemistry, too, faded into the background: I was in training as a business man, and my father was a diligent and exigent teacher. At the beginning of 1899, when I was eighteen, he died suddenly, and a week later I applied for a job on the old Baltimore *Herald*, now no more. I was put on trial immediately, and in a few months had a regular assignment. I remained with the *Herald* until it suspended publication, in 1906, becoming in succession Sunday editor, city editor, managing editor and editor-in-chief.

During my early days as a reporter, in 1900, my manner of writing news attracted the attention of the late Col. A. B. Cunningham, then chief editor of the *Herald*, and he proposed that I take over a weekly column on the editorial page, and therein disport myself in prose and verse.[1] In that remote day columnists were still rare, and their present imperial honoraria were unheard of. My stipend was $14 a week, and my heavy duties as a somewhat starrish reporter kept on. Naturally enough, it was sometimes hard for me to fill my column, especially after it began to run twice a week instead of once. So I had recourse to my drawer full of schoolboy verse, and a great deal of it got into the *Herald* in 1900 and 1901. It was mainly banal, but so was nearly all the other newspaper verse of that time. Col. Cunningham liked it, and early in 1900 raised my wages to $18.

There was in those days an artist on the *Herald* named John Siegel, a youngster of my own age. Not infrequently he illustrated my column, and so we became good friends. In 1902, when I was made Sunday editor, we were thrown together constantly. Another artist on the staff was Charles S. Gordon, and he too became one of my intimates. A third young man who hung about the place was Jim Beek, who knew something about advertising and engraving, and he in turn had a friend named Marshall, a printer. The five of us—Siegel, Gordon, Beek, Marshall and I—met often, both at the *Herald* office and in the adjacent saloons. We were all young and full of schemes. Siegel was preparing to go to Paris to study painting. Gordon chafed at his routine duties on the *Herald*. Beek and Marshall dreamed of owning a printing plant. And I was beginning to harbor literary ambitions, for some of my verse, too pretentious for the *Herald*, had been getting into the magazines, and with it a number of short stories.

One night, while we were drinking beer in a saloon, Marshall said he thought the time was ripe for setting up his printing office. The town printers, he said, were all old-fashioned; they seemed to know nothing about the new typography that was making a stir elsewhere. He had with him some specimens of that new typography, and they made a vast impression on all of us. In half an hour Marshall, Beek and Gordon had formed a partnership, with Marshall told off to do the printing, Beek to fetch the customers, and Gordon to do the art work. Siegel was left out because he was going to Paris, and I because I was neither a printer, a man of business nor an artist.

Within a week a small office was rented, presses and type were put in, and Beek was on the street soliciting trade. At once he found that potential customers wanted to be shown. It was all well enough to tell them that the new style of printing was swell, and to show them specimens of it from New York, England and Germany; what they demanded to see was what the firm of Marshall, Beek and Gordon could do. So it became necessary to print something for their delectation, and that involved finding suitable copy. The three came to me for counsel, and I at once suggested that they do a book of my short stories: I had printed enough in the magazines to make a lovely volume. But there were obvious objections to that. The first was that short stories were straight copy, and would give Marshall little chance to display his talent for beautiful composition. The second was that such a book as I proposed would run to 250 pages, and would cost more than the new firm had to invest. Moreover, it would take more type than lay in the cases. The thing, obviously, had to be hand-set. It would not do to abandon that lovely Caslon for the poor faces which the linotype then offered.

Someone, as a way out, suggested that a book of verse be substituted for the short stories—a book of no more than 50 pages, elegantly hand-set by Marshall and decorated by Siegel and Gordon. It seemed a good idea, but I was inclined to balk. Most of my verse, I protested, was poor newspaper stuff; I had written only a few better things for the magazines. But there were plenty of arguments against that. No one read verse, anyhow—and certainly not business men. The thing would not go any further than Baltimore—and Baltimore had already digested and survived my worst. Marshall allowed that he fairly itched to fall upon the composition. The irregular lines would give him a grand chance, and he would produce a masterpiece. Siegel and Gordon promised to do their damnedest. Next morning the project was under way, and within a week the book was set up. I spent two hours confecting the title-page and two more pasting clippings on copy-paper. It was a quick job, and the critical faculty was in abeyance. At twenty-two I was to see my first book! It came out toward the end of April, 1903. I was not twenty-three until the following September.

Unfortunately, it cost more than Marshall had estimated, and when the time came to buy paper the infant firm found itself somewhat embarrassed. Thirty dollars, it appeared, stood between the book and disaster. I supplied the thirty dollars, and took half of the edition as my share. How many copies that ran to I can't recall, but it was certainly not much beyond a hundred.[2] Most of them were bound in brown paper, with labels printed red on white, but a few—probably forty altogether—were bound by Marshall in binder's boards, with red backs and the same labels. Beek distributed the firm's copies among potential customers, and took some orders on the strength of them. Mine I divided into two halves, presenting the first half to friends and sending out the other to reviewers. Perhaps it deserves to be remembered by the historians of critical science in America that every paper which noticed the book at all praised it as good! One of them, I remember, was the New York *Sun,* then the most intelligent newspaper in the land!

How many copies survive I don't know—probably not many. The same one tends to bob up over and over again, bringing a larger price each time. Eight or ten years ago occasional copies were to be encountered in Baltimore, dredged out of lumber-rooms, but then the alert Baltimore dealer, Meredith Janvier, issuing from his lair in picturesque Hamilton Street, made a thorough search of the town, and when he had finished the supply was exhausted. It was about that time that the copies in the public libraries—perhaps five or six in all—were neatly stolen. One day, just as the news began to go about that the book could be sold, I met an old acquaintance on the street in Baltimore and he told me that he had a copy. He asked me if I would be offended if he turned it into cash. I told him no, and urged him to go to Janvier immediately, for the buying price was then $20, and I believed it would shrink to fifty cents, once the cackle over my dreadful verse had died down. Lately this punctilious Baltimorean got news of a sale at $140, and he has been giving me black looks ever since. Obviously, he shares the common belief that an author gains something when his dead books bring high prices. Ah, that it were so! I'd be richer than I am, and maybe chaster. As it is, all I get is the uneasy feeling that many a collector, bled by the current price, consoles himself by roaring over my youthful follies.

Let him console himself also with the assurance that there will never be a second edition.[3] The copyright expires on April 30, 1931. Promptly at high noon of April 30, 1930, I shall make application in due form of law for a renewal for twenty-eight years. And if, before that time, my colloids turn to gas, then my executors will make the application for me.

WALTER ABELL AND THE *SUN*

When I hung up my hat in the *Sun* office on July 30, 1906, the grandsons of Arunah S. Abell, the Founder, were in active control of the paper. They were Walter W. Abell, who died last Monday; Arunah S. Abell II, who died on July 28, 1914; and their cousin, Charles S. Abell, who is now living in Washington. I came to the paper to edit the Sunday edition, which was then but five years old and still more or less vague in contents and aim, and in that capacity I naturally had constant business with the three Abells. They were all young men in that remote era, the oldest, Arunah, being barely past forty.

They differed enormously in character and mien, and especially the two brothers, Walter and Arunah. Arunah, the treasurer of the A. S. Abell Company, was one of the most jovial men I have ever known, and I can't recall ever seeing him in bad humor—not even when he caught an office boy stealing books from the *Sun* library. Charles S., the secretary, seemed almost austere by comparison, but he too was extremely amiable, and he got much closer to the members of the staff than the other two. But Walter, the president, was genuinely on the formal side, and there were not a few *Sun* men, including several of the older ones, who regarded him as unapproachable, and even forbidding.

He was, in fact, nothing of the sort, as I soon found by almost daily palavers with him. What gave him his false appearance of aloofness was simply a sort of boyish shyness—a charming weakness, if weakness it be called, that seems to have been born in him, but got encouragement from the circumstances of his situation. He was in command over men who, in many cases, were much his elders in years and experience, and some of them had been trained under his grandfather. He was thus very diffident about pitting his judgment against theirs, but nevertheless he had to do it constantly, and so there was conflict between his native courtesy, which was marked, and his responsibility as captain of the ship. He solved the problem by concealing his authority beneath a grave reserve, and the impression got about that it was difficult to penetrate.

There was another conflict, too, and that was between his filial devotion to the *Sun* tradition and his intelligent appreciation that when times change traditions must be modified. It was a day of revolution in journalism, largely due to the increasing efficiency of the linotype, and he had before him in Charles H. Grasty, of the *Evening News,* a competitor who became more formidable every day. Mr. Abell never allowed that competition to hurry him, but he was acutely aware of it, and if he met it quietly he also met it boldly. Some of his reforms were so radical that, to the oldsters of the staff, they seemed almost catastrophic, but he put them through resolutely, and it is apparent today, looking back over a generation, that all of them were sound.

In this business he had the eager support of his cousin, who was always for any novelty that was actually improvement, and the ready acquiescence of his brother, who preferred administration to grand strategy, and kept rather to the sidelines. But there was active opposition in other quarters, and not infrequently it impeded the flow of events. Some of the old-timers, bred in hand-set days, were constitutionally unable to go along, and they had the zealous reinforcement of a large body of old subscribers, many of whom held as a cardinal article of faith that the *Sun* of 1887 could never be surpassed on this or any earth, and that any attempt to change it was a sin against the Holy Ghost.

I well remember the uproar when the first large illustrations began to appear in the Sunday edition. It was not illustrations *qua* illustrations that outraged the guardians of tradition, for a few had been printed even in the Founder's time; it was their size. One column—yes, and maybe even two. But four, five, six—God help us all! When, on a fateful Sunday, Mr. Abell gave me *pratique* for one running the full width of the page, and dropping down to half its depth, there was a moan that reverberated throughout the Sun Building, and next morning the president's office was jammed with complainants and objurgators.

But it was not only in the editorial rooms that the old Sunpaper suffered a face-lifting at the hands of that quiet and determined man; in the business office (then called the counting room) there were operations of even more serious nature and import. What Baltimore thought when the paper put its first advertising solicitor on the street should have been taken down in shorthand and embalmed in history, for it was surely aplenty. And when this revolution was followed by the publication of circulation figures (at first, to be sure, only confidentially, and to a select few) the whole town was aghast. It was almost as if the Johns Hopkins University had sent out sandwich-men whooping up courses in meat-cutting and chiropractic.

But Mr. Abell, if he was deliberate, was also sure-footed, and I can recall none of his innovations that turned out, on trial, to be a mistake. Nor were any mistakes made during the administration of his cousin and successor, Charles S. The whole *Sun* organization was renovated from top to bottom, and not only renovated but also reoriented. When these youngsters took the paper in hand at the death of Edwin F. Abell in 1904, just after the great Baltimore fire, it still looked back toward the days of the Founder. When they handed it over to a new management in 1910 it was headed for the future, and well prepared for the notable advances, both in editorial enterprise and in business prosperity, which followed the World War.

Life in the *Sun* office in the era of the Abells was comfortable and leisurely, and I once described the atmosphere as that of a good club. There was a stately courtesy that is uncommon in the dens of journalism, and indeed in any other working place of busy men. All hands save the office boys were mistered by the proprietors, and even by most of their other superiors, and no one was ever upbraided for a dereliction of duty, however inconvenient. The worst a culprit ever encountered was a mild expostulation, usually couched in very general terms.

I recall with blushes a day when my own carelessness admitted to the *Sunday Sun* an unhappy sentence which made the issue a collector's item in the barrooms of Baltimore the next day, with the price approaching $1. When I got to the office Monday morning a note was on my desk, saying that Walter Abell wanted to see me. There was no defense imaginable, so I entered his office as jauntily as possible, saying "I am not here for trial, but for sentence." But there was no sentence, nor even any trial. Mr. Abell, in fact, referred to the matter in hand only obliquely, and with great politeness. All his talk was about the paramount necessity, on a paper as ancient and honorable as the *Sun*, for the utmost care in copy-reading. He discoursed on that theme at length, but always in broad philosophical terms. Finding his argument unanswerable, I offered no caveat, and withdrew quietly at the first chance.

Not many of the old-timers are left. O. P. Baldwin, the managing editor when I came to the office, is gone, and so are all his editorial writers. Of the repertorial staff, only four remain. The city editor, the telegraph editor, the State editor and all the straw-bosses under them are departed. But the corps of poets, consisting of one man in 1906, still consists of the same man, to wit, the Bentztown Bard, and he remains as unchanged as Mont Blanc. When he joined the staff, a month before my own advent, I printed an editorial in the *Evening Herald* congratulating the *Sun* on hiring him. "Hire a poet!" replied Baldwin in the *Sun* the next day. "Perish the expression! *Poeta nascitur,*[4] not hired. You might as well talk of hiring a zephyr."

TWENTY-FIVE YEARS OF THE *EVENING SUN*

It would be natural, I suppose, to say that the day when the *Evening Sun* was hatched seems only yesterday, but if I were on oath it would certainly be perjury, or something else of like wickedness and the same name. The truth is that, as I look back upon the birthday of this great moral organ, it appears infinitely remote in time, and very vague in outline. I simply can't remember what happened; it was a day like any other. We got out the first issue without any of the pangs and dubieties that seem to be proper on such occasions. We knew in advance that it was going to be bad, and it *was* bad, so we put it out of our minds as quickly as possible. Later on, I am glad to add, the paper improved.

I became a member of the staff by a sort of accident, and never had any recognized office or title. I had come to the Sunpaper in 1906 when the old *Evening Herald,* of which I was editor, succumbed, and for three years I enjoyed the placid and lordly life of a *Sun* man under the Abell régime. There was never on this earth a more pleasant newspaper office. It was full of charming fellows, and the Abells carried it on as if it were a good club rather than a great industrial plant. I began as Sunday editor, but by 1910 I was writing editorials.[5]

Then came Charles H. Grasty, an apparition from a strange planet. I knew him, but had reason for believing that he didn't like me, so I prepared to shuffle on. But he sent me word that he had no intention of canning me, whereupon I consented coyly to stay, and in a little while we were very friendly. It wasn't long before he began to make plans for an evening edition. Inasmuch as I was one of the few men in the editorial rooms who had had any experience on an evening paper, I was naturally taken into his councils, and when the paper came out at last, on April 18, 1910, I found myself a sort of first mate to J. H. Adams, the editor.

My duties, at the start, were rather complicated. I was supposed to be at my desk at 8 o'clock every morning, and to write two editorials before 11 o'clock.[6] In addition, I had to read all the letters received from correspondents, and to translate into English those that seemed suitable for the *Evening Sun* Forum. If any nuts came in with proposals for new laws or unearthly schemes to beat Taft in 1912, I usually had to listen to them for Adams was busy in his cage, damning the telephone and trying to write his own leaders. If he was still busy at 11.30 I made up the editorial page for him. Then to the Rennert for lunch.

Of an afternoon I devoted myself to a long signed article for the next day. It was printed in the column next to the editorials, and was set in such crowded type that it consumed a great many words. When I undertook this job it seemed easy enough, for I was busting with ideas in those days, and eager to work them off. But in a little while I found that writing 2,000 or 3,000 words a day was really a killing chore, and one day I remember especially, when sitting at the typewriter became suddenly unendurable, and I turned to pen and ink for relief.

When Adams found me using such paleozoic implements he was horrified and, with his usual decency, let me off some of the editorial writing. But soon after that his health began to be indifferent, and he was sometimes disabled, and at such times I had to do a double stint. I don't remember ever having a disagreement with him, though the only thing we had in common, politically speaking, was our belief in the Bill of Rights. But rows are very rare in newspaper offices. Men of all sorts of ideas somehow manage to get along together.

One rather curious incident of our association I recall. At the end of a busy afternoon Adams called me into his office and asked me to find out what I could about airships. "It looks to me," he said, "as if they were actually coming in, and we ought to have somebody in the place who knows something about them. You are a graduate of the Polytechnic, and should be able to find out how they work." I agreed to do it, but had to report my failure a few weeks later.[7] To this day my knowledge of airships is precisely nil. I never see one in the air without expecting it to fall.

How long my job lasted I don't remember exactly, but it wasn't very long. By the end of 1910 I was transferred to the last column of the editorial page, and turned loose upon the town under the style and appellation of The Free Lance, and there I performed daily for five years, with only two intervals out for brief trips abroad. This work was a lot of fun, but it brought me so many visitors and so much mail that editorial writing on the side became impossible, and I have never done any since.

I apologize for talking so much more about myself than about the *Evening Sun*. My share in it, in fact, has always been small, and since its first days I have given a good part of my time to other enterprises. But a newspaper man always thinks of his paper in terms of his own job, and that must be my excuse. Some of these days, I hope, the history of this one will be told in more or less detail.

It will be a story of a hard and long fight against depressing odds, carried on with magnificent devotion by a gang of strictly non-messianic and very amusing fellows, and ending in an extraordinary success.

The changes that have come over American journalism during the twenty-five years of the *Evening Sun* have been marked and many, and nearly all of them, it seems to me, have been for the good. There are old-timers who pine for the days when every considerable American city had eight or ten newspapers, but I am not one of them. The truth is that the majority of those newspapers were shabby rags that printed very little news, and fell far below the chastity proper to Cæsar's wife. They overworked and underpaid their men, and were constantly blowing up. That their treadmills produced some extremely competent journalists is a fact, but it is also a fact that they polluted the craft with a great many shady quacks.

In my early days, I confess, some of these quacks enchanted me, for the romance of journalism—and to a youngster, in that era, it surely was romantic—had me by the ear, and the quacks themselves, in many cases, were picturesque characters, and not without a certain cadaverous glow. But chance threw me, when I was still in my early twenties, into the post of city editor, and as such I had to get out a paper with their aid. The experience convinced me that the newspaper business was in need of a wholesale disinfection, and I am glad to be able to say that it came anon, and has left apparently permanent good effects.

The improvement in newspapers has been general, and very great. Their machinery for gathering news is enormously better than it was when I was a young recruit. More news now comes into the Sunpaper office every night than came into it in two weeks back in 1900, and that news is better written and more accurate. It is almost impossible today for an event of any significance to be missed, but in my nonage it happened every day. The New York *Sun* was, in many ways, the best of the American papers a generation ago, but it had only the most meager news service, and at the time of the San Francisco earthquake, in 1906, it came out with nothing save a few brief bulletins and a fine obituary of the town by Will Irwin, written in the office.

Newspapers are a great deal more honest than they used to be, and a great deal more intelligent. Some of the Stone Age editorial writers survive in legend as masters of prose and publicists of the first chop, but the truth is that most of them were only third-rate rhetoricians itching for public office. Nothing that any of them wrote, on public questions, whether in their papers or elsewhere, is worth reading today, or is remembered by anyone. Even the prose of William Cullen Bryant, perhaps the most respectable of them, is as deadly and as dead as that of Donald G. Mitchell or Edmund Clarence Stedman.

The improvement in newspapers I ascribe mainly to the increased cost of operating them. When a new one could be set up by any adventurer with a hand press and a few cases of type, the trade naturally attracted a great many dubious persons, and their competition kept even the best papers on a low level. But the invention of the linotype made large capital investments necessary, and in a little while the weaker and more vulnerable sheets begin to disappear. Those papers that survive today, whatever their faults otherwise, are at least safely solvent, and they show the virtues that always go with solvency, that is to say, they are not purchasable, they spend money freely in discharging their public responsibilities, they stand aloof from the corruptions of party politics, and they are able to attract to their service a well-educated and self-respecting corps of men. Here, as in so many other fields, capitalism shames the mountebanks who deride it.

A WORD ABOUT THE *SMART SET*

George Jean Nathan and I took over the editorial direction of the *Smart Set* in the Summer of 1914, just after the outbreak of the late war. I had been doing my monthly book article since November, 1908, and Nathan had been doing his article about the theaters since a month or two later. It never occurred to me, in those years, that I should ever assume a larger share of editorial responsibility for the magazine. John Adams Thayer, then the publisher and majority stock-holder, had offered me the editorship several times, but I had always refused it for a single and simple reason: I didn't want to live in New York, which seemed to me then and seems to me now a most uncomfortable city. My home was and is in Baltimore, which I like much better.

But in the Summer of 1914 that impediment was removed. Thayer disposed of the magazine to Eltinge F. Warner, publisher of The Warner Publications, and his associates. Some time before this, by one of the trivial accidents of life, Warner had met Nathan on a ship bound home from England; the two happened to be wearing overcoats of the same kind, and stopped to gabble idly, as fellow passengers will, on deck one morning. They had a few drinks together, parted at the dock and never thought to meet again. But when Warner looked into the magazine that he was to manage, he found the name of Nathan on the list of regular contributors, and, recalling their brief meeting, sought him out and asked him to take the editorship. Nathan said that he would do it if I agreed to help him. There ensued negotiations, and the upshot was an arrangement that is still in force.

Our authority as editors is exactly equal; nevertheless, we are never in conflict. I read all manuscripts that are sent to us, and send Nathan those that I think are fit to print. If he agrees, they go into type at once; if he dissents, they are rejected forthwith. This veto is absolute, and works both ways. It saves us a great many useless and possibly acrimonious discussions. It takes two yeses to get a poem or essay or story into the magazine, but one no is sufficient to keep it out. In practice, we do not disagree sharply more than once in a hundred times, and even then, as I say, the debate is over as soon as it begins. I doubt that this scheme has ever lost us a manuscript genuinely worth printing. It admits prejudices into the matter, but they are at least the prejudices of the responsible editors, and not those of subordinate manuscript readers. We employ no readers, and take no advice. Every piece of manuscript that comes into the office passes through my hands, or those of Nathan, and usually through the hands of both of us. I live in Baltimore, but come to New York every other week.

So much for editorial management. Our financial organization is equally simple. Warner made over some of the capital stock of the magazine to Nathan and me, and we three continue in joint control today. Warner's problem, when we took charge, was to pay off the somewhat heavy floating debt of the property, and put it on a sound basis. This he accomplished before the end of 1915. From the moment he came into the office the *Smart Set* has paid all authors immediately on the acceptance of their manuscripts, paid all printers' and paper bills promptly—and absorbed not a cent of new capital. Warner operates all of his enterprises in that manner. We trust his judgment in all business matters, as he trusts ours in editorial matters. The usual conflict between the editorial room and the business office is never heard of here.

[II]

An impression seems to be abroad that the *Smart Set,* selling at 35 cents, makes an enormous profit, and that Warner, Nathan and I have got rich running it. This is not true. Warner is a man of many enterprises and has made a great deal of money, and Nathan and I are both able to exist comfortably without looking to the magazine. Had we been inclined, we might have turned it into a very productive money-maker. This is not merely tall-talk; we actually did the thing with three other magazines.[8] But from the start we viewed the *Smart Set* as, in some sense, a luxury rather than a means of profit, and this view of it has always conditioned our management of it. We have never made any effort to attract readers in large numbers; we have always sought to print, not the most popular stuff we could find, but the best stuff. And we have never made any effort to load the magazine with advertising: it prints less than any other magazine of its class. This desire to be free—to run the thing to suit ourselves without regard to either popular taste or the prejudices of advertisers—has cost us much revenue, and the fact has not only deprived us of good profits, but also made it impossible for us to compete with the more popular magazines in bidding for manuscripts. But we have never regretted our policy. The authors who expect and demand enormous prices for their wares—the Carusos and Babe Ruths of letters—are but seldom the sort of authors we are interested in. It has been our endeavor, not to startle the booboisie with such gaudy stars, but to maintain a hospitable welcome for the talented newcomer—to give him his first chance in good company, and to pay him, if not the wages of a moving-picture actor, then at least enough to reward him decently for his labor. We believe that this scheme has cost us very few manuscripts worth printing. We have not only brought out by it more novices of first-rate ability than any other American magazine; we have also had the pleasure of printing some of the best work of contemporary American authors of assured position, including Dreiser, Cabell, Sherwood Anderson and Miss Cather. Such authors, we believe, regard the atmosphere of the *Smart Set* as different form that of the commercial magazines.

But our purpose, of course, has not been altruistic. We are surely not uplifters, either as critics or as editors. We have run our magazine as we have written our books—primarily to please ourselves, and secondarily to entertain those Americans who happen, in general, to be of our minds. We differ radically in many ways. For example, Nathan is greatly amused by the theater, even when it is bad, whereas I regard it as a bore, even when it is good. Contrariwise, I am much interested in politics, whereas Nathan scarcely knows who is Vice-President of the United States. But on certain fundamentals we are thoroughly agreed, and it is on the plane of these fundamentals that we conduct the *Smart Set,* and try to interest a small minority of Americans. Both of us are against the sentimental, the obvious, the trite, the maudlin. Both of us are opposed to all such ideas as come from the mob, and are polluted by its stupidity: Puritanism, Prohibition, Comstockery, evangelical Christianity, tin-pot patriotism, the whole sham of democracy. Both of us, though against socialism and in favor of capitalism, believe that capitalism in the United States is ignorant, disreputable and degraded, and that its heroes are bounders. Both of us believe in the dignity of the fine arts, and regard Beethoven and Brahms as far greater men than Wilson and Harding. Both of us stand aloof from the childish nationalism that now afflicts the world, and regard all of its chief spokesmen, in all countries, as scoundrels.

We believe that there are enough other Americans of our general trend of mind to give a reasonable support to a magazine voicing such notions. We believe that such men and women have the tolerance that is never encountered in the nether majority—that they like a certain amount of free experimentation in the arts. We thus try to assemble for them the novelties that seem to us to be genuinely worth while—not the tawdry monkey-shines of Greenwich Village, but the new work of the writers who actually know how to write. Thus we printed the plays of Eugene O'Neill when he was still an unknown newcomer, and the strange, sardonic short stories of Ben Hecht before ever he started to write "Erik Dorn," and the sketches of Lord Dunsany before his vogue began. As I say, we do not pursue neologism for its own sake: the *Smart Set* avoided all the extravagances of the free verse movement, as it is now avoiding the extravagances of such foreign crazes as Expressionismus and Dadaism. We try to entertain the reader who can distinguish between genuine ideas and mere blather. It is for this reason, perhaps, that our poetry, to some readers—and especially to many of the new poets—seems excessively conservative. But here conservatism, we believe, has served a good purpose, for we have certainly printed as much sound poetry, during the past seven or eight years, as any of the magazines devoted to *vers libre,* and a great deal more than most. Practically all the genuine poets of the country have been in the magazine during that time, and most of them have been in it very often.

[III]

Needless to say, what we print does not always correspond exactly with what we'd like to print. We buy the best stuff that we can find, and that is within our means—and sometimes the supply of such stuff is distressingly short. There have been months when we felt that only a small portion of the contents of the magazine was really fit to set before the readers we have in mind—when the larger part of those contents, read in manuscript and proof, filled us with depression. In particular, we have often found it difficult to obtain suitable novelettes.[9] The ordinary novelettes of commerce are fearful things, indeed; once or twice, failing to discover anything better, we have had to print one. Invariably there came protests from many readers—a thing that pleased us, despite our distress, for it showed clearly that we were reaching a public that was not content with the average magazine fare. But in the face of this chronic scarcity we have printed many novelettes of quite extraordinary merit, including W. Somerset Maugham's "Miss Thompson," Miss Willa Cather's "Coming, Eden Bower!" Thyra Samter Winslow's "Cycle of Manhattan,"[10] and several capital pieces by other writers. Essays have also given us much concern. Practically all of the essayists who flourish in the United States devote themselves to whimsical fluff in imitation of Charles Lamb—stuff that is poor in ideas and conventional in execution. We have tried hard to find and encourage writers with more to say, but so far without much success. However, even in this bleak field we have unearthed an occasional piece of sound quality—for example, Stephen Ta Van's "Tante Manhattan" and Thomas Beer's "The Rural Soul" and "The Mauve Decade"[11]—and we have hopes of doing much better hereafter. In the field of the short story we believe that we have presented a great deal of genuinely first-rate work. The stories we print are not reprinted in the annual anthologies issued by admirers of the late O. Henry, but in a good many cases the authors of them—for example, Mr. Hecht, Sherwood Anderson and F. Scott Fitzgerald—have later shown their quality by brilliant successes in the larger form of the novel. Our own contributions to the magazine I need not discuss: opinion about them seems to be very sharply divided. But I have reason to believe that they are read rather widely, both when they are serious and when they are not serious, and I know that, when reprinted in books, they have sold far better than such books usually sell, and got a great deal more notice, both at home and abroad. Of my own books since 1914, all those save "The American Language" have consisted in large part of matter reworked from articles first printed in the *Smart Set*. So with all of Nathan's books.

I have mentioned the difficulty of filling the magazine each month with stuff that is wholly up to the mark we try to set; we print what we can get, but we can't print it until it is written. Various other handicaps have beset us, and still beset us. One lies in the fact that we are determined to make the magazine pay its own way—that we are convinced that a subsidized magazine, conducted at a loss, is unsound in principle, and very apt to be led astray by all the current æsthetic crazes, to the dismay of the sort of readers we try to reach. This policy, during the days of the wartime and post-bellum paper famine, reduced us to printing on a paper that was frankly atrocious. It was too thick and rough, it would not take the ink cleanly, and its stiffness made the magazine hard to open. Hundreds of readers denounced us for using it, and with justice. We abandoned it as soon as possible, and have since improved the quality of our paper steadily, as the market price has fallen. I am also inclined to think that for a while we neglected our covers, and that many readers found them out of harmony with the general contents of the magazine. If so, the matter has been remedied, and will be further remedied hereafter. But the worst of all our handicaps lies in the name of the magazine. A great many persons, unfamiliar with its contents, assume that it is a society paper, or that it is chiefly devoted to tales of high life. Unluckily, changing the name is not a simple matter. We inherited a bond issue with the property, and by the terms of the mortgage no change may be made without the consent of the bondholders—and inasmuch as they are scattered and view all such radical innovations with distrust, that consent is not easy to obtain. The matter is further complicated by the fact that there is an English Smart Set Company, reprinting most of the contents of the magazine under the same name in England. Our contract with that company is of such character that a change in the name of the magazine would cause serious difficulties, and perhaps subject us to great loss. So we have to continue the *Smart Set* on the flagstaff, though both Nathan and I believe that the name loses us many readers who might otherwise buy the magazine. At some time or other in the future we may solve the problem.

Finally, there is the fact that, in the days before we acquired editorial control, the *Smart Set* passed through the hands of many editors,[12] some of them sharply at odds with the others on questions of general policy, and that the resultant aberrations alienated a good many readers. There was a time when the magazine ran to "daring" stuff, often of a highly sexual and sophomoric character. That was before our day, and the experiment was soon abandoned, but there are many old readers, scared off then, who still believe that the magazine is full of *risqué* stories. This, of course, is not true. We do not aim to astonish sucklings; the readers we address are assumed to be of adult growth, and hence capable of bearing occasional plain-speaking without damage. But neither do we devote ourself to providing diversion for the dirty old men of the vice societies. One more misunderstanding remains. The *Smart Set* is often spoken of as a fiction magazine, and there are persons who seem to think that it prints nothing else. This was true years ago, but it is certainly not true now. In our average number fully half of the contents is not fiction. Very soon we hope to make that proportion even larger.

[IV]

Now for the lesson of the day. Most of our circulation, at the moment, is what is called news-stand circulation. That is to say, it tends to be irregular. A reader buys the magazine for three or four months running at some news-stand he passes now and then, and perhaps likes it enough to look forward to each new number. But soon or late he finds that his dealer has sold out—or he looks for it at some stand that doesn't keep it. Then, for a few months, he drops out. Meanwhile, the dealer of whom he has inquired for it has ordered some extra copies, or begun to stock it. The result is easily seen. There are 60,000 news-stands in the United States. Some of them, of course, carry only the cheap magazines, but perhaps 20,000 of them have a sufficiently civilized clientele to stock such publications as the *Smart Set*. To cover all of them on this hit-or-miss plan subjects us to inevitable heavy losses—for we must take back copies that are unsold. In consequence, our printing and paper costs are a good deal larger than they ought to be, and we have that much less to spend upon the contents of the magazine.

The conversion of a substantial part of our news-stand circulation into subscriptions would lead us into easier waters. Not only would our readers get a better magazine, but they would get it regularly and surely, with no need to look for it at the corner stand, and no chance of not finding it. Finally, they would save something every year—not much, but something. I thus make the suggestion that you who read this send in your subscription on the blank herewith. I assume that you already know the magazine—that you have read at least a few numbers, and found them not altogether stupid. If you like my own writings you will find them regularly in the *Smart Set*—and seldom anywhere else. So far as I know, there is no other American magazine that is trying to do precisely what we are trying to do. We offer every year, at a total cost of $4, 1728 pages of the best stuff we can write or find. This is the cost of two ordinary novels. We believe that you will go far before you find two novels that are more amusing.

FOREWORD TO *A BIBLIOGRAPHY OF THE WRITINGS OF H. L. MENCKEN*

An air of finality always hangs about a bibliography. To me, the author dealt with, it hangs especially about this one, for I have a feeling that most of the books listed are of a sort that I shall not write again—that whatever I do hereafter, if I do anything at all, will differ materially from what has gone before. It is not that I have changed my fundamental ideas; it is simply that my interests have changed. In other words, it is simply that I have passed into the middle forties, and am no longer the artless youth that I once was. That youth was chiefly interested in the gaudy spectacle of human life in this world, *i.e.*, in the superficial effects of ideas. The somewhat oxidized fellow who now confronts you is chiefly interested in the immemorial instincts and emotions that lie under them. So this is a good time, perhaps, to draw a line and take stock. I certainly hope that the show is not over, but there is, I suspect, a climax and a new beginning.[13]

As I ponder somewhat gloomily the books here listed the thing that most arrests me is the accidental origin and character of most of them. Scarcely one of them was deliberately planned. My early volume of dreadful verse got itself into type simply because two young fellows that I knew were setting up a printing-office and wanted a manuscript to exercise their art upon. They came to me for suggestions, and I naturally suggested a book of my own compositions. They preferred verse to prose, and so verse it was.

Two years later, when Brentano began printing Shaw in America, I was greatly delighted by the format he gave to "The Quintessence of Ibsenism," and decided forthwith to write a book on Shaw himself in the same form. But Brentano rejected it, and so it fell into the hands of H. H. Schaff, then an active publisher in Boston, and he published it. Schaff then suggested a similar work on Nietzsche: the result was "The Philosophy of Friedrich Nietzsche."

"The Artist," first published as a separate book in 1912, was written in response to a request for copy from Theodore Dreiser, then editor of the *Bohemian Magazine*. That was in 1909. "A Little Book in C Major" and "A Book of Burlesques" were by-products of my early work for the *Smart Set*. "Damn" and "In Defense of Women" were put together at the suggestion of Philip Goodman, now a theatrical producer but in 1918 a beginning publisher.

"The American Language" grew out of a satirical article on American grammar, written for the Baltimore *Evening Sun* in 1910 or thereabout:[14] it brought in so many letters from readers that I was presently engrossed in the subject, and began to study the history of the English language and to acquire a vast and disorderly stock of other philological learning, most of it useless.

"A Book of Prefaces" was done for A. A. Knopf, and at his request, when he set up business as a publisher. The whole series of "Prejudices" books was suggested by Richard Laukhuff, the Cleveland book seller. He told Knopf that he believed that an occasional volume of my magazine essays would have a satisfactory sale, and Knopf agreed with him. I was full of doubts myself, but it turned out that Laukhuff was right, and the "Prejudices" books are still coming out every two years.

"Men vs. The Man" was suggested by my collaborator, La Monte, and he arranged for the publication of the book by Henry Holt. "Europe After 8.15" was suggested and managed by Wright. "The American Credo" was Nathan's idea, not mine; I did only the preface. "The Player's Ibsen" and "The Gist of Nietzsche" were suggested by Schaff, and the "Free Lance Series" by Knopf.[15]

"Heliogabalus," I believe, is the only book I ever wrote deliberately, and of that I wrote only part. One afternoon Nathan and I were sitting in his apartment at the Royalton, in Forty-fourth Street, New York, and fell into a discussion of playwriting. We came to the conclusion that writing a play was a much smaller job than writing a book, and decided to write one to prove it. I contended that a so-called plot was unnecessary; that all that was needed was an amusing character. "Very well," said Nathan, "but where is your character?" I had just been re-reading Edgar Saltus' "Imperial Purple," and Heliogabalus came to mind. We then went to Rogers', in Sixth Avenue, for dinner. By the time we got it down "Heliogabalus" was planned, and six weeks later it was finished. I still believe somehow that, as plays go, it is not a bad one. Writing it turned out to be absurdly easy—in fact, a sort of holiday from criticism. I ceased to respect dramatists from that time. Their work, I am convinced, is child's play.

But the several books I now have in mind, to be done, God willing, during the next five or six years, will not be child's play, at all events to me. They have been rolling around in my mind for a long while, and they will harass me painfully until I get them on paper. One will be—but this is not an advance notice. I bespeak the prayers of the faithful.

FIVE YEARS OF THE *AMERICAN MERCURY*

With this issue the *American Mercury* completes its fifth year. Its friends, no doubt, will be glad to hear that it comes to this interesting age in the best of health, and with every hope of afflicting the right-thinking for a long while to come. It has paid off every cent of the capital invested in it, it has no debts, and it is showing a profit—not large, but still safe, steady and sufficient. Its circulation has now gone beyond that of any save a few magazines of its class, and its readers show a charming disposition to stick to it, so that the turnover is small. That portion of its circulation which is represented by annual subscribers continues to grow, both absolutely and in relation to the total monthly sale. Its advertisers, having discovered by experience that it reaches a class of readers who want things of merit and are able to buy them, patronize it faithfully, and many of them increase their bookings of space. In brief, the position of the magazine is sound and satisfactory. It does not presume to rival *True Stories*[16] or *The Saturday Evening Post*, but within its own field it is well fortified, and the hopes of those volunteer morticians who have so often announced or pre-dicted its failure seem doomed to disappointment. Several flattering but naïve imitations of it have appeared, and it has obviously influenced the format and contents of more than one of its elders, but so far there is no sign that its readers fail to distinguish between the simon pure article and the second best.

The basic programme of the magazine continues to be as it was at the start. Its appeal is not to the great mass of Americans, but to the minority which stands clear of the prevailing national superstitions. It has no desire to organize the members of that minority in any way, either as to ideas or as to acts; it simply aims to give them accurate and realistic news of what is going on in the country, with as much good humor as possible, and to entertain them pleasantly with competent writing. Because of the fact that many of the men and ideas it has brought to autopsy enjoy the protection, in the general press of the nation, of somewhat formidable taboos, the impression has gained some ground that it is engaged in a lofty campaign of iconoclasm, or, as the barbaric phrase now goes, debunkification. In this there is a considerable inaccuracy. The *American Mercury* is not dedicated to reforming the United States or to saving the human race. It believes, indeed, that most reformers are frauds, and it has given over a great deal of its space to setting forth the evidence against this or that one. But it holds that even reformers have human juices in them, and so it has tried to exhibit their fraudulence, and that of the other varieties of quacks, without indignation, and above all without any bawling for the police.

In this benign work it has covered a considerable range, and tried to proceed with a reasonable impartiality. The chiropractors and the Socialists, the Holy Rollers and the homeopaths, the pacifists and the spiritualists have all taken their turns upon its operating table. It has exhibited, mainly in their own words, the dreams and imbecilities of the prophets of high-powered salesmanship, vocational guidance, osteopathy, comstockery and pedagogy. It has brought to notice, in the chaste, dispassionate manner of the clinic, the hallucinations of Rotary, the Gideons, the D. A. R., the American Legion, the League of American Penwomen, the Methodist Board of Temperance, Prohibition and Public Morals and a multitude of other such klans and sodalities, many of them highly influential and all of them amusing.

Its theory is that quacks give good shows, and offer salubrious instruction, if only in the immemorial childishness of mankind. Nor are all of them clad in obvious motley. They exist within the circle of the American Medical Association as well as under rustic flambeaux, and in the great universities as well as beneath the banners of Communism, Kiwanis and the New Thought. To these austerely respectable quacks, in particular, loving attention has been given.

Naturally enough, there have been outbursts of rage against this free-and-easy flouting of idealists, and sometimes that rage has gone to the extent of reprisals. The wowsers of Boston, offended by certain animadversions upon their chicaneries, tried to bar the magazine from that great city, and when their effort failed sought the reinforcement of the Postoffice Department, with its crew of pious Coolidge men.[17] But the magazine continues to circulate in Boston, and to go through the mails.

The Methodist brethren, characteristically, have turned for revenge to lying: their various *Christian Advocates* lately announced that the magazine was on the rocks and for sale. But it continues to be printed and to prosper. Rotary and Kiwanis began by hinting broadly that it was backed by Russian gold, but of late their orators have invented the doctrine that what they call its "attacks" are sanitary and hence to be welcomed—that the effect of "Americana"[18] will be to purge all the tin-pot luncheon-clubs of folly and false pretenses, and so make them bigger and better.

This last is an unkind cut, but the *American Mercury* will survive. It surely has no desire to improve Rotary. The lily is gilt enough. All it asks is that the brothers do as well hereafter as they have done in the past.

[II]

But this business of setting forth pleasantly the aims and achievements of the national zanies, æsthetic, commercial, patriotic, political, scientific, military, theological and philosophical—this business, after all, has been one of the least of the magazine's concerns. It has given a great deal more space to something quite different, namely, to introducing one kind of American to another. It has ranged the country for interesting men and women, and it has let them, when they were articulate, tell their own stories. Not many of them have been persons of any prominence and very few of them have had any previous experience as writers. They have run the whole scale from visionaries to criminals, from heroes to poor fish. But all of them, writing out of their own lives, have written with that earnest simplicity which is beyond all art, and some of their papers have been among the most interesting and moving things the magazine has printed.

The case of Mr. James Stevens is in point. His first contribution dealt with his adventures and observations as a lumberman in the Northwest. He was working at the time in a lumber-mill, and there was a sharp reality in his story that no professional writer save the most adept could have hoped to match. The response of readers was immediate, and he was encouraged to try his hand further. Presently he was retelling the legends of Paul Bunyan, the fabulous hero of the Western lumberman, and those legends, a bit later, made a book. It was a substantial success, and since then he has written other books and shown marked and rapid progress as a writer. But when he made his first appearance in the *American Mercury* it was as a workman in a lumber-mill.

The magazine, since its beginning, has steadily sought out such unspoiled and amusing men, and has not hesitated to employ spies to track them down. Several of its most interesting contributors have been gentlemen suffering imprisonment for lamentable crimes. One of them, Mr. Ernest Booth, is serving a life sentence. His first article, "We Rob a Bank,"[19] was a fascinating and brilliant piece of self-revelation. More effectively than a hundred somber tomes on crime and its causes, it threw a light into the mind of the professional criminal. It was not only a good story; it was a capital piece of writing. Mr. Booth followed it with several other excellent articles, but is unable to go further because of a rule adopted by the California prison authorities, forbidding prisoners to send out MSS. This rule has also greatly damaged another man of promise, Mr. Robert J. Tasker, whose two articles, "The First Day" and "A Man Is Hanged," will be remembered. But Mr. Tasker had finished his first book, "Grimhaven," before the rule was promulgated, and it has just been published.[20]

Many other personal narratives have been printed. They have ranged from a charmingly philosophical essay, by a country doctor, upon the difficulties and compensations of his modest situation to a poignant paper by the daughter of an evangelical clergyman, discussing realistically the pains of life in a Southern parsonage. Mrs. Sanger, the birth controller, has described her adventures with the Puritans who have sought to put her down. An architect has told of his encounters with prehensile union leaders. Mr. Owen P. White has recalled the Texas of his youth, now standardized and gone. Mr. Walt McDougall, the veteran cartoonist, has done the story of the old Park Row. Men of business and affairs—for example, Mr. Dane Yorke, and Mr. Henry Tetlow—have discussed the arts and mysteries they know. Mr. Gregory Mason has contributed the gay reminiscences of a Chautauqua lecturer. Bishop Charles Fiske has discoursed gloomily upon the sorrows of his exalted office. Messrs. Jim Tully and Henri Tascheraud have told their barbaric tales of the road. Mr. Herbert Asbury has shaken the adherents of a great communion and delighted the rest of us with his "Up from Methodism."

The roll is a long one, and it will be extended hereafter. Despite the ironing out process life in America continues to be infinitely various. There are thousands of back-waters that remain to be explored. There are many adventures that have yet to find their bards.

[III]

The *American Mercury* has not neglected *belles lettres*, but it makes no apology for devoting relatively little space to mere writing. Its fundamental purpose is to depict and interpret the America that is in being; not to speculate moonily about Americas that might be, or ought to be. It would print more short stories if more good ones could be found. But not many are being written in the United States today. There are, or would seem to be, two reasons for this. One is that the form is probably in decay—that all of its potentialities have been worked out, and nothing remains save to chase tails. Various ardent experimentalists try to overcome or evade its natural limitations, but none of them, so far, has solved the problem. The other reason is that the market for bad short stories is so wide and lucrative at the moment that only romantic idealists try to write good ones. On the one hand there is the demand of the magazines of huge circulation for standardized stuff that will interest their vast herds of morons and offend no one—in other words, for trash that may be turned into movie scenarios. And on the other hand there is the demand of the innumerable all-fiction magazines for trade goods on an even lower level—stories, indeed, for readers who are just able to read at all.

These markets offer good livings to multitudes of diligent hacks. They inevitably lure and debauch the young writer, save he be of extraordinary resolution. He may get ready money for any MS. in the guise of fiction, however bad it may be; if he is able to put a certain low plausibility into it he may get a very handsome honorarium. Thus the flow of stories of any honesty and dignity is less than it used to be, and it seems doomed to be still less hereafter. The *American Mercury* prints good ones when it can find them, but finding them is not an easy task. Of a hundred that come to it from volunteer contributors, not five are even second-rate; yet many of them appear later on in other magazines—sometimes in magazines of considerable pretensions—, and apparently they are consumed with satisfaction. But the *American Mercury* is not addressed to the sort of reader who consumes them.

In the field of poetry there are similar doldrums. An immense mass of verse is being written, but not one per cent. of it has any merit whatsoever. The poets, after a long and bitter battle over forms, now devote themselves mainly to pawing over the debris of the combat. At intervals a thing as sound and brilliant as Mr. James Weldon Johnson's "Go Down, Death," makes its appearance, but the intervals seem to grow longer. There was a time, nine or ten years ago, when poetry appeared to be enjoying a renaissance in America, but the promise of that time has not been fulfilled. The new poets who were then thrown up did all their best work in the swing of the movement; the moment it began to lose momentum they took refuge in formulæ, and of late little of any interest has come from them.

But in this direction the *American Mercury* still cherishes certain hopes. Poets are always the forerunners of a literature. Its first lispings are done in numbers. Thus an effort has been made to induce some of the poets of yesterday to experiment in prose, and not infrequently the result has been very gratifying. Meanwhile, the later bards, in so far as they show any skill at all, are accorded a certain hospitality—perhaps rather more than they deserve. The magazine, more than once, has printed passable poetry. It will print better when better is written.

[IV]

The five years have been busy ones, but amusing. The charm of the grab-bag is in every editor's daily toil. For weeks he plows hopelessly through heaps of dull and depressing stuff, and then, on some gloomy morn, there arrives the pearl of great price. It may come in wholly unheralded, or it may come in as the end-product of long months of effort and negotiation. Not uncommonly an article is rewritten four or five times before it takes on a pleasing shape, and even then it may need a great deal of editorial work before it is ready for type. Worse, it may be rewritten four or five times, and grow progressively more hopeless. Such are the hazards of an editor's life. Its compensations come when a new note, clear and charming, is sounded in the office—when there appears out of nowhere the ever-enchanting marvel of a new writer who has something really interesting to say and knows how to say it.

The *American Mercury* has been more fortunate than most magazines in this respect. Its departures from the old formulæ have naturally attracted to it a great many contributors with novel and striking ideas. Some of them have been old hands and some of them have been novices. It owes its substantial success to their collaboration. It has tried to repay them by finding a civilized and highly intelligent audience for them, sufficiently large to get them something approaching general notice.

The response of its readers has been hearty and generous. They have borne its occasional vagaries patiently, and they have supported it with extraordinary fidelity. I can only assure them, at the end of five years, that there is no letting down of the original striving. Plans of improvement are in contemplation, and they will be executed as the chance offers. The *American Mercury* will be a great deal better magazine hereafter than it has ever been in the past.

TEN YEARS OF THE *AMERICAN MERCURY*

My retirement from the editorship of the *American Mercury,* to take effect at the end of the present year, was announced on October 6, and is thus stale news to the readers of these pages. A good many of them, in fact, have long since sent me pleasant words of farewell, and from several I have received more material certificates of goodwill, including two cases of beer. My thankfulness to all of them needs no saying, nor my natural regret on severing so charming and stimulating a relationship. But I am firmly convinced that magazines, like governments, are benefited by rotation in office, and I am carrying out that principle by yielding to Mr. Henry Hazlitt.

Of his qualifications for the post there will be plenty of evidence immediately. He is fourteen years younger than I am, but he has behind him a varied and rich experience in the editorial chair, and that experience fits him peculiarly for the work ahead of him. He is the only competent critic of the arts that I have ever heard of who was at the same time a competent economist, of practical as well as theoretical training, and he is one of the few economists in human history who could really write. Thus he is extraordinarily well equipped for the business which faces him, for the big show in America, during the next few years, will be carried on mainly in the economic ring, and if it is to be dealt with according to the taste of the readers of the *American Mercury* it must be dealt with boldly, gracefully and with not too much solemnity.

In case there be any among those readers who fear that the change of editorial administration will convert the magazine into something that it is not they may put their minds at ease. In its basic aims and principles there will be little change. Hereafter, as in the past, it will try to play a bright light over the national scene, revealing whatever is amusing and instructive, but avoiding mere moral indignation as much as possible. There are reasons for believing that the United States, as it stands, might be improved, but there is certainly no reason for complaining of it as a spectacle. That spectacle fascinates Mr. Hazlitt as it has always fascinated me. He will try to discern and set forth its changing phases as I have done. The only difference will be that he will bring a fresher eye to the enterprise, and kinds of discernment that lie outside my equipment. He was my first and only choice for the post he takes, and I am completely convinced that he will make a first-rate magazine.

My reasons for clearing out are not, of course, purely theoretical—that is, they are not based wholly upon the doctrine that ten years is long enough for one editor to serve. I believe in that doctrine thoroughly, and have put it into practice twice, once in the case of the *Smart Set* and now with the *American Mercury;* but I am also moved by an eager desire to devote more of my time to other undertakings, some of which have been luring me for a long while, often to my acute impatience and discomfort.

The main one is the writing of some books. There was a time when all of my books were simply reworkings of magazine and newspaper articles, and putting them together was thus a relatively easy matter. But with my "Treatise on the Gods," begun in 1927, I ventured into fields outside the periodical range, and it soon became apparent that the hard study and continuous application that such work demanded were hardly compatible with the daily duties of a magazine editor. It took me three years to write "Treatise on the Gods," for the only time

I had to give it was an occasional evening, and books of its kind cannot be written comfortably on occasional evenings. Its successor, "Treatise on Right and Wrong," has been under way since 1930, and should have been finished long ago. Now I'll be free to push it to quick completion, for despite my difficulties three-fifths of it is done, and the rest is blocked out.

I go into these details because many readers of the *American Mercury* have been polite enough to show some interest in my plans for the future, and my gratitude to them for their ten years of unfailing support induces me to think of them as friends. I have a schedule of writing that will keep me busy for at least five years to come, and at fifty-three it is perhaps imprudent for any man to look further ahead. The books, I hope, will roll out without any more delay, some of them new ones, long planned, and the rest extensive revisions and amplifications of old ones—for example, "The American Language," which promises to run to two volumes in its next incarnation.[21] For recreation in the intervals of labor I propose to travel, for the world grows more interesting to me every day, and though I have seen rather more of it than most I am still eager to see and savor what is left.

My obligations are many—to the capable and diligent staff of the magazine, to its large corps of contributors (more than 600 in all), to the advertisers who have sustained it in fair weather and foul, and above all, to its body of faithful readers, many of whom have been on its books since the first issue in January, 1924. I have had the pleasure of meeting some of these readers, and have been in correspondence with many more. I have marvelled at times at their patience with my aberrations, and can only offer them my thanks for keeping the magazine going, and for giving me, these ten years, the fun of editing it.

The *American Mercury* started out as something considerably more modest than what it has become. When Mr. Knopf and I made our first plans for it we had in mind a magazine of about 20,000 circulation, appealing to a relatively small class of readers, and devoting its attention mainly to the arts. But after the first issue it was plain that many more people were interested in it than we had counted on, and since then it has made a secure place for itself in what may be called the upper bracket of American magazines, and as its scope has widened it has increased in circulation. Not many of its contemporaries have been quoted so often in the newspapers, and none other has got so much attention in foreign countries.

I am naturally glad that I can leave it in such good hands. It may be that, from time to time, Mr. Hazlitt will be hospitable and enlightened enough to print me, but that is a matter for the future to determine. He is to be editor in fact as well as in name, and my position will be precisely that of any other contributor. My conduct of The Library ceases with this issue, and I won't pretend to be sorry, for it began in the *Smart Set* in 1908, and has thus been running twenty-five years.[22] How many books I have reviewed in that time, God alone knows—probably at least four thousand, for I used to plow through whole shelves of them in an issue. My belief is that I have endured enough for the swell letters of my native land. It is now time for other, and perhaps even worse critics to take over the job.

MEMOIRS OF AN EDITOR

Magazine editors, I gather, are generally regarded as very enviable fellows: certainly there seems to be a wide impression that their office is pleasant beyond the average. In this notion, somewhat unexpectedly, there is a good deal of truth. The editorial chair may not be exactly soft, but it is at least tolerable to the hinder parts, and it is propped high enough above the common level to keep the ego fanned with the heady airs it craves. An editor, within the limits of his reach and sway, is almost as puissant as a bishop, and may bind and loose with the same freehand and authoritative strokes. All the contributors to his magazine are carefully polite to him, at any rate to his face, and he soon learns—indeed, it is the first lesson in the First Reader of his art—that the only subscribers who write in to damn him are idiots. Thus he leads what must be set down, by every fair standard, as an easy and elegant life, and if it were not for his work, of which more anon, he would be as happy and as pleased with himself as a college president.

My mention of idiots may seem a trope, but it is to be taken almost literally. I elucidate it with an anecdote borrowed from my old friend, Colonel Patrick H. Callahan of Louisville, the only Irish Catholic Prohibitionist ever actually seen and measured by scientists. In the high days of the late William Jennings Bryan the colonel was one of his torpedoes, and used to travel with him, now and then, through the Bible country. He found that poor Jennings was horribly beset by letters and telegrams from customers, and especially by telegrams. No matter how remote the region in which he operated they pursued him at the rate of forty or fifty a day, and dealing with them was a chore he dreaded worse than booze or Darwin. So when Bryan discovered that the colonel had a slick epistolary style he put off on him the job of reading and answering them.

"In my first day's work," says the colonel, "I found that Bryan really received only *two* telegrams, and save for an occasional message from his family or a personal friend that was all he got thereafter. The first telegram ran about as follows:

"'Before retiring to rest tonight my husband and I are going on our knees to thank our Heavenly Father that you have been spared for your great work. So long as you are with us the American Republic and the Christian religion will be safe.'

"The other was somewhat shorter. It ran:

"'You mangy old fake, why don't you jump into a sewer? I hope you break your neck.'"

There were, of course, some slight variations in the phraseology, but the substance, says the colonel, was always the same. Two-thirds of a magazine editor's mail may be divided into the same halves. One half comes from readers who have been struck all of a heap by something that he has printed, and write in to say that he is the greatest ornament of his mystery since Jeffrey,[23] and the other half comes from readers who are of the opinion that he is a jackass, and say so with greater frankness. What is he to think? He thinks precisely what, in like case, a President would think, or a radio crooner, or the bishop aforesaid. That is to say, he thinks that half of his correspondents are persons with an extraordinarily high development of the critical faculty, and that the rest are morons. Perhaps morons is too harsh a term to apply to some of them: they are simply fools carried away by an excessive development of the lust to teach: their communications are furiously hortatory. But in the group there are also some who are downright loony, and so we strike a fair balance.

This leaves us a third of the editor's mail. Out of it comes all the pleasure of his job, and most of its woe. After twenty years of hard service I am surely fed up on unsolicited letters, but all the same I can imagine nothing more pleasant, even to this day, than receiving one from a stranger who really has something to say, and who says it with force and charm. Looking back, I can recall hundreds of that sort, and out of them have issued some exhilarating acquaintanceships, and even a few friendships. The notion that all the good writers are engaged in writing professionally is very far from true; some of the best that the Republic has produced in my time are too modest to bust into print, or too wise. From an American engineer marooned in a remote camp in Mexico I have received from time to time comments on current affairs that show him to be an editorial writer of the highest skill, though he probably doesn't know it, and from a man laid low by tuberculosis in South Africa I once received a series of letters on biological topics that revealed a first-rate scientific intelligence going to waste.

One day about ten years ago I had a long communication from a man who began by describing himself as a workman—he used the more forthright word laborer—in a lumber-mill in the Northwest. What he had to say I forget, but the direct and excellent way in which he said it is still brilliantly in mind. I replied at once, suggesting that he try an article, and after some shy hemming and hawing he did so. I embalmed it in print at once, and called for more, and within six months he had enough orders from other editors to deliver him from the sawmill and set him up as a professional writer. He is one to this day, with half a dozen books behind him—but I have an uneasy feeling that I did him a disservice in encouraging him, for life in his sawmill, judging by his accounts of it, must have been immensely amusing, whereas the life of a professional writer is at best a hard and dull one, and at worst an agony. I add this man's name and crave his forgiveness: it is James Stevens.

Another day the mail brought a bundle of short stories from a young man incarcerated at San Quentin Prison. They were bad stories, but there was some good writing in them, and I suggested to my correspondent that he throw them away and try an article. He made a couple of bad starts but finally produced a good one, and after it four or five more, and eventually they made a book, and it had its brief day, and out of it came the author's release on parole. At last accounts he was writing movie scenarios—surely a sad destiny for a man of talent, and a model prisoner.

His first article, published, brought me a flood of MSS. from other felons— most of them horrible rubbish, but among them some very diverting and instructive stuff. In the course of eight years I published eighteen such sagas and lucubrations of the damned—an average of less than 0.2 a month; unfortunately, it turned out to be more than a moral people could digest comfortably, and I was denounced in the newspapers for editing a magazine *wholly* written by criminals. My private adventures with these brethren were not reassuring. One of them—not a contributor to the series, but only an aspirant—called at my home one day, exhibited a revolver, boasted that he had killed two men, and scared my wife half to death. Another, paroled at the solicitation of literati, including myself, was soon taken in the company of burglars, with a kit of professional instruments upon him. His defense was that some unnamed magazine owed him a lot of money, and he had been driven back to crime by its failure to pay. The newspapers naturally hinted that it was *my* magazine, and at the same time announced, somewhat inconsistently, that I was the culprit's intimate.

How many candidates for the literary shroud are housed in the United States, either in prison or out, I don't know, but surely the number must run to tens of thousands. There are at least forty correspondence-schools devoted to luring them from the gasoline-pump and washtub, and convincing them that, if they only send on sufficient money, they can be converted into Dreisers and Cathers. In addition, all of the colleges offer courses in journalism and in fiction and drama, and there are hundreds more in the high schools. The last-named appear to be mainly snap courses set up to entertain pupils too stupid to take on the ordinary branches, but some colleges offer what seems to be very useful instruction. I believe that such instruction, if it were actually what it looks to be, might do some good, if only by saving the more promising aspirants the pains of trial and error. Unluckily, the gogues told off to impart it are competent only rarely, and some of them are complete frauds, as are most of the mail-order professors. In consequence, the good students get no benefit and the bad are made worse.

From the latter comes the vast flow of MSS. which inundates every magazine office in the land. I have long toyed with plans for a machine to sort it out, based on the selenium cell and the notorious fact that the bookworm (*Sitodrepa panicea*) prefers good books to bad, but my other concerns have prevented me from pursuing the matter, and so the sorting is still done by hand. It is an expensive business, for despite the conviction of every Vassar girl that reading MSS. is as simple as mixing gin rickeys, it actually takes a great deal of skill and judgment; but expensive as it is, it must be carried on, for concealed among the rubbish is some stuff of promise, and once in a great while the alert reader discovers the pearl of great price. I happened upon several such pearls in my first days as a magazine editor, and in consequence I kept fishing in the MS. stream to the end, hoping always. But the chances against another good haul ran at least 10,000 to 1.

The magazine editor faces odds almost as depressing in far more likely waters. His mail is full of letters from obviously literate persons, offering articles that fit into his scheme precisely, and give every assurance of delighting his customers. He orders them all—but he receives only ten in every five hundred, and of the ten only one is fit to print. Even professional writers, in this matter, are far from dependable. I could tell some strange tales, beginning with Anderson and going through to Zangwill, but avoid litigation by citing only my own case. Since retiring from the editorial hot-spot I have been doing a little writing myself, and some time ago the editor of the eminent periodical you are now reading suggested to me that I do this article. I agreed at once, and promised to deliver it on a Tuesday. On the Thursday following he received a notice of postponement, and on the Friday of the next week another. When, after several more weeks had passed, he finally saw the MS, it was a complete surprise to him.

In Poe's time, I take it, editing a magazine had a flavor of romance in it. There was never any certainty that the editor would get his day's victuals, and there was always the chance that a rich female poet would break into his office unannounced and carry him off to Brooklyn, the Palm Beach and Gomorrah of that time. But in these days most magazines are quite solvent and pay salaries punctually, and so many ingenious traps for catching and hamstringing female poets have been invented that it is a rare editor who ever really sees one. Printing magazines may still be an adventure in Greenwich Village and its literary and sexual succession-states, but on higher levels it has been lifted to the solid dignity and security of the moving and hauling business. The wise editor no longer professes to disdain his colleagues of circulation and advertising. He knows that they practise far more exact sciences than he does, and he has found by experience that they are usually very shrewd and amusing fellows, with no yen to take over his own gloomy responsibilities. As for amour, it has gone out of magazine offices. I can recall but one lady during my last two years in service who indicated that I might make havoc with her amiability, and she turned out, on investigation, to be insane.

An editor, poor fellow, is always shooting into the space-time continuum. Between the time he snares a good story or article and the time the magazine containing it comes off the stands there is an immense reach of waiting—to him, indeed, it seems almost a geological epoch. He is always loading cannon to bombard targets that may not be there when he fires at them at last. By dismal experience he learns that only the chance shots ever bring down any substantial bag of game. Something that he has counted on to fetch the universe turns out to be a dud, and some inconsidered trifle sets off lovely fireworks.

The survivors, as I have hinted, deserve a good deal of the envy that seems to bathe them. They have much more freedom than most men, and enough power in their somewhat shadowy and meager world to keep them respecting themselves fiercely. So long as they do their work with reasonable competence, no one cares how they do it, or when: the only thing asked of them is that they get their magazines out on time, and fill them with stuff that is generally endurable, and thrilling now and then. If they crave society it is at their door, for invitations to all the bad public luncheons and worse dinners go with their trade. And if they incline toward retirement they may have their wish just as readily, for no man whose name is constantly before the public is so thoroughly obscure as a magazine editor, or so little missed when the time comes to let go his hold.

THE WORST TRADE OF THEM ALL

It is, of course, the trade of the author. To judge by the immense numbers of persons who try to horn into it, it seems to be generally viewed as easy, and certainly there is a widespread impression that it is lucrative and full of honor. But in reality it is one of the most vexatious and laborious crafts ever undertaken by presumably sane men, and its rewards, however vast, are seldom commensurate with its pains. I have been at it myself for more than forty years, and I can only report that it has left me, at sixty, a mere museum of pathology, and that I'd make off for Beulah Land at once if it were not for my patriotic reluctance to leave my country in the lurch.

A man writing must sit in a room alone, tortured by every sensation that flits through his carcass, and with his mind a prey to all the fears and hallucinations that have haunted humanity since the Ice Age. Every other man who uses his head professionally has other people in front of him to divert and console him—the doctor, the pedagogue, the clergyman, the business man, the lawyer (save when he is writing a brief, which he usually farms out to a law student). But the poor author, like the deep-sea diver, must fight it out alone. Into his room he goes with the heavy step of a felon approaching the electric chair, and there he sits in solitary wretchedness until his day's stint is finished, and he emerges in misery to meditate upon its badness, and to pray that in his next incarnation he will be a band leader, a baseball umpire or a traffic cop.

Is there a suggestion from the gallery that he resort to dictation? Then it comes from some one whose ignorance of the literary process is only too manifest. In the whole history of the world, at all events since Old Testament days, no really good book has ever been dictated—and by good I do not mean masterly, perfect, immortal, but simply good enough, tolerable, up to the average of the author who did it.

The truth is that being alone is of the very essence of competent writing. Let some one else be in the room, and you will get, at best, journalism. It will be a mirror, not of the author himself, which all sound literature is, but of his mere environment.

The case of John Milton had better be disposed of at once, for every schoolboy knows that he dictated "Paradise Lost," partly to hired secretaries and partly to his suffering and rebellious daughters. But every schoolboy also knows that Milton, by that time, was stone-blind—and there is the easy answer to the paradox. He could hear his poor daughters mouthing bad Latin and worse Greek, but he could not see them, and so he could not be distracted by their shining morning faces, and their possibly intolerable clothes and coiffures, their glares and glowers when he went too fast or too slow. Moreover, it is not to be forgotten that what he dictated was not the "Areopagitica" but "Paradise Lost," which is to say, the dullest poem ever written.

I do not argue that an author needs solitude in order to think, for he can think in company as well as any other man, and as a matter of fact all of his really productive thinking is so done. More than others, indeed, he must keep contact with his fellows; for his writing must be about them when it is not about himself, and even an author tires of himself soon or late, as his customers do even sooner than soon.

But thinking and writing are not the same thing—not by any means. Thinking is simply a free and easy ramble through the woods of ideas, but writing is chopping down and piling up the trees. Any one can think; but to reduce thought to orderly chains of nouns, verbs, adjectives, pronouns, adverbs, prepositions and all the rest, and to fill the ensuing sentences and paragraphs with sweet music and an air of ingratiating reasonableness, and to induce some publisher to print them and circulate them, and a sufficiency of readers to buy them and read them—to do all this is something else again. As I have intimated, it demands the stark, insulated solitude of a monk in his cell.

Such solitude, of course, is hard to bear. Thus the author in his agony seizes upon every chance to break it. If a parade comes down the street, he hangs out of the window; if the neighbors start a quarrel, he listens like a Broadway journalist; if there is a fire or a bomb explosion, he is on his way to it before the police.

Failing such excuses to knock off his almost impossible work, he invents all sorts of banal entertainments to escape it, if only for a few moments. If there is a book in his room, he dips into it; if there is only a circular from a bond house explaining that the bondholders' committee hopes to recover 8 per cent., he reads that, and with pathetic attention; if there is no reading matter at all, he counts matches, or sharpens lead pencils, or reties his necktie, or refills his pipe, or carves his initials on his desk.

But even these devices are not enough, for he must have something to do, not only in the intervals of his writing, but also while he is actually at it. Henrik Ibsen, as his chambermaid has told us, used to chew tobacco; many other authors chew gum. And all the rest, male and female, smoke. A few exceptions occur to me—for example, Tolstoy and Nietzsche. But such anomalies always end mashuggah.

Any other man, once he learns his trade, is able to carry it on with reasonable competence day in and day out, without any considerable variations. There may be days, to be sure, when a surgeon, say, feels low in mind and gets relatively little private stimulation out of excavating an appendix; but nevertheless he is able to do it well enough to satisfy his patient, or the patient's heirs and assigns. In the same way, a lawyer in good health can perform in court almost as facilely on one day as on another, and a banker can take in and pay out, and a business executive can harass and upset his subordinates. Even an actor, so long as he remains on his legs, can get through his part. But an author is the victim of moods that come and go with no apparent reason, and while the bad ones are on him he is as useless and helpless as a juggler without hands.

The origin of these moods, I suppose, lies in the endocrine system—the current refuge of all the psychic horrors that yesterday inhabited the Freudian unconscious. When it is in prime working order the author performs his labors with a kind of ease that seems to him to be almost magical. Even his solitude ceases to afflict him, for in the heat of composition he quite forgets it. Rough spots in his manuscript that have afflicted him for days and even weeks are ironed out with a few strokes, and he achieves phrases that make him drunk with paternal pride. There is, I believe, no happier creature on earth than an author who is thus hitting on all eight cylinders. He renews his faith in the metaphysical banshee called inspiration. He begins to believe that he has been chosen by the gods to inform and inflame humanity.

So far his error is of no great magnitude, judging by its consequences. It may make him vain, but vanity is not painful. But when he proceeds, as he always does, to the false inference that this imaginary inspiration was set loose not by some fortuitous concatenation of insensate hormones but by his own free motion or by some combination of external circumstances under his control—when he goes so far, and then assumes that he can renew the set-up at will, he lets himself in for much grief. For what he hits upon as the agent—a new kind of lead pencil, a whiff of band music down the street, a kind word from his wife, less coffee at breakfast, or what not—is never really responsible. The miracle actually sprang out of his most secret recesses, and pencils, wives, bands and coffee had nothing whatever to do with it. But he remembers only what was visibly before him, and so he spends many a bitter day trying to reconstruct it.

I have a large acquaintance among authors, and have made discreet inquiries· about their ideas in this direction. They show a vast and protean imbecility. There is, for example, the poet who once concocted some saucy dithyrambs, since much praised, on a day when it happened to be hailing, and has since searched the world for a place where it hails every day. There is the novelist who thinks he can't write unless he has a green ribbon in his typewriter and his dog nestling at his feet. There is the art critic who gets his inspiration from a ten-cent print of Rosa Bonheur's "Horse Fair" hung upside down. There is the writer on music who, when he is stuck for hard words, puts "The Star-Spangled Banner" on his phonograph and plays it fortissimo. I myself, in my character of author, have such fetishes, like my betters, though my scientific conscience prompts me to pooh-pooh them. I simply can't work by daylight; unless the curtains are drawn and an electric light is burning, I am sunk. Nor can I work with a coat on, or within sound of a radio, or with rheumatism entertaining me, or after eating forty or fifty oysters, or on the day a war is declared. But here, perhaps, I slide into the domain of authentic cause and effect.

Mostly, of course, an author can't work at all. No man on earth has fewer good days or puts in less time at productive labor. It seems to be a sheer physical impossibility for any one to write for more than three hours at a time. I know authors who say they work longer, but their belief that they do, though it may be honest enough, is only self-deception. They actually work three hours and no more—if, indeed, they work that long; the rest of the time they simply endure patiently the horrors that I have been describing. An hour for sharpening lead pencils and tearing up old letters; an hour for reading a last month's magazine; an hour for gazing at the menacing ceiling, the oppressive walls, the hard, implacable floor—and so the day goes. At the end of it, if it has been lucky, there is three hours' work to show. If not, there is a sheet or two of spoiled paper, ghastly and accusing.

Why, then, do men and women take to literary endeavor? The answer must be another question: Why does a hen lay eggs? The impulse to say something to make people sit up and take notice is universal in humankind. The ego craves attention almost as violently as it craves life. Well, who can think of an easier, safer and more effective way to give it what it wants than by writing? Alone in his gloomy cage, the writer addresses, at least potentially, the whole human race, not only of the living generation but also of all generations to come. He may be poor and drunken like Poe, or a brawler and nuisance like Marlowe, or an obscure nonentity like Emily Dickinson, but he knows that, if the fates are with him, he may yet attain a kind of fame that not even the most competent lawyer or doctor or banker or business man may hope to match. No wonder so many are at it! One success, however slight, and they are incurable.

"The life of a man of letters," said Gustave Flaubert, "is a dog's life, but the only one worth living." His judgment was probably sound on both counts. Rewards of the author at their best are stupendous—and every one knows they are. His troubles are only too easily forgotten.

I have tried in these paragraphs to set forth a few of them. If I printed the whole list, the readers of this magazine would drown the nation with their tears, and many would curse the day they learned to read and write.

WHY I AM NOT A BOOK COLLECTOR

If there are such things as inadvertent book collectors, then I seem to belong to the clan. Never in this life have I bought a book for its age or rarity or elegance alone, yet I have managed to amass, at different times, three collections, and two of them were of some value. The first was a long run of Ibseniana—at the time I got rid of it, apparently the largest in the Western World. The second was a run of autographed presentation copies, mainly American but also including some volumes from England, Germany and France—a run enriched and embellished with manuscripts, proof-sheets and other such association items. The third was (or is, for I still have it) a collection of books and pamphlets by Menckens other than myself. Beyond this I have never collected anything save working tools; indeed, there are not two hundred books in my house this minute, barring the Menckeniana, that are not in use.

The Ibsen collection was the outgrowth of the fact that, in my early newspaper days, I served two of the great Baltimore journals as dramatic critic. This was during the years 1903 to 1908, and Ibsen was then still a novelty and a sensation in the American theater. Very few of the more cerebral actresses of the time failed to take a hack, if under fifty, at Nora Helmer, or, if older, at Hedda Gabler. They began, commonly, with what were then called special matinées, but if the going happened to be good, which was not too often, they branched out upon road tours. One of these ladies, Mary Shaw, put on "Ghosts" in Baltimore, in 1905 or thereabout, to great scandal and success, and afterward played Mrs. Alving along a route stretching from Boston to Tucson, Ariz., for no less than three years.

It was part of my official duty to wait upon, interview and encourage or console all such female fosterers of the intellectual drama, and in the course of my discharge of it I heard from many of them that the English versions of the Ibsen plays, mainly made by William Archer, were hard going. Some of the crucial speeches, in fact, were so stiff and improbable that it was almost impossible to speak them. This seemed to me to be a situation calling for reform, and I sought the aid and counsel of an old friend who knew the originals thoroughly. He was the late Holger A. Koppel, then Danish consul in Baltimore, and he confirmed what the nascent Duses had told me. Ibsen, he said, wrote a beautiful colloquial Dano-Norwegian, and did not hesitate to resort to occasional slang. But the Archer translations, as anyone could see, had no truck with such loose language, and some of the purple passages in them were far more suitable for intoning by English schoolma'ms than by Scandinavian hussies.

I proposed to Koppel that the two of us undertake revised and better versions, and he fell in with the idea at once. In a little while I interested Harrison Hale Schaff, head of the Boston publishing firm of John W. Luce and Company, which had brought out several of my early books, and Koppel and I were hard at it. He worked with the original text before him, and a French translation beside it. I worked with the Archer text and one or more of the numerous German translations. These cribs helped us somewhat, but in the main we labored with naked hands. Koppel, who knew English very well and Dano-Norwegian perfectly, made a literal translation of each succeeding speech, and I then tried to put it into smooth and colloquial phrases. In 1908 we finished "A Doll's House," and early in 1909 we finished "Little Eyolf." Each was brought out by Schaff separately, in a handsome little volume in scarlet and gold, selling for a dollar. We planned to do all the prose plays one by one, and actually finished "Hedda Gabler," but by that time Schaff had discovered that his price of a dollar a play could not meet the Archer price of three for a dollar, and the project blew up.

But meanwhile I had collected a considerable stock of Ibsen literature, hoping to make use of it in our work, and when we downed tools I kept on with it. That literature was very extensive in those days, and kept on growing steadily. Every critic on earth, it appeared, had something to say about the Norwegian.

My collecting took but little of my time and next to none of my energy, for the news that I was interested in Ibseniana quickly spread to the booksellers of the whole earth, and I was presently receiving we-offer postcards in every mail. Nor did the enterprise run into much money, for no other millionaire seemed to be hunting along the same trail, and many of the rarest items that I amassed cost me as little as a couple of shillings, marks, francs, or crowns.

By 1920 I was beginning to tire of the business, for I am not a collector at heart, and my accumulation was already occupying a long length of shelves that I needed for other books. But it was hard to cut off the flow of offers, and whenever they were cheap, which was nearly always, I could not resist them. By 1925 I had got together all the Ibsen firsts, most of them in duplicate and not a few in triplicate and even quadruplicate, and a huge mass of commentaries. Also, I had three or four hundred translations of the plays in no less than thirty languages, including Esperanto, Volapük and Modern Greek. The whole collection ran to more than 2,000 items.

It was now high time to strike for emancipation, and the chance fortunately offered in 1928. I had a friend in Leipzig, Professor Otto Glauning, librarian of the university library there, and one day he let fall the news that he was trying to get together some early Ibseniana for the use of the university department of Nordic studies. This was my chance, and early in 1929 a North German Lloyd freighter sailing from Baltimore for Bremen had in its hold two huge boxes containing my whole collection. They weighed, taken together, more than 350 pounds, and a few weeks later they arrived safely in Leipzig. Whether or not their contents survived the bombs of World War II I do not know. All I can report is that the Ibseniana that once jammed a large bookcase in my small house is now reduced to a dusty card-index—unhappily, very far from complete.

My collection of autographed firsts was the natural fruit of my twenty-five years as a book reviewer. I became acquainted with many of the principal American and English authors of the 1908–1933 era, and some of them were kind enough to send me their new books, usually inscribed. These things accumulated until in the end they swamped me. But in 1940 Dr. Joseph L. Wheeler, then librarian of the Enoch Pratt Free Library in Baltimore, offered amiably to house them in his fine new library building, and there they are now, waiting the judgment day. So long as I live they will remain at my orders, but on my departure for bliss eternal they will be thrown open to the literary historians and scavengers of the world.

My collection of Menckeniana is still in my house. It shows a dozen or more authors of my name and family stretching back over 270 years, and runs to about 150 items. Many of these books and pamphlets are in Latin, and have been long forgotten, but there is one item on the list, published 1715, that remained in print for nearly a century. Then it died at last, but I revived it myself in 1937 by bringing out the first translation into English.[24] This was 222 years after the first edition. If anyone resurrects a book of my own in 2167 I shall, from my pew in Gehenna, be powerfully surprised.

THINKER

OFF THE GRAND BANKS

Come Saturday I shall be forty-five—older than my father was when he died, almost up to the average span of the Menckenii for three hundred years. We are, I suspect, a somewhat feverish race, launching out into life prematurely and wearing out before most are full grown. My grandfather was married at nineteen; my father had a business of his own at twenty-one; I was the city editor of a daily newspaper at twenty-three. Exigent enterprises, and mine, perhaps, the most exigent of the three. I have known what hard work is. At the time of the Baltimore fire I worked continuously from eleven o'clock Sunday morning until the dawn of Wednesday. Another time, for six months running, I ran an average of 5,000 words of news copy a day, getting the news myself and writing it myself. The reporters of today lead lordly, voluptuous lives. There were no taxicabs in my time, and the telephone was a toy. One man did the work of two, three, four. If it was a boozy day in the office, and he was young and eager, of five, six, seven.

Theoretically, I suppose, I am in the *Landsturm*,[1] and even ready to pass out of it. But where are the subjective symptoms? I search for them a bit fearfully, and rejoice that they are not to be found. Now and then it seems to me that I tire more easily than I used to, that my capacity for work is diminishing. The next day I do twelve hours straight. Moreover, didn't I tire back in 1902? God knows I did. There were nights when I reached bed scarcely able to put out the gas. It was a gaudy life, but it was killing. It taught me, perforce, a useful and perhaps life-saving trick: that of snatching a nap between rounds. If the pressure is heavy, I stretch out half an hour before dinner and depart to nothingness like a man hit with an ax. If there is more time, an hour or two of heavy exercise goes before—not your diabetic golfing, but work with hammer, saw and shovel, fit for a longshoreman. In the evening, after that, I am full of notions, and in excellent humor.

What keeps me going at my trade, I suppose, is my continuous curiosity, my endless interest in the stupendous farce of human existence. It is the principal and perhaps only stock of a journalist; when it begins to slip from him he is fit only for the knacker's yard. To be short of ideas is an experience that I have yet to suffer; it is, indeed, almost incomprehensible to me. Short of ideas in the Republic of today? As well try to imagine a Prohibition enforcement officer short of money! They dart and bang about one's ears like electrons in a molecule. A thousand new ones are born every day.

The hard job is to choose from among them, to get some coherence into them, to weave them into more or less orderly chains. In other words, the hard job is to reduce them to plausible and ingratiating words, to make them charming, to turn them into works of art. After thirty years of incessant endeavor in that direction I come to two conclusions about it: skill at it is never (or only miraculously) inborn, and it cannot be taught. How, then, is it to be acquired? By one method only; by hard work. By trial and error. By endless experiment. Is what was done today better than what was done last year? Does it move more gracefully? Is it better organized? Then keep on. But is it still clumsy, still stiff, still dull? Then back to the office stool!

Fortunately, the quest is without end. Of the other languages I know little, but of English I have learned something. Its charm is its infinite complexity, its impenetrable mystery. Do not suspect me of rhetoric when I say that it seems to change from year to year. Or maybe those of us who write it change. We hear new melodies, sometimes far below the staff. We are tripped by strange, occult surprises. A new and rich color appears. There is here something magnificently fascinating. The lesson is never quite learned.

Schoolmarms, of course, profess to teach it. To the lions with them! I am no pedagogue myself, assuredly, but at forty-five a man naturally yearns to wave his beard at the apprentices to his trade. My advice, brethren, if you would do honor to our incomparable tongue, is that you pay little heed to books, even the best. Listen to it on the street. It is there that it is alive.

In a moral Republic, a man engaged in controversy is naturally assumed to seek moral ends. That is, he is assumed to be a reformer. If he is palpably innocent of all the orthodox reforms, inspired by the angels, then he is guilty of sinister reforms of a downward trend, inspired by the devil. The first passion of a good Americano is to make his fellow-primates do something that they don't want to do. His second is to convince them that doing it will improve the world and please God.

Here, I believe, I lie outside the stream, happily at ease upon the bank. I can't imagine a man with less public spirit in him. Every day I receive an invitation to join this movement or that, sometimes toward consummations most laudable, and every day the invitation goes into my waste-basket. If I had it in my power to put down Prohibition overnight, or to scotch the Fundamentalists, or to hang all Men of Vision, I'd not have to flee from the temptation, for there would be no temptation. The lust to improve the world is simply not in me.

This attitude, I find, is incomprehensible to most Americans, and so they assume that it is a mere cloak for a secret altruism. If I describe the Fundamentalists *con amore,* dwelling luxuriously upon their astounding imbecilities, their pathetic exploitation by mountebanks,[2] I am set down at once as one full of indignation against them, and eager to drag them to the light. Indignation? Is one indignant at a monkey doing his tricks? Or at a dry Congressman down with delirium tremens? Such spectacles do not make me indignant; they simply interest me immensely, as a pathologist, say, is interested by a beautiful gastric ulcer. It is, perhaps, a strange taste—that is, in a country of reformers. But there it is.

No doubt it keeps me from understanding reformers, as they are unable to understand me. But what are the odds? I do not argue that they should be put down; I simply presume to be unconvinced by their reforms. They are free to go on, convincing others if they can. All I ask is equal freedom. When it is denied, as it always is, I take it anyhow.

Quod est veritas?[3] I know the answer no more than Pilate did. But this, at least, I have observed in forty-five years: that there are men who search for it, whatever it is, wherever it may lie, patiently, honestly, with due humility, and that there are other men who battle endlessly to put it down, even though they don't know what it is. To the first class belong the scientists, the experimenters, the men of curiosity. To the second belong politicians, bishops, professors, mullahs, tinpot messiahs, frauds and exploiters of all sorts—in brief, the men of authority.

My inclination, I suspect, makes me lean heavily in favor of the former. I am, as the phrase is, prejudiced in their favor. They fall, now and then, into grievous errors, but in their fall there is still something creditable, something that takes away all shame. What fetches them is the common weakness of humanity, imperfectly made by a God whose humor has been greatly underestimated. They have, at least, the virtue of fairness. And that of courage. Unhorsed, they pick themselves up and try again. They do not call for the police.

In the other camp I find no such virtues. All I find there is a vast enmity to the free functioning of the spirit of man. There may be, for all I know, some truth there, but it is truth made into whips, rolled into bitter pills. It is truth that has somehow lost all dignity, all beauty, all eloquence and charm. More often, it is not truth at all, but simply folly horribly bedizened. Whatever it is, it is guarded by the common enemies of mankind: theologians, lawyers, policemen, men armed with books, guns, clubs, goads, ropes.

I find myself out of sympathy with such men. I shall keep on challenging them until the last galoot's ashore.

MEDITATIONS AT VESPERS

After a quarter of a century of active and sometimes gaudy controversy, literary, political, ethical, legal and theological, I find myself, at the brim of senility, cherishing the following facts: (a) that I can't recall ever attacking an adversary who was not free to make a reply, and in tones as blistering as he liked, and (b) that I can't recall ever calling for quarter, or indulging in any maneuvers to get it. Such are the banal satisfactions that must content a rat-catcher in his declining years. Like all other satisfactions, they are probably largely delusory—in fine, Freudian phenomena. That is to say, I suspect that an impartial inquiry would show that I have hit below the belt more than once, and ducked more than once. Do I forget it grandly, and flap my wings? Then it is for the same reason that a Sunday-school superintendent forgets stealing 15 cents from his blind grandmother back in 1885.

But if I thus have to lie a little, if only unconsciously, to make my record clear, I can at least say with complete honesty that the uproars I have been engaged in from time to time have been very agreeable, and left me without any rancor. Speaking generally, I am of a somber disposition and get very little happiness out of life, though I am often merry; but what little I have got has come mainly out of some form of combat. Why this should be so I don't know. Maybe it indicates that I am only half civilized. But if so, then Huxley was also only half civilized, and Voltaire before him, and St. Paul before Voltaire.

The truth is that life without combat would be unbearable, and that men function freest and most gloriously under stress. Every effort to make humanity peaceable has failed, and I believe that all the efforts to come will fail. The colossal failure of Christianity must have been noticed, by this time, even by the clergy, a singularly naïve and deluded body of men. It came into the world to make an end of war; it has made more wars than avarice, or even than hunger. To this day, it is difficult for a Christian clergyman to rise in his pulpit without excoriating something, if that something be only war.

I surely do not complain of the fact, for on the whole the brethren of the cloth have contributed more to my mild and phosphorescent happiness in this life than any other class of men. There was a time when I had almost constant differences with them, and learnt to have a high respect for their dialectic talents. What makes them so formidable is their familiarity with weapons of a dreadful potency. They handle hell-fire as freely and easily as a barber handles his shears: it is their everyday arm. No other men are so formidably equipped. The most a lawyer ever demands of the victim before him is that he be hanged, but even the meekest clergyman is constantly proposing to doom his opponents to endless tortures in lakes of boiling brimstone.

This habit of playing daily with horrible weapons makes clergymen extraordinarily violent in controversy, and violence is what makes that great art charming. I can recall being tackled by them, for trivial errors in political science—if, indeed, they were errors at all—in a manner almost suitable for flooring the appalling beasts described in the Book of Revelation. Once, when I argued that chasing poor harlots up and down the alleys of Baltimore would not make the town chaste, some of them accused me of having a proprietary interest in bawdy-houses. Another time, when I argued more or less calmly that Prohibition could never be enforced, they alleged that I was in the pay of the Whiskey Trust, and pledged to besot and ruin the youth of Republic.

I don't recall ever having a controversy with a man of God that did not end in dreadful bawling. It is impossible to discuss them at all without getting an eye full of sulphur, though surely they are important men, and hence worth discussing. For years it was my high privilege to devote myself mainly to the follies of the Protestant pastors, and so many of them denounced me as an agent of the Pope. This got me friends in Catholic circles, and one of my constant visitors was a venerable monsignor who insisted very charmingly upon treating me as a servant of the True Faith. But of late, for uttering certain platitudes about the American hierarchy, I have been violently denounced by Catholic clergymen, led by the Paulist Fathers. This makes me feel fair again. I am no longer biased.

The ecclesiastical habit of conducting all controversies à *outrance*—of assuming and insisting that every opponent is a scoundrel, and ought to be boiled and fried in hell forever—this habit, as everyone knows, also marks those laymen whose convictions have a theological color—for example, Prohibitionists and anti-evolutionists. It has been my fortune to have many combats with such fellows: I can recall only one who ever showed any sign of good humor. That one was the Hon. William H. Anderson. He liked controversy for its own sake, and hence could carry it out without bile. The fact later undid him, for when the New York wets took him in some insignificant misdemeanor his brother drys deserted him, and he went to prison.

The rest of the drys all hit below the belt habitually, and as a matter of pious devotion. They saddled Prohibition upon the country, indeed, at a time when hitting below the belt was official, and any who refused to do it got the attention of the *Polizei*. The anti-evolutionists are quite as bad. I know several of them who, in their private lives, are amiable enough, but when they mount the tub they get out all the weapons in the theological arsenal, and employ them with great gusto. I have been denounced in my time more than most, but never so violently as by anti-evolutionists.

Some time ago one of the most influential of them printed a long philippic damning me as a paretic, and alleging flatly that my sad state was due to transactions forbidden by Holy Writ. The charge, of course, was not new. It had been whispered here in Baltimore more than once, and by Christians of high tone, along with the hint that I was incessantly in my cups. But here the thing was plainly stated in print, and by a gentleman notorious for his solvency. It was a temptation, indeed! The libel laws are very harsh in such matters. But, intrenched behind my lifelong principles, I somehow resisted, and soon afterward the gentleman was called to bliss eternal, and the tenements and hereditaments that I might have collared are now enjoyed by his heirs and assigns.

Is controversy of any use? Obviously, it is the only device so far invented that actually spreads the enlightenment. Exposition, persuasion, homiletics, exegesis—these devices are all plainly inferior, for you must first get your crowd. How difficult that is every preacher knows. But a combat brings the crowd instanter, and if that combat is furious enough, and over an issue of any importance at all, the crowd will stay to the end.

True enough, what it gets out of the immediate uproar is often only folly. It is, save in extreme circumstances, in favor of whoever takes and holds the offensive. The chief desideratum in practical controversy, indeed, is to do that, and the second is to make your opponent angry: the moment he begins to fume he is lost. But though the immediate victory may thus go simply to the better gladiator, I believe it is safe to say that he often ruins his cause, if it is intrinsically a bad one, by winning. The Prohibitionists scored a glorious triumph in 1920. They not only got their law; they also converted at least four-fifths of all the morons in America. But they began to go downhill from that moment.

The history of controversy, in truth, is a long history of winners losing and losers winning. There is more to the thing than the concrete battle. Ideas are shot into the air, and some of them keep on flying. The first ecclesiastical rush in the 60's apparently overwhelmed Huxley—but it also gave him his chance. Voltaire had to flee from France in 1726, but he scattered seeds as he fled, and they are still sprouting and making fruit. I believe that the long battle over Prohibition and its allied imbecilities will come to an excellent issue in the end, though the wrong side appears to be triumphant now. Slowly but surely, as the fundamental questions are thrashed out, common sense will sort out what is sound and workable from what is merely sound and fury, signifying nothing. In the long run, more than Prohibition may be cleared off the board. The American people, grown reasonably enlightened at last, may also sweep away the whole hocus-pocus of law worship.

WHAT IS THIS TALK ABOUT UTOPIA?

As a native and citizen of the Maryland Free State I am, of course, a subject of the United States—but that is about as far as it goes. For the Republic as a whole, I confess, I have very little affection: it amuses and delights me, but never touches me. If the Huns of Japan should launch themselves upon the Pacific Coast tomorrow and begin burning down the chiropractic hospitals and movie cathedrals of Los Angeles, the news would strike me as interesting but not poignant, for I have no investments in that appalling region, and few friends. (San Francisco, to be sure, is something else again, but the Japs are well aware of the fact: they would not burn it.) And if the Huns of the Motherland, assisted by the usual horde of chromatic allies, should take New York, or even Baltimore, it would not perturb me greatly, for the English scheme of things, when all is said and done, is far closer to the Maryland scheme than the American scheme. I was, no doubt, a patriot as a boy, just as I was a teetotaler; I remember glowing, or at all events yelling, when Dewey sank the tin fleet of the Spanish Huns in 1898. But since Good Friday of 1917[4] such thrills have missed me. It is difficult, indeed, for a man not born a Puritan to glow over the obscene, or even to yell. Moreover, the doctrine was promulgated in those gallant days that, as an American not of British blood and allegiance, I had lost certain of my constitutional rights. I let them go without repining, and sent a flock of duties after them.

Today, whenever my thoughts stray to such lofty and occult matters, I think of myself as a Marylander, not as an Americano. My forebears for three generations lie buried in the Free State, and I was born there myself, and have lived there all my life. I like to dwell upon the fact, and am proud of it. So far as I have been able to find out, no man has ever been jailed in Maryland for his opinions—that is, in my time. Even during the late struggle for human freedom, with the rest of the country handed over bodily to the blacklegs of the Department of Justice, a reasonable liberty survived there. It survives to this day, and even tends to increase. The present Governor of the State (he has served for nine years, and has three more to go) is an enlightened and civilized man, and as far from the Fullers as he is from the McCrays.[5] There is no Webster Thayer[6] on the State bench, and there never has been. The mayor of Baltimore is an honest Moose, and favors fewer laws and lower taxes. Even the State Legislature, though it is ignorant and corrupt, is less ignorant and corrupt than any other State Legislature that I know of, and immensely less so than Congress. There is no State Volstead Act in the *Sáorstat*.[7] There is no Comstock society. There is no Methodist Board of Morals. The Klan survives only in a few mountain counties, and even there its only recorded tar party landed its whole local membership, along with the wives thereof, in the House of Correction. In the entire United States there are but five great newspapers that are liberal, wet, sinful and intelligent; two of them are in Baltimore.

I could go on thus for columns; maybe even for acres. But the sad, alas, must go with the sweet. The Maryland Free State, by its own misguided generosity, lies adjacent to the District of Columbia, and in the District of Columbia is the city of Washington, and in the city of Washington are gigantic factories for making chains. These chains rattle, ever and anon, over the boundary. They are fastened upon the legs and arms of free Marylanders. Hordes of mercenaries wearing government badges tote them; it is a facile matter to cross the imaginary line. But the free man, despite the chains, manages somehow to remain a free man. He hopes, and he resists. The two federal courts in Baltimore spend more and more of their time rescuing Prohibition gunmen from the clutches of the State courts; on some blest tomorrow that benign evasion of the Fourteenth Amendment will break down, and there will be an old-time Maryland hanging, with fireworks in the cool of the evening. I must know thousands of Marylanders, old and young, rich and poor, virtuous and damned. I can recall but two who would honestly deplore that hanging. One is a bootlegger who is also a Quaker. The other is an elderly evangelist who professes to believe every word of the Bible, including the warning against witches, and who alleges that God once appeared to him personally, surrounded by glaring headlights.

This proximity of Washington, the citadel of scoundrels, only makes life in the Free State sweeter to the born and incurable Marylander. It throws up into tremendous relief the difference between the new *mores* of the United States and the traditional *mores* of Maryland. It makes him intensely conscious of his citizenship, and fills him with a vast satisfaction. He is an American legally, but not, thank God, by his own free act. Duties go with his predicament, and he discharges them, but where they end he stops. No heat of 100 per cent. Americanism is in him. He harbors no great, brave urge to snout out, jail and burn a Sacco and Vanzetti. He observes the local Anita Whitneys at their depressing business without feeling any lust to clap them behind the bars. He views the Klan and the I. W. W.[8] with equal indifference, so long as they keep to rhetoric. There is no law in Maryland against red flags or red oratory. Birth-controllers are free of the air. Even during the war Socialists whooped from their soap-boxes, and went unscathed. Hearst reporters have been jailed in Baltimore for photographing, against his will, a gunman on trial for his life, but on the public street even Hearst reporters are safe, and the cops protect them in their ancient rights. I proceed to marvels: the American Legion, in the Free State, is polite, modest, intelligent and soldierly. Its grand dragons are men who actually served in the war, and it has made but one attempt to blow up the Bill of Rights. That attempt ended in swift and ignominious disaster, and since then it has been tamer than a tabby cat.

In all this gabble of Maryland notions of the true and the good, of course, I allude to the notions entertained by those Marylanders whose IQ's run well above the middle line. The nether brethren exist there, too, but it is not the Maryland tradition to pay too much heed to them. If, assembled in the legislature, they enact laws designed to convert Sunday into a day of woe and mourning, there is happily no disposition, save in a few remote and malarious counties, to enforce those laws. The city of Baltimore, as a body corporate, breaks them deliberately and officially, and the grand jury winks at the crime. The Rev. Dr. John Roach Straton tried Baltimore, and gave it up. The Rev. Dr. Billy Sunday was sent in to launch Prohibition, and the price of sound Scotch has been falling ever since. The town wowsers lead the dreary lives of town clowns. Evangelical pastors roar in tin tabernacles behind the railroad tracks, but there is not one of them whose public influence or dignity matches that of an imperial wizard of the Elks.

Do I limn Utopia? Well, why not? Utopia, like virtue, is a concept shot through with relativity. To men in jail, I daresay, the radio is a boon. To men doomed to be Americans the existence of such an asylum as the Free State ought to be comforting. How the more enlightened and self-respecting citizens of Massachusetts, Pennsylvania, Ohio, Mississippi and California can sleep at night is more than I can make out. I always feel vaguely uneasy when my literary apostolate takes me into their ghastly States, as I feel uneasy when I have to go to Washington, or to Paterson, New Jersey, or down in a coal mine. What would follow if the Ohio *Polizei* got a sniff of my baggage? How would it fare, in Mississippi, with one who has publicly argued that Aframericans accused of felony should be tried before being hanged? It is a solace, I assure you, to reflect that numerous swift and swell trains are still running, and that the tariff even from California is less than the cost of trephining a skull, broken by agents of what the heroic open-shoppers out there call the law.

When I cross the line I feel safer and happier. The low moan of Methodist divines comes from the swamps of the Chesapeake littoral, but it is only a moan, not a bark of "Attention!" Even coming from New York, that great city, I notice a change of air. The cops grow polite, and hold their cavalry charges for cases of foreign invasion. The Governor writes his own state papers, disdaining the aid of the reverend clergy. When a still blows up, no one is alarmed. The very Babbitts walk lightly, with eager eyes upon their betters. It could be better, to be sure—but remember what country it is in!

WHAT I BELIEVE

[I]

"Faith," said the unknown author of the Epistle to the Hebrews, "is the substance of things hoped for, the evidence of things not seen."[9]

The definition, in these later days, seems to be pretty well forgotten, especially by those master forgetters, the Christian theologians, for it is common to hear them discussing (and denouncing) the beliefs of men of science as if they were mere articles of faith. The two things, of course, are quite distinct. Belief is faith in something that is known; faith is belief in something that is not known. In my own credo there are few articles of faith; in fact, I have been quite unable, in ten days and nights of prayer and self-examination, to discover a single one.

What I believe is mainly what has been established by plausible and impartial evidence, *e.g.,* that the square on the hypotenuse of a right triangle is equal to the squares on the other two sides, that water is composed of oxygen and hydrogen, and that man is a close cousin to the ape. Further than that I do not care to go. Is there a life after death, as so many allege, wherein the corruptible puts on incorruption and the mortal immortality? I can only answer that I do not know. My private inclination is to hope that it is not so, but that hope is only a hope, and hopes and beliefs, it seems to me, can have nothing in common. If, while the taxidermists are stuffing my integument for some fortunate museum of anatomy, a celestial catchpoll summons my psyche to Heaven, I shall be very gravely disappointed, but (unless my habits of mind change radically at death) I shall accept the command as calmly as possible, and face eternity without repining.

Most of the sorrows of man, I incline to think, are caused by just such repining. Alone among the animals, he is dowered with the capacity to invent imaginary worlds, and he is always making himself unhappy by trying to move into them. Thus he underrates the world in which he actually lives, and so misses most of the fun that is in it. That world, I am convinced, could be materially improved, but even as it stands it is good enough to keep any reasonable man entertained for a lifetime.

As for me, I roll out of my couch every morning with the most agreeable expectations. In the morning paper there is always massive and exhilarating evidence that the human race, despite its ages-long effort to imitate the seraphim, is still doomed to be irrevocably human, and in my morning mail I always get soothing proof that there are men left who are even worse asses than I am.

It may be urged that such satisfactions are lowly; nevertheless, the fact remains that they are satisfactions. Would the tinsel world that idealists pant for be better? Would it be really habitable at all? I am ready to doubt it formally. It would be swept, at best, by chill winds; there would be no warming glow of human folly. There would be no Lindberghs in it, to risk their necks preposterously and charmingly; there would be no Comstocks and Wayne B. Wheelers, no Hoovers and Coolidges; there would be no poets with their pretty bellyaches; above all, there would be no theologians. And maybe no Americans.

[II]

One hears complaint that the existing world is being Americanized, and hence ruined. It may be that my steadfast refusal to join in that complaint is patriotism; if so, make the most of it. Here in these States, if we have accomplished nothing else, we have at least brought down all the more impossible varieties of human aspiration to absurdity, and so made life the more endurable. Alone among the great nations of history we have got rid of religion as a serious scourge—and by the simple process of reducing it to a petty nuisance. Alone again, we have rid ourselves of the worst curses that lie in politics—and by the easy and obvious device of making politics comic.

The Fathers of the Republic, I believe, were far cleverer fellows than they are commonly represented to be, even in the schoolbooks. If it was not divine inspiration that moved them, then they must have drunk better liquor than is now obtainable on earth. For when they made religion a free-for-all, they prepared the way for making it ridiculous; and when they opened the doors of office to the mob, they disposed forever of the delusion that government is a solemn and noble thing, by wisdom out of altruism. The bald facts stand before every eye today; it is a joyous and instructive business to contemplate them. And it is even more joyous and instructive to contemplate the sad heavings of those who still refuse to face them, but try to get rid of them by the arts of the prestidigitator and the rhetorician.

When I travel abroad, which is no oftener than I can help it, I am always depressed by the gloom of the so-called intellectuals. My acquaintance among them, in most of the countries of Europe, is somewhat large, and so I can't escape their agonies. Everywhere they fret themselves to death over the problem of government. Everywhere they plan to bring in Utopia by turning this gang out and putting that gang in. Everywhere they believe in wizards and messiahs. It seems to me that we in America—that is, those of us who have become immune to rhetoric—have got beyond that naïveté, and that we are the sounder and happier for it. Reconciling ourselves to the incurable swinishness of government, and to the inevitable stupidity and roguery of its agents, we discover that both stupidity and roguery are bearable—nay, that there is in them a certain assurance against something worse.

The principle is surely not new in the world: everyone ought to know by this time that a mountebank, thinking only of tomorrow's cakes, is far safer with power in his hands than a prophet and martyr, his eyes fixed frantically upon the rewards beyond the grave. So a prudent man prefers Hoover to Stalin or Mussolini, or even to Ramsay MacDonald, a Scotsman and hence a fanatic. No doubt Al Smith would have been better, if only on Burke's theory that politics is at its best when it is most closely adjusted, not to reason, but to human nature. But Hoover is natural enough for all everyday purposes; and where his timidity makes him fall short, his failure is concealed by the glorious labors of such corn-doctors as Borah, Jim Watson, Charlie Curtis, Andy Mellon and Old Joe Grundy.

Here I do not argue that mountebanks are more admirable than honest men; I merely argue that, in such fields as those of politics and religion—to which, of course, the master-quackery of pedagogy ought to be added—they are socially safer and more useful. The question before us is a practical one: how are we to get through life with a maximum of entertainment and a minimum of pain? I believe that the answer lies, at least in part, in ridding solemn ponderosities of their solemn ponderosity, in putting red noses on all the traditional fee-faw-fo-fums.

That enterprise, by the cunning of the Fathers, we have been able to carry further in the United States than it is carried anywhere else. Do strong men blubber against the outrage of Prohibition? Then smell their breaths to see how real their grievance is. Are there protests against the clubs of the police? Then compare a few amiable bumps on the head to a quart of Mussolini's castor oil. Do jobholders consume the substance of the people? Then ask the next Englishman you meet to show you his income tax bill. And are the high places of the land held by trashy and ignoble fellows, bent only upon their own benefit? Then take a look at the scoundrels who constitute the state in France.

[III]

I have said that the Fathers, by making religion a free-for-all, reduced it to innocuous absurdity. No doubt many a saddened patriot will enter a caveat to that, thinking of Cardinal O'Connell and his effort to make Boston a Dublin slum, and Bishop Cannon and his bold attempt to run the whole United States. But these rev. gentlemen really prove my case. For after all, Monsignor Cannon, even with both White House and Capitol quaking every time he looks up from the stock ticker, has *not* succeeded in forcing Prohibition upon the country: all he has succeeded in doing is to make his whole moral system odious and the theology behind it infamous. Nor has His Eminence of South Boston achieved anything better. When he came into his princely dignity, the church he serves was plainly making progress in America, and there was a steady infiltration of intellectuals into it. But now it is headed in the other direction, and every time he arises to denounce Einstein or to launch his janissaries against a new book, its momentum is accelerated.

In this department I have myself been an eyewitness of a large and salubrious change—and it is a pleasure, from the opposition bench, to offer it as a set-off to all the public skullduggery that the tender-minded complain of. That change has to do with the general American attitude toward ecclesiastical organizations, and especially toward the one that Dr. Cannon adorns. I well remember the uproar that followed a polite allegation I chanced to make, now nearly twenty years ago, that the Methodist Church, at least in the South, was operated by charlatans and manned by ignoramuses. The editor of the paper in which it appeared—his dark, innocent eyes wet with tears—stared at me as if I had denounced female chastity or advocated cannibalism. His office was overrun for weeks by prancing pastors, threatening him with disaster. They met in conclave and passed resolutions against him and me; some of them, with their fingers carefully crossed, prayed publicly for my salvation.

Fortunately, they also challenged my facts, and under the pretense of meeting that challenge it was possible for me to renew and reiterate my allegation. But it went down very badly, and for a long while I was under the displeasure of so-called fair men for raising a religious rumpus, and for failing in that respect which, so it appeared, was due to all bodies of believers. Even when, five or six years later, the Anti-Saloon League began running its trails of corruption across the country; and I ventured to point out the patent fact that it was the offspring of Methodism and as anti-social as its parent—even then such charges were generally felt to be somewhat advanced. So again when the Ku Klux emerged from the swamps and began trying to put down civilization. The first article in which I spoke of it as no more than the secular arm of the Methodist-Baptist Inquisition was badly received, and I was widely advised to confine myself to constructive criticism.

This advice made some impression on me: I became, in fact, more or less constructive. But meanwhile Bishop Cannon and his friends went into politics full tilt, brandishing clubs and howling for blood, and before long what had once seemed scandalous became only too self-evident. The Southern editors, for a time, had very hard sledding; they had to discuss politics without mentioning the principal current politicians. But that was soon a sheer impossibility, even to publicists so subtle, and presently they were ventilating the facts with candor, and politics in their dismal section became realistic again, and very lively. Today they all belabor the Methodist Crokers and Charlie Murphys[10] in a hearty and open manner, and have their say about the whole evangelical camorra in precisely the same terms they use against the Italian Black Hand, the Vice Trust and the American Civil Liberties Union.

Nor is this new frankness confined to the South. The last presidential campaign brought the subject of evangelical theology into open discussion everywhere, and the result, as I see it, is a great increase in public pleasure, and, to some extent at least, in public enlightenment. With all the old taboos got rid of, that theology is being revealed as what it actually is—a decadent form of Puritanism, preposterous in its ideology and brutal and dishonest in its practices. If the hinds of the farms and villages still cling to it, then certainly it is fast losing its hold upon all the ranks above them. To confess to a belief in it today is to confess not only to stupidity, but also to a kind of malignancy—a delight in opposing decent ideas and harrowing honest men.

For that change, so swift and so sanitary, we have to thank Bishop Cannon and his colleagues of the Anti-Saloon League, the Ku Klux Klan and the Methodist Board of Temperance, Prohibition and Public Morals. They have gained (at least transiently) a formidable power over politicians even worse than they are, but they have wrecked their church. They have won a battle and lost a war.

The wrecking of such churches as these, whether they be spiritual or secular, seems to me to be an excellent gauge of the progress of civilization. For men become civilized, not in proportion to their willingness to believe, but in proportion to their readiness to doubt. The more stupid the man, the larger his stock of adamantine assurances, the heavier his load of faith.

[IV]

There is a darky living in the alley behind my house who knows a great deal more than I do, and is far more positive and confident in his kind of knowledge than I am in mine. He knows that he will be snow-white in the life beyond the grave, and that the Twelve Apostles will be very polite to him. He knows that a rabbit-foot carried in his pocket will protect him against thieves, warts and the police. He knows that the fall of the die may be conditioned by verbal formulas, mainly theological in character. He knows that meeting a black cat on a dark night is comparable, practically speaking, to meeting a locomotive head-on. He knows precisely why the stars were hung in the sky, and how they are kept there, and what their influence is upon the destiny of man. He knows what Moses said to Abraham, and what Abraham said to Pontius Pilate. He is the proprietor of a perfect epistemology, and his cosmogony, pathology and political science are neat, well-rounded and completely sufficient for his standards of judgment. To find his match as a wiseacre one must resort to the Rev. Billy Sunday, to Arthur Brisbane or to the Pope.

Nevertheless, I am iconoclast enough to doubt his whole stock of wisdom, as I doubt, indeed, that of his three colleagues in omniscience. His certainty that cancer is caused by incantations seems to me to be somehow dubious. I prefer to believe that no one knows what causes it, and to reckon that belief a kind of knowledge.

The common view of science is that it is a sort of machine for increasing the race's store of dependable facts. It is that only in part; in even larger part it is a machine for upsetting *un*dependable facts. When Copernicus proved that the earth revolved around the sun, he did not simply prove that the earth revolved around the sun; he also proved that the so-called revelation of God, as contained in the Old Testament, was rubbish. The first fact was relatively trivial: it made no difference to the average man then, as it makes no difference to him today. But the second fact was of stupendous importance, for it disposed at one stroke of a mass of bogus facts that had been choking the intelligence and retarding the progress of humanity for a millennium and a half.

So with every other great discovery in the physical world: it had immediate repercussions in the world of ideas, and often they were far more important than its immediate effect. The long line of glorious workers in medicine are not to be regarded merely as cheaters of the grave, for the grave, in the long run, has cheated every one of them in turn; their service to man was that they dissuaded him from laying vain blames for his ills and making vain and ignominious appeals for aid against them, and set him to examining them, and himself with them, in a rational and self-respecting manner. That medicine saves today thousands who must have died yesterday is a fact of small significance, for most of them will leave no more marks upon the history of the race than so many June bugs; but that all of us have been persuaded thereby to turn from priests and magicians when we are ill to doctors and nurses—that is a fact of massive and permanent importance. It benefits everybody worthy of being called human at all. It rids the thinking of mankind of immense accumulations of intellectual garbage. It increases the dignity of every honest man and it diminishes the puissance of every fraud.

To believe in frauds, it seems to me, is incompatible with any sort of dignity. It may be held, by the sorry standards which prevail in certain quarters, to be virtuous, but it is plainly not dignified. Is it a fact that the authors of the New Testament were inspired by God, and compiled a record that is innocent of error? It is not a fact. They were ignorant and credulous men, and they put together a narrative that is as discordant and preposterous, at least in material parts, as the testimony of six darkies in a police court. Is it a fact that believing that narrative is an act of merit, and that its reward is deliverance from Hell and entrance upon an eternity of bliss? It is not a fact. More, it is not even an innocent fiction. For its necessary implication is that the test of a proposition is something unrelated to its truth—that lying is virtuous so long as it brings a reward.

There, it seems to me, pragmatism is run to earth at last and turns out to be, not a lion, but only a fox. I can imagine no self-respecting man haggling for advantage on any such terms. It involves not only a repudiation of every rational criterion of truth; it also involves a repudiation of every sort of decency. Whenever such an idea is unhorsed in the world, the integrity of man increases.

The supply, unluckily, still remains very large. Its reservoir is the mob, uneducable and irrational, and along the banks of that reservoir many enterprising frauds—theological, political and philosophical—find profitable fishing. There are impatient men who long to heave the whole company overboard at one swoop: they are the fashioners of Utopias. But human progress, of course, can never be so facile. It must be carried on, not with the cosmic engines of gods, but with the puny machinery at hand; and that machinery, as everyone knows, is always breaking down.

The Fathers of the Republic, despite the sagacity that I have been praising, were a bit too confident and impatient. I suppose they believed that by setting religion adrift they had got rid of it, but all they had really done was to make it ready for self-wrecking years after their day was done. Again and even worse, they bent their hardest endeavors to setting up a government of the most sagacious, the most honorable, the most fit—but all they actually achieved was to let in the least fit, and a century and a half afterward we are still struggling to get rid of the Hardings, Coolidges and Hoovers.

[V]

Things would move faster if there were a general agreement as to the goal, but that is too much to hope for. There are men in the world, and some of them not unintelligent men, who have a natural appetite for the untrue, just as there are others who have a natural appetite for the ugly. A bald fact somehow affrights them: they long to swathe it in comforting illusions. Thus one hears from them that it is somehow immoral for an artist to depict human life as it actually is: the spectacle of the real must be ameliorated by an evocation of the ideal, which is to say, of the unreal. So Thomas Hardy becomes a bad artist, and the author of "Pollyanna" a good one.[11]

One hears again, and from the same men, that religious faith is a valuable thing per se, even if it be faith in propositions revolting to the most elementary intelligence. And one hears that it is an evil business to dwell upon the gross and intolerable failures of democracy, lest the general belief in democracy itself be converted into doubt. The facts, it appears, are nothing; the important thing is to retain a hopeful and pleasant frame of mind. The most valuable philosopher is that one who conjures up glittering universes in which two and two make five, six or even ten; the most despicable is the fellow who keeps on insisting that they make only four.

Of such sort are the reconcilers of science and religion, the more naïve variety of Liberals in politics, and the various disciples of Hamilton Wright Mabie and Edward W. Bok in the arts. I daresay the first-named were an active and expectant party in the day of Copernicus; if so, they must have given a great deal less comfort to Pope Paul III. They continue energetically today, proving that Genesis and the Darwinian hypothesis are not in conflict, that curved space is still reconcilable with the Book of Revelation, and that, in any case, it is better to go to church on Sunday than to stay away.

The tragedy of such men is that, in the long run, they are bound to find that they are holding empty bags. The Popes, soon or late, always go over to Copernicus, as Dr. Andrew D. White once proved in two noble tomes. The truth, battered and torn, yet survives all the petty nothings that beset it. Out of the welter of hopes and fears, of cautions and evasions, there always arises in the end the gaunt, immovable figure of a solid fact.

Certainly the Liberals in our midst should have learned long ago how dangerous it is to tackle such facts with no better weapons than hosannas. Is it so soon forgotten that they once believed in Roosevelt? And then in Wilson? And then in the War to End War? And then in a long series of other impostures, ranging from the initiative and referendum to the direct primary, and from woman suffrage to Prohibition? There is more here than mere innocence; there is also, it seems to me, a downright libido for the improbable, a thirst to believe what can scarcely be imagined as true.

Certainly something of the sort must be sought in the current Liberal crush upon Holmes, J., an upright judge but no more fit to be a hero of Liberals than his predecessor in their adoration, the limber Borah. I have been vastly diverted of late by reading the volume of Dr. Holmes's dissenting opinions, so conveniently arranged by Mr. George Lief. It shows that his juridic theory, taking it by and large, is hardly to be distinguished from that of the late Mr. Chief Justice Taft, and that not a few of his dissenting opinions have been launched against a more liberal majority! Yet the Liberals, with their craving for unrealities, continue to hail him as one of them, and when disillusionment overtakes them at last, as overtake them it must, they will no doubt turn to some even more impossible hero—maybe even to Mr. Chief Justice Hughes or Old Joe Grundy.

Such is the will to believe. Holding it to be a great nuisance in the world, and worse even than the will to power, I try to keep myself as free of it as I can. On gloomy days I speculate as to the probable state of modern man if it had ever been universal. We'd still be following Pope Paul; nay, not the Pope of that name but the Saint, with his cocksure ignorance and his Little Bethel moral scheme. Perhaps we'd be even further back than that—among the sheiks of the Palestine plateau and the primitive shamans of the Central Asian wilderness. It seems to me that such prophets as Dr. Robert A. Millikan, when they flirt gravely with the rev. clergy, ask us to go back almost that far.

Are the clergy true teachers or false? Is the body of ideas that they merchant true or not true? If it is not true, then I can imagine no prudent and profitable traffic with them. They have a right, of course, to be heard, but they have no more right to be attended to than the astrologers and necromancers who were once their colleagues and rivals.

There is only one man who has a right to be attended to, and that is the man who is trying, patiently, fairly, earnestly, diligently, to find out the truth. I am willing to give him my ear at any time of the day or night, year in and year out. But I am not willing to listen to the man who argues that what might be or ought to be true is somehow superior to what is true. One Copernicus, it seems to me, is worth all the Popes who ever lived, and all the bishops and archbishops, and all save a baker's dozen of the holy saints.

[VI]

The title of this article is far too wide. No man, within the bounds of a magazine, could make anything approaching a complete or even a fair statement of his credo. I must content myself, after the foregoing prolegomenon, with a few random notes.

I believe that religion, generally speaking, has been a curse to mankind— that its modest and greatly overestimated services on the ethical side have been more than overborne by the damage it has done to clear and honest thinking.

I believe that no discovery of fact, however trivial, can be wholly useless to the race, and that no trumpeting of falsehood, however virtuous in intent, can be anything but vicious.

I believe that all government is evil, in that all government must necessarily make war upon liberty; and that the democratic form is at least as bad as any of the other forms.

I believe that an artist, fashioning his imaginary worlds out of his own agony and ecstasy, is a benefactor to all of us, but that the worst error we can commit is to mistake his imaginary worlds for the real one.

I believe that the evidence for immortality is no better than the evidence for witches, and deserves no more respect.

I believe in complete freedom of thought and speech, alike for the humblest man and the mightiest, and in the utmost freedom of conduct that is consistent with living in organized society.

I believe in the capacity of man to conquer his world, and to find out what it is made of, and how it is run.

I believe in the reality of progress.

I—

But the whole thing, after all, may be put very simply. I believe that it is better to tell the truth than to lie. I believe that it is better to be free than to be a slave. And I believe that it is better to know than to be ignorant.

ON THE MEANING OF LIFE

You ask me, in brief, what satisfaction I get out of life, and why I go on working. I go on working for the same reason that a hen goes on laying eggs. There is in every living creature an obscure but powerful impulse to active functioning. Life demands to be lived. Inaction, save as a measure of recuperation between bursts of activity, is painful and dangerous to the healthy organism—in fact, it is almost impossible. Only the dying can be really idle.

The precise form of an individual's activity is determined, of course, by the equipment with which he came into the world. In other words, it is determined by his heredity. I do not lay eggs, as a hen does, because I was born without any equipment for it. For the same reason I do not get myself elected to Congress, or play the violoncello, or teach metaphysics in a college, or work in a steel mill. What I do is simply what lies easiest to my hand. It happens that I was born with an intense and insatiable interest in ideas, and thus like to play with them. It happens also that I was born with rather more than the average facility for putting them into words. In consequence, I am a writer and editor, which is to say, a dealer in them and concoctor of them.

There is very little conscious volition in all this. What I do was ordained by the inscrutable fates, not chosen by me. In my boyhood, yielding to a powerful but still subordinate interest in exact facts, I wanted to be a chemist, and at the same time my poor father tried to make me a business man. At other times, like any other relatively poor man, I have longed to make a lot of money by some easy swindle. But I became a writer all the same, and shall remain one until the end of the chapter, just as a cow goes on giving milk all her life, even though what appears to be her self-interest urges her to give gin.

I am far luckier than most men, for I have been able since boyhood to make a good living doing precisely what I have wanted to do—what I would have done for nothing, and very gladly, if there had been no reward for it. Not many men, I believe, are so fortunate. Millions of them have to make their livings at tasks which really do not interest them. As for me, I have had an extraordinarily pleasant life, despite the fact that I have had the usual share of woes. For in the midst of those woes I still enjoyed the immense satisfaction which goes with free activity. I have done, in the main, exactly what I wanted to do. Its possible effects upon other people have interested me very little. I have not written and published to please other people, but to satisfy myself, just as a cow gives milk, not to profit the dairyman, but to satisfy herself. I like to think that most of my ideas have been sound ones, but I really don't care. The world may take them or leave them. I have had my fun hatching them.

Next to agreeable work as a means of attaining happiness I put what Huxley called the domestic affections—the day to day intercourse with family and friends. My home has seen bitter sorrow, but it has never seen any serious disputes, and it has never seen poverty. I was completely happy with my mother and sister, and I am completely happy with my wife. Most of the men I commonly associate with are friends of very old standing. I have known some of them for more than thirty years. I seldom see anyone, intimately, whom I have known for less than ten years. These friends delight me. I turn to them when work is done with unfailing eagerness. We have the same general tastes, and see the world much alike. Most of them are interested in music, as I am. It has given me more pleasure in this life than any other external thing. I love it more every year.

As for religion, I am quite devoid of it. Never in my adult life have I experienced anything that could be plausibly called a religious impulse. My father and grandfather were agnostics before me, and though I was sent to Sunday-school as a boy and exposed to the Christian theology I was never taught to believe it. My father thought that I should learn what it was, but it apparently never occurred to him that I would accept it. He was a good psychologist. What I got in Sunday-school—beside a wide acquaintance with Christian hymnology—was simply a firm conviction that the Christian faith was full of palpable absurdities, and the Christian God preposterous. Since that time I have read a great deal in theology—perhaps much more than the average clergyman—but I have never discovered any reason to change my mind.

The act of worship, as carried on by Christians, seems to me to be debasing rather than ennobling. It involves grovelling before a Being who, if He really exists, deserves to be denounced instead of respected. I see little evidence in this world of the so-called goodness of God. On the contrary, it seems to me that, on the strength of His daily acts, He must be set down a most stupid, cruel and villainous fellow. I can say this with a clear conscience, for He has treated me very well—in fact, with vast politeness. But I can't help thinking of his barbaric torture of most of the rest of humanity. I simply can't imagine revering the God of war and politics, theology and cancer.

I do not believe in immortality, and have no desire for it. The belief in it issues from the puerile egos of inferior men. In its Christian form it is little more than a device for getting revenge upon those who are having a better time on this earth. What the meaning of human life may be I don't know: I incline to suspect that it has none. All I know about it is that, to me at least, it is very amusing while it lasts. Even its troubles, indeed, can be amusing. Moreover, they tend to foster the human qualities that I admire most—courage and its analogues. The noblest man, I think, is that one who fights God, and triumphs over Him. I have had little of this to do. When I die I shall be content to vanish into nothingness. No show, however good, could conceivably be good forever.

"GENERALLY POLITICAL"

After damning politicians up hill and down dale for forty years, as rogues and vagabonds, frauds and scoundrels, I sometimes suspect that, like everyone else, I often expect too much of them. Though faith and confidence are surely more or less foreign to my nature, I not infrequently find myself looking to them to be able, diligent, candid and even honest. Plainly enough, that is too large an order, as anyone must realize who reflects upon the manner in which they reach public office. They seldom if ever get there by merit alone, at least in democratic states. Sometimes, to be sure, it happens, but only by a kind of miracle. They are chosen normally for quite different reasons, the chief of which is simply their power to impress and enchant the intellectually underprivileged. It is a talent like any other, and when it is exercised by a radio crooner, a movie actor or a bishop, it even takes on a certain austere and sorry respectability. But it is obviously not identical with a capacity for the intricate problems of statecraft. Those problems demand for their solution—when they are soluble at all, which is not often—a high degree of technical proficiency, and with it there should go an adamantine kind of integrity, for the temptations of a public official are almost as cruel as those of a glamour girl or a dipsomaniac. But we train a man for facing them, not by locking him up in a monastery and stuffing him with wisdom and virtue, but by turning him loose on the stump. If he is a smart and enterprising fellow, which he usually is, he quickly discovers there that hooey pleases the boobs a great deal more than sense. Indeed, he finds that sense really disquiets and alarms them—that it makes them, at best, intolerably uncomfortable, just as a tight collar makes them uncomfortable, or a speck of dust in the eye, or the thought of Hell. The truth, to the overwhelming majority of mankind, is indistinguishable from a headache. As I once defined it in a moment of despair, it is something somehow discreditable to someone.[12] After trying a few shots of it on his customers, the larval statesman concludes sadly that it must hurt them, and after that he taps a more humane keg, and in a little while the whole audience is singing "Glory, glory, hallelujah," and when the returns come in the candidate is on his way to the White House.

I hope no one will mistake this brief account of the political process under democracy for exaggeration. It is almost literally true. I do not mean to argue, remember, that all politicians are villains in the sense that a burglar, a child-stealer or an atheist are villains. Far from it. Many of them, in their private characters, are very excellent persons, and I have known plenty that I'd trust with my diamonds, my daughter or my liberty, if I had any such things. I happen to be acquainted to some extent with nearly all the gentlemen, both Democrats and Republicans, who are currently itching for the Presidency, including the present incumbent, and I testify freely that they are all charming fellows, with merits above rather than below the common. One of them, as you all know, has been praised publicly as a labor-baiting, whiskey-drinking, poker-playing, evil old man—which is certainly no small encomium, considering his advanced age. If I am still that sinful at seventy-one it will be a grand joke on my pastor, and I'll enjoy it much more than anyone else.[13] So with all the other candidates, young and old. The worst of them is a great deal better company than most generals in the army, or writers of murder mysteries, or astrophysicists, and the best is a really superior and wholly delightful man—full of sound knowledge, competent and prudent, frank and courageous, and quite as honest as any American can be without being clapped into a madhouse. Don't ask me what his name is, for I am not in politics. I can only tell you that he has been in public life a long while, and has not been caught yet.

But will this prodigy, or any of the other candidates, really unload any appreciable amount of sagacity on the stump? Will any of them venture to tell the plain truth, the whole truth and nothing but the truth about the situation of the country, foreign and domestic? Will any of them refrain from promises that he knows he can't fulfill—that no human being *could* fulfill? Will any of them utter a word, however obvious, that will alarm and alienate any of the huge packs of morons who now cluster at the public trough, wallowing in the pap that grows thinner and thinner, hoping against hope? Answer: maybe for a few weeks at the start. Maybe before the campaign really begins. Maybe behind the door. But not after the issue is fairly joined, and the struggle is on in earnest. From that moment they will all resort to demagogy, and by the middle of June the only choice among them will be a choice between amateurs of that science and professionals. They will all promise every man, woman and child in the country whatever he, she or it wants. They'll all be roving the land looking for chances to make the rich poor, to remedy the irremediable, to succor the unsuccorable, to unscramble the unscrambleable, to dephlogisticate the undephlogisticable. They will all be curing warts by saying words over them, and paying off the national debt with money that no one will have to earn. They will dispose of Hitler and Stalin with one hand, and the law of natural selection with the other. When one of them demonstrates that twice two is five, another will prove that it is six, six-and-a-half, ten, twenty, n. In brief, they will divest themselves of their character as sensible, candid and truthful men, and become simply candidates for office, bent only on collaring votes. They will all know by then, even supposing that some of them don't know it now, that votes are collared under democracy, not by talking sense but by talking nonsense, and they will apply themselves to the job with a hearty yo-heave-ho. Most of them, before the uproar is over, will actually convince themselves. The winner will be whoever promises the most with the least probability of delivering anything.

Many years ago—in fact, a ponderable part of a century—I accompanied a candidate for the Presidency on his campaign-tour.[14] He was, like all such rascals, an amusing fellow, and I came to like him very much. His speeches, at the start, were full of fire. He was going to save the country from all the stupendous frauds and false pretenses of his rival. Every time that rival offered to rescue another million of poor fish from the neglects and oversights of God he howled his derision from the back platform of his train. I noticed at once that these blasts

of common sense got very little applause, and after a while the candidate began
to notice it too. Worse, he began to get word from his spies on the train of his
rival that the rival was wowing them, panicking them, laying them in the aisles.
They threw flowers, hot-dogs and five-cent cigars at him. In places where the
times were especially hard they tried to unhook the locomotive from his train,
so that he'd have to stay with them awhile longer, and promise them some more.
There were no Gallup polls in those innocent days, but the local politicians had
ways of their own for finding out how the cat was jumping, and they began to
join my candidate's train in the middle of the night, and wake him up to tell him
that all was lost, including honor. This had some effect upon him—in truth,
an effect almost as powerful as that of sitting in the electric chair. He lost his
intelligent manner, and became something you could hardly distinguish from
an idealist. Instead of mocking he began to promise, and in a little while he was
promising everything that his rival was promising, and a good deal more.

One night out in the Bible country, after the hullabaloo of the day was over,
I went into his private car along with several other newspaper reporters, and we
sat down to gabble with him. One of these reporters, a faithful member of the
candidate's own party, began to upbraid him, at first very gently, for letting off
so much hokum. What did he mean by making promises that no human being
on this earth, and not many of the angels in heaven, could ever hope to carry
out? In particular, what was his idea in trying to work off all those preposterous
bile-beans and snake-oils on the poor farmers, a class of men who had been
fooled and rooked by every fresh wave of politicians since Apostolic times? Did
he really believe that the Utopia he had begun so fervently to preach would
ever come to pass? Did he honestly think that farmers, as a body, would ever
see their rosy but insane dreams come true, or that the share-croppers in their
lower ranks would ever be more than a hop, skip and jump from starvation? The
candidate thought a while, took a long swallow of the coffin-varnish he carried
with him and then replied that the answer in every case was no. He was well
aware, he said, that the plight of the farmers was almost hopeless, and would
probably continue so for centuries to come. He had no notion that anything
could be done about it by merely human means, and certainly not by political
means: it would take a new Moses, and a whole series of miracles. "But you
forget, Mr. Blank," he concluded sadly, "that our agreement in the premises
must remain purely personal. You are not a candidate for office. I am." As we
left him the oldest of the reporters, a gentleman grown gray in Washington and
long ago lost to every decency, pointed the moral of the episode. "In politics,"

he said, "a man must learn to rise above principle." Then he drove it in with another: "When the water reaches the upper deck," he said, "follow the rats."

Some time ago I told this story to one of the men who is often mentioned for the Presidency today, usually by himself. Rather to my surprise, he was not at all upset, but proceeded to defend his predecessor of long ago. "Such things always happen," he said, "in political campaigns. One party tends inevitably to steal the thunder of the other. I believe that in the long run this is a good thing. It keeps the two major parties from flying too far apart, and so converting every change of control into a revolution. We had a good example of the dangers of really radical overturns at the time Mr. Roosevelt became converted to the New Deal, shortly after his inauguration. He tried to launch so many reforms at once that the effect was that of an earthquake, and we were lucky to escape bloodshed. The consequences are still visible. The country is almost in the state of mind that would have followed if he had been made President, not by votes but by bayonets. If the Republicans come in next November they'll have a dreadful time liquidating the New Deal without setting huge armies to marching on Washington, led by jobholders."

So far I have been quoting. My own belief is that there is something in this argument. Whenever democracy really functions, and a new majority proceeds to inflict its ideas on a new minority, without compromise or concession, we have what is really a revolution, and there is a good deal of trouble. This happened with Prohibition, and it happened again with the New Deal. Fortunately for all of us, our usual way is less drastic. Each party steals so many articles of faith from the other, and the candidates spend so much time making each other's speeches, that by the time election day is past there is nothing much to do save turn the sitting rascals out and let a new gang in. This is not theoretical democracy, but it is actual democracy. When the theoretical kind gets a bite at us we always suffer horribly, for theories and theorists are almost as unpleasant as the truth and those who tell it. It is much more comfortable to go on compromising, stalling, talking through hats. The men who get into high office under this system are sometimes anything but museum pieces of conscience, but they are at least better than fanatics. What it means to be run by fanatics was demonstrated during the thirteen dreadful years of Prohibition. Once the Prohibitionists got control, two-thirds of the professional politicians of the country leaped on their bandwagon, and for some years thereafter the United States was one of the Balkan States, and a great deal worse than most.

A long while ago John C. Calhoun wrote a "Discourse on the Constitution and Government of the United States" that has been completely forgotten, but deserves to be resurrected. In it he argued with great plausibility that actual democracy is almost as bad as government by divine right—that giving a chance majority an unrestricted franchise to work its wicked will upon the whole country, regardless of the interests and desires of the minority, is simply setting up an irrational and irresponsible tyranny. Other sages have pointed out the same thing, but we are lucky that our actual political system saves us, in ordinary times, from such evil consequences. The majority, despite its theoretical omnipotence, is hobbled by various practical considerations. One is the fact that the public, having only a very feeble development of the mind, changes what little it has very often. That threat is always present, and every politician is constantly conscious of it. Another thing is the fact that the public always tires of its messiahs, and soon or late invariably turns them out, whether they be good, which is uncommon, or bad, which is the rule. Indeed, it usually tries to lynch them in the long run, as the cases of Washington, Wilson and the elder Roosevelt well exhibited. Even Abraham Lincoln, if he had lived, would have ended as a kind of Hoover, distrusted and disliked by whites and blacks alike. He was saved by the bullet of John Wilkes Booth, which made him a martyr and hence beyond the reach of justice. There is enough material in Carl Sandburg's life of Lincoln to make forty Hoovers, with a dozen Hardings and Coolidges to boot.[15]

The third factor that saves us from being saved too often, and at too great expense, is the fact that professional politicians seldom believe in reform, and almost never in the reforms they advocate. This was demonstrated on a grandiose scale during Prohibition. Probably not a quarter of the statesmen who voted for the Eighteenth Amendment in Congress had any belief in it whatsoever—except, of course, as a means of collaring moron votes. Some of these official drys were the real master boozers of the thirteen dreadful years, headed by the sainted Harding. I knew not a few of them who got down so much alcohol that it was impossible to freeze them in Winter, even though they lay in the gutter outside a Washington speakeasy, with five feet of snow over them. When Prohibition finally blew up with a bang they went wet overnight, and with almost as much fervor publicly as they had been showing privately. As I recall it, more than 200 of them were converted instantly and in a body—a magnificent example of the power of reason upon inanimate matter. One day they were taking orders from Bishop Cannon, and the next day they were talking of hanging him. The Bishop himself, an agreeable fellow despite his sepulchral office and his dislike of the human race, was not surprised. In fact, he was less surprised than I was, though I had been predicting such a wholesale conversion for some years. He had been in politics up to his ears for a generation, and was well aware of the nature of politicians. He knew that they were chronic antidotes to the great boons and usufructs they whooped up.

The same thing is now happening in Washington all over again, and if there had been no war in Europe it would have been plainly visible today. Not half of the Senators and Congressmen who were lately supporting the New Deal really believed in it, or made any effort to conceal that fact behind the curtain. They went along simply because it seemed the smart and profitable thing to do. They would have been in favor of Fascism, Communism, Zoroastrianism or even cannibalism under the same circumstances. A year or so ago, when it began to appear that the New Deal was making heavy weather of it, and that the great masses of the plain people had got an overdose of Roosevelt and were longing for another and worse, these statesmen lost a great deal of their former enthusiasm for Utopia, and took to sabotage. The Hon. John Nance Garner was certainly not the worst; he was simply the first. After a while he became so bold that he actually began to talk treason with the door *open.*

Well, if you think that all this is pessimism, then you are mistaken. For democracy in general, I have no great taste, just as I have no great taste for other forms of virtue. But there are some things in it that seem to me to be very valuable—at all events, to me personally. I enjoy living in a country where government is a creature of purely delegated powers, with no inherent rights of its own. And I enjoy the right of free speech, even when it is employed to argue—and prove—that I am in the pay of Wall Street. For the rest I care little. Having no desire for public office and being by birth a member of the bloated and nefarious bourgeoisie, well crammed with vitamins from the age of two or three hours, I am not interested in the fact that any poor boy may become President. Nor does it give me any thrill to hear that my vote is as good as that of the president of Harvard—and no better than that of a share-cropper in Arkansas. But, as I have said, I enjoy talking, and I agree with Thomas Jefferson that the best government is the weakest. Unfortunately, Jefferson's idea is now out of the window, along with his idea that public debts are public misfortunes, and will have to be repaid soon or late in either money or blood. How long the right to free speech will last I don't know, but if the New Dealers try to save their hides by horning into the war it probably won't be long.

In this country, as everywhere else, government is only a sorry compromise, a half loaf that is better, so we assume, than no bread at all. The human race has never succeeded in fashioning a government that was even 20 per cent. good. The effort is always a failure, here, there and everywhere. It is mankind's most gorgeous flop. In some respects our own failure is worse than the average, but in other respects it is probably better. Our system of checks and balances, the pride of our trusting hearts, is really not between the executive, the legislature and the judiciary, but between the people and the politicians of the country, which is to say, between its fools and its rogues. The people keep the politicians from stealing too much, and the politicians keep the people from getting too crazy. If it were not for the knavery of politicians the Townsend Plan would be the law of the land at this moment. Old Dr. Townsend, a couple of years ago, had more than half the candidates for Congress, regardless of party, on his mourners' bench. But the moment his back was turned most of them bolted, and so the country was saved once more from being saved. On the other hand, the people perform a valuable service every time they rise up for some possibly good but usually bad reason, and throw the politicians of a whole party out. It doesn't make much difference whether the victims are Democrats or Republicans, Liberals or Tories, mere pickpockets or downright burglars. The essential thing is they are thrown out. The experience chastens them, at least until they can get back.

It is thus, under democracy, that we live and have our being. It is thus that the imperishable ideals of the Founding Fathers are preserved, or, at all events, embalmed. The process, described in cold and rigid scientific terms, as I have described it here, is not a pretty one, but neither is any other biological process pretty. Certainly those that have been set going in other countries are no better. We shudder as we think of them—though most of us have a sneaking yearning for some element of one or another of them. Let us be content with what we have, and thank God that it is no worse. Say what you will against it, you must always admit in the end that it makes a great show. A national campaign is better than the best circus ever heard of, with a mass baptism and a couple of hangings thrown in. It is better, even, than war. If I am alive come September, I'll follow the next one from the opening prayer of the first national convention to the terminal cries of fraud, and with unfailing zest and edification. I have been doing so since 1904, and am still thirsty for more. But one war was enough to content me for life, just as I was satisfied by one attack of delirium tremens.

WORLD TRAVELER

AT THE EDGE OF THE SPANISH MAIN

Port Antonio, Jamaica, Aug. 13 [1900].—If you look at the map of the West Indies you will note that to the southward of Cuba, and separated from it by a loop of the Caribbean Sea, there is a small island shaped like the elongated skull of a Flathead Indian. If you look closer and have a good map you will further note that the coastline of the island is pitted by the sea, in a hundred score of places, as if the owner of the skull during his time upon earth had fought frequent boxing club fights with his friends.

The name of this little patch of land is Jamaica, and since the 11th day of May in the year 1655 it has been a colony of the British Empire. Before that date it was owned by the Spanish, who had obtained it from its original owners, the Caribbean Indians, by the simple process of executing all persons who opposed the transfer. When Oliver Cromwell pitched his tent upon the spot where the throne of England had been he began to cast longing glances upon it. Finally he dispatched a certain Admiral Penn and a certain General Venables[1] to the West to investigate its resources. Finding the Spaniards inhospitable, the Britishers killed them and hoisted the Union Jack. During all of the 245 years since that day no one has seen fit to lower it.

Jamaica is one of those lotus-grown corners of the earth whereat man may emulate the lilies of the field. The wind from the glimmering sea sings a lullaby and the spice-laden zephyr from the dim blue mountains seems to bear the caressing music of a half-heard blumenlied. There is restfulness in the sparkle of the myriad streams and contentment in the glare of the sun upon the palms. "Lay down your labors" whispers the hummingbird, as he glides among the trees. "Forget your woes and dream" sighs the green sea, as it rolls over and over in mad joy upon the sand.

And the Jamaican, who is black and lazy and sleepy, obeys them.

For two hours before the lookout on the steamer from the North sights Folly Point light the passengers beneath the awning upon the upper deck have watched the green gray mountains rise out of the sea. First the tip of the highest peak shows above the horizon, like a low-lying rock in the haze. Then the land seems to grow as if it were some giant sea plant, higher and higher, and greener and greener. Slowly it takes form and color and stretches out toward the east and west. Suddenly the lookout sings "Light four points on th' stabbard bow!" the wheel goes over a point or two, the second mate appears on deck in his best new uniform and the Harbor of Port Antonio is dead ahead.

Then the ensign flutters above the taffrail, the house flag creeps up to the foremast and the pilot climbs over the side. A half hour later the steamer is at her dock, and an army of roustabouts and bumboatmen and idlers are swarming over her deck. All around her rise the foothills, and upon them wave the palms.

There are dozens of words in the dictionary which express very well the superlative of beauty. Enchanting, charming, majestic and beautiful, for instance, serve admirably to describe the Black Forest and Niagara and the Alps. But below the tropic of cancer they are as meaningless as the word zero. There is a something about the tropics which is unlike anything real or imaginable in the North. The sea, the mountains, the flowers, the trees are so different, so fairy-like, so isolated in their loveliness. It might well be supposed that where the sun glares with ten-fold power everything would be garish and gaudy and lacking in the finer and more lasting kinds of beauty. But this is not true. Instead, the staring white light seems to soften the colors and make them fade into each other like the red and blue of a sunset. A hotel-keeper in the mountains near Kingston, in one of his advertisements, has unconsciously hit upon an extraordinarily vivid sentence descriptive of this characteristic of the southland. "The air," he says, "is beautiful." This is rather free English, but it tells the story better than any other combination of words in the language. The air is beautiful, and everything that walks or grows upon the earth or exists in the heavens above or the waters around the earth partakes of its beauty.

Blasé globe-trotters become silent when they enter the Harbor of Port Antonio, and travelers of lesser miles stare and stare and stare. Land-locked, with hills about it and bending palms starting up from its water's edge, it is so unreal that for hours one takes no note of its detail. The rooftops in the bit of town along the beach glare redly in the green, and far up the mountain-side the white roofs of plantation-houses and thatch-huts glimmer in the sun like huge day stars. As the ship swings idly round her anchor a bit of showy roadway flashes into view, and far away the light pea-green of a field of bananas breaks the darker emerald of the hills. Over the side the water is greener than the greenest tree that ever grew, and clearer than the clearest crystal of a woodland spring. Far below, among the seaweed and purple coral a silvery fish makes his lazy way, and far above a curious John crow idly flaps along. Peace is abroad in the land and the sky and the water. It is always afternoon.

When you sail into the Harbor of Port Antonio and spy the half-hundred inky banana handlers waiting for your ship to touch the dock, you will think, if you can blind yourself to the palms and the hills and the sky, that you are about to be landed at Bewley's Wharf. For, between the 'longshoremen, who swarmed over the vessel's side in Baltimore, and the roustabouts, who await her in Jamaica, the eye can detect no difference. They are alike ragged, rugged, lazy and prone to fall asleep as soon as their bosses turn away.

But when the steamer touches the landing place and you begin to distinguish individual voices from among the babble of shouts and yells, the realization that you are a stranger in a strange land comes to you with a sudden shock. When you hear a coal black darky yell: "Cawn't H'i hailp you weeth yo' luggidge?" it will jar you. When another informs you that his "kerridge" goes "pawst the 'otel," you will rush below and stuff your Kipling into the galley fire. By and by, however, you will become accustomed to the weird dialect, and in the course of a week or two you will be able to understand and hold converse with all sorts and conditions of Jamaicans, white and black, with the possible exception of the darkies from the mountains. The speech of the latter sounds like the plaintive shrieking of a $4 mandolin with two strings.

Of course, it is impossible to describe a dialect and very difficult to represent it, even approximately, in writing. That of the average black Jamaican, who is guiltless of learning and careless of grammar, is full of surprises to the newcomer. In the first place he uses an *a* nearly three times as broad as it is long. This disgusting practice he learned years ago from the English, as he did the equally reprehensible vice of dropping his h's. Beside these Britishisms, which, after all, are comparatively harmless, he indulges in the habits of rolling his r's, mixing his vowels and dropping at intervals into a nasal twang. These crimes the Cubans have taught him.

Finally, in addition to his numerous acquired philological blunders, he daily invents new ones of his own. As a result his speech is like the rattle of hexagonal brass doorknobs rolling down a galvanized iron chute. To reproduce it it would be necessary to hire a Spaniard from the backwoods of the Pyrenees, have him learn English from a Cockney, make him read a ton of "Hoot, mon!" novels and send him to live at Cape Cod. Unless his consequent insanity were of a violent kind, he would be able, in the course of fifteen or twenty years, to give a very fair imitation of an Afro-Jamaican.

Putting aside the industrious thousands who make their living by petty larceny, half of the inhabitants of Northern Jamaica live by selling fruits and bread to the other half. As the other half can purchase fruit at wholesale for the same price paid by the merchants—to wit, nothing—it is difficult to discern any possibility of financial success in the business. Within the shadow of the banana wharf warehouses, where undersized and nearly ripe "rejects" lie in foot-deep piles for the free feeding of the hungry, plaid-turbaned old women sit cross-legged by the roadside and offer fruit to the fruit-laden passerby.

And it is very noticeable that the bananas selected from the "reject" heaps by the banana women are, by long odds, the worst to be found. Big ones they seem to pass by; undamaged ones they seem to scorn. Some day a native philosopher will arise and explain the wherefore and why of this. Until he does so it will remain a mystery like unto that concerning Maloney's assault upon McCarthy.

As has been mentioned, petty thieving is a favorite occupation among the black Jamaicans. Because of the soft influence of the tropic sky and the color of their skins they covet their neighbor's yams and his cocoanuts and his bananas. It must be remembered that there are few chickens and fewer watermelons in the island. If their neighbor surprises them with a pound's worth of his produce in their possession he is debarred by the ready-made British laws of the land from the pleasure and satisfaction of abraiding their inky hides. Consequently, he has them arrested and pays for their support until the law has properly punished them. In recent years the burden he is thus called upon to bear has become exceedingly heavy, and in hopes of finding some relief from it he takes frequent counsel with his fellow sufferers. The Jamaican newspapers are daily filled with long accounts of district and parish meetings held for the purpose of considering the "praedial larceny" question. Some ingenious citizens advocate fining the petty thief an amount sufficient to reimburse the owner of the stolen property for his loss. But as the former seldom counts as much as a shilling in his pocket at one time, this plan is plainly wanting in practicability. Others favor flogging, and still others long imprisonment. But there are serious objections to both. The efficacy of a shotgun, loaded with rock salt, seems to have never suggested itself to the minds of the unfortunates who are compelled to wrestle with the problem. Neither has the moralizing influence of the spring gun and the hickory club with big knots.

Some day a Georgian or South Carolinian will alight in Jamaica, and teach the Jamaicans a thing or two about the noble science of scaring all craving for forbidden fruits from the colored kleptomaniac's brain. Until then they will continue to write letters to the papers and to listen to senseless speeches by country curates and other enemies of physical argument.

It is easier to write a small-arm drill book than to give any idea of the beauty of Northern Jamaica. Only about one-tenth of 1 per cent. of the colors of a Caribbean sunset have names. The rest are too beautiful to be burdened with verbal tags. It would be sacrilege to baptize them. Usually the sun goes down like a white-hot ball of iron sinking into a lake of blue-green dye. Huge clouds of steam seem to rise to the zenith, and if you have a little imagination you will almost fancy that you hear the splutter and hiss.

Now, the dying light, breaking upon these clouds, is itself broken into a million rainbows. In the spot where the sun was last seen there is a big splash of red—not the common, tame and rusty red seen in the North, but a wild and woolly scarlet, which seems to fairly scream. Blood is brown compared to it, and vermilion a dirty yellow. There is nothing else like it between pole and pole.

From this staring daub in every direction run streaks of blue and purple and violet and pink. When one of them strikes a bunch of cloud the latter looks like the inside of a shell. Up toward the zenith they fade into nothingness. Ten minutes after the sun is out of sight the east is misty and dark.

Gradually this darkness creeps across the sky, and, like falling soldiers, the yellows and pinks and blues go down before it. Finally it reaches the splash of red, and there is a battle royal. But the red doesn't last long. In a minute it is plain scarlet. In another minute it is maroon. Then it is purple and garnet and brown and black. Then it has faded into the night. There is no twilight in latitude 18.

THE BEERIAD

Let the most important facts come first. The best beer in Munich is the Spaten-bräu; the best place to get it is at the Hoftheater Café in the Residenzstrasse; the best time to drink it is after 10 P.M., and the best of all girls to serve it is Fräulein Sophie, that tall and resilient creature, with her appetizing smile, her distinguished bearing and her superbly manicured hands.

I have, in my time, sat under many and many superior *kellnerin,*[2] some as regal as grand duchesses, some as demure as shoplifters, some as graceful as *prima ballerini,* but none reaching so high a general level of merit, none so thoroughly satisfying to eye and soul as Fräulein Sophie. She is a lady, every inch of her, a lady presenting to all gentlemanly clients the ideal blend of cordiality and dignity, and she serves the best beer in Christendom. Take away that beer, and it is possible, of course, that Sophie would lose some minute granule or globule of her charm; but take away Sophie and I fear the beer would lose even more.

In fact, I know it, for I have drunk that same beer in the Spatenbräukeller in the Bayerstrasse, at all hours of the day and night, and always the ultimate thrill was missing. Good beer, to be sure, and a hundred times better than the common brews, even in Munich, but not perfect beer, not beer *de luxe*, not super-beer. It is the human equation that counts, in the *bierhalle* as on the battlefield. One resents, somehow, a *kellnerin* with the figure of a taxicab, no matter how good her intentions and fluent her technique, just as one resents a trained nurse with a double chin or a glass eye. When a personal office that a man might perform, or even an intelligent machine, is put into the hands of a woman, it is put there simply and solely because the woman can bring charm to it and irradiate it with romance. If, now, she fails to do so—if she brings, not charm, not beauty, not romance, but the gross curves of an aurochs and a voice of brass—if she offers bulk when the heart cries for grace and adenoids when the order is for music, then the whole thing becomes a hissing and a mocking, and a gray fog is on the world.

But to get back to the Hoftheater Café. It stands, as I have said, in the Residenzstrasse, where that narrow street bulges out into the Max-Joseph-platz, and facing it, as its name suggests, is the Hoftheater, the most solemn-looking playhouse in Europe, but the scene of appalling tone debaucheries within. The supreme idea at the Hoftheater is to get the curtain down at ten o'clock. If the bill happens to be a short one, say "Hansel und Gretel" or "Elektra," the three thumps of the starting mallet may not come until eight o'clock, or even 8.30, but if it is a long one, say "Parsifal" or "Les Huguenots,"[3] a beginning is made far back in the afternoon. Always the end arrives at ten, with perhaps a moment or two leeway in one direction or the other. And two minutes afterward, without further ceremony or delay, the truly epicurean auditor has his feet under the mahogany at the Hoftheater Café across the platz, with the seidel of that incomparable brew tilted elegantly toward his face and his glad eyes smiling at Fräulein Sophie through the glass bottom.

How many women could stand that test? How many could bear the ribald distortions of that lens-like seidel bottom and yet keep their charm? How many, thus caricatured and vivisected, could command this free reading notice from a casual American, dictating against time and space to a red-haired stenographer, three thousand and five hundred miles away? And yet Sophie does it, and not only Sophie, but also Frida, Elsa, Lili, Kunigunde, Märtchen, Thérèse and Lottchen, her confrères and aides, and even little Rosa, who is half Bavarian and half Japanese, and one of the prettiest girls in Munich, in or out of uniform. It is a pleasure to say a kind word for little Rosa, with her coal black hair and her slanting eyes, for she is too fragile a fräulein to be toting around those gigantic German schnitzels and bifsteks, those mighty double portions of sauerbraten and rostbif, those staggering drinking urns, overballasted and awash.

Let us not, however, be unjust to the estimable Herr Wirt of the Hoftheater Café, with his pneumatic tread, his chaste side whiskers and his long-tailed coat, for his drinking urns, when all is said and done, are quite the smallest in Munich. And not only the smallest, but also the shapeliest. In the Hofbräuhaus and in the open air *bierkneipen*[4] (for instance, the Mathäser joint, of which more anon) one drinks out of earthen cylinders which resemble nothing so much as the gaunt towers of Munich cathedral; and elsewhere the orthodox goblet is a glass edifice following the lines of an old-fashioned silver water pitcher—you know the sort the innocently criminal used to give as wedding presents!—but at the Hoftheater there is a vessel of special design, hexagonal in cross section and unusually graceful in general aspect. On top, a pewter lid, ground to an optical fit and highly polished—by Sophie, Rosa *et al.,* poor girls! To starboard, a stout handle, apparently of reinforced onyx. Above the handle, and attached to the lid, a metal flange or thumbpiece. Grasp the handle, press your thumb on the thumbpiece—and presto, the lid heaves up. And then, to the tune of a Strauss waltz, played passionately by tone artists in oleaginous dress suits, down goes the Spatenbräu—gurgle, gurgle—burble, burble—down goes the Spatenbräu— exquisite, ineffable!—to drench the heart in its nut brown flood and fill the arteries with its benign alkaloids and antitoxins.

Well, well, maybe I grow too eloquent! Such memories loose and craze the tongue. A man pulls himself up suddenly, to find that he has been vulgar. If so here, so be it! I refuse to plead to the indictment: sentence me and be hanged to you! I am by nature a vulgar fellow. I prefer "Tom Jones" to "The Rosary," Rabelais to the Elsie books,[5] the Old Testament to the New, the expurgated parts of "Gulliver's Travels" to those that are left. I delight in beef stews, limericks, burlesque shows, New York City and the music of Haydn, that beery and delightful old rascal! I swear in the presence of ladies and archdeacons. When the mercury is above ninety-five I dine in my shirt sleeves and write poetry naked.

I associate habitually with dramatists, bartenders, medical men and musicians. I once, in early youth, kissed a waitress at Dennett's. So don't accuse me of vulgarity: I admit it and flout you. Not, of course, that I have no pruderies, no fastidious metes and bounds. Far from it. Babies, for example, are too vulgar for me; I cannot bring myself to touch them. And actors. And evangelists. And the obstetrical anecdotes of ancient dames. But in general, as I have said, I joy in vulgarity, whether it take the form of divorce proceedings or of "Tristan und Isolde,"[6] of an Odd Fellows' funeral or of Munich beer.

But here, perhaps, I go too far again. That is to say, I have no right to admit that Munich beer is vulgar. On the contrary, it is my obvious duty to deny it, and not only to deny it, but also to support my denial with an overwhelming mass of evidence and a shrill cadenza of casuistry. But the time and the place, unluckily enough, are not quite fit for the dialectic, and so I content myself with a few pertinent observations. *Imprimis,* a thing that is unique, incomparable, *sui generis,* cannot be vulgar. Munich beer is unique, incomparable, *sui generis.* More, it is consummate, transcendental, *übernatürlich.* Therefore it cannot be vulgar. Secondly, the folk who drink it day after day do not die of vulgar diseases. Turn to the subhead *Todesursachen* in the instructive *Statistischer Monatsbericht der Stadt München,*[7] and you will find records of few if any deaths from delirium tremens, boils, hookworm, smallpox, distemper, measles or what the *Monatsbericht* calls "liver sickness." The Müncheners perish more elegantly, more charmingly than that. When their time comes it is gout that fetches them, or appendicitis, or neurasthenia, or angina pectoris; or perchance they cut their throats.

Thirdly, and, to make it short, lastly, the late Henrik Ibsen, nourished upon Munich beer, wrote "Hedda Gabler," not to mention "Rosmersholm" and "The Lady from the Sea"[8]—wrote them in his flat in the Maximilianstrasse, overlooking the palace and the afternoon promenaders, in the late eighties of the present, or Christian era—wrote them there and then took them to the Café Luitpold, in the Briennerstrasse, to ponder them, polish them and make them perfect. I myself have sat in old Henrik's chair and victualed from his table. It is far back in the main hall of the café, to the right as you come in, and hidden from the incomer by the glass vestibule which guards the pantry. Ibsen used to appear every afternoon at three o'clock, to drink his vahze of Löwenbräu and read the papers. The latter done, he would sit in silence, thinking, thinking, planning, planning. Not often did he say a word, even to Fräulein Mizzi, his favorite *kellnerin.* So taciturn was he, in truth, that his rare utterances were carefully entered in the archives of the café and are now preserved there. By the courtesy of Dr. Adolf Himmelheber,[9] the present curator, I am permitted to transcribe a few, the imperfect German of the poet being preserved:

NOVEMBER 18, 1889, 4.15 P.M. —*Giebt es kein Feuer in diese verfluchte Bierstube? Meine Füsse sind so kall wie Eiszapfen!*
    APRIL 12, 1890, 5.20 P.M.—*Der Kerl ist verrückt!* (Said of an American who entered with the Stars and Stripes flying from his hat.)
    MAY 22, 1890, 4.40 P.M. —*Sie sind so eselhaft wie ein Schauspieler!* (To an assistant of Herr Wirt who brought him a Socialist paper in mistake for the London *Times*.)[10]

Now and then the great man would condescend to play a game of billiards in the hall to the rear, usually with some total stranger. He would point out the stranger to Fräulein Mizzi and she would carry his card. The game would proceed, as a rule, in utter silence. But it was for the Löwenbräu and not for the billiards that Ibsen came to the Luitpold, for the Löwenbräu and the high flights of soul that it engendered. He had no great liking for Munich as a city; his prime favorite was always Vienna, with Rome second. But he knew that the incomparable malt liquor of Munich was full of the inspiration that he needed, and so he kept near it, not to bathe in it, not to frivol with it, but to take it discreetly and prophylactically, and as the exigencies of his art demanded.

Ibsen's inherent fastidiousness, a quality which urged him to spend hours shining his shoes, was revealed by his choice of the Café Luitpold, for of all the cafés in Munich the Luitpold is undoubtedly the most elegant. Its walls are adorned with frescos by Albrecht Hildebrandt. The ceiling of the main hall is supported by columns of colored marble. The tables are of carved mahogany. The forks and spoons, before Americans began to steal them, were of real silver. The chocolate with whipped cream, served late in the afternoon, is famous throughout Europe. The Herr Wirt has the suave sneak of John Drew and is a privy councillor to the Prince Regent of Bavaria. All the tables along the east wall, which is one vast mirror, are reserved from 8 P.M. to 2 A.M. nightly by the faculty of the University of Munich, which there entertains the eminent scientists who constantly visit the city. No orchestra arouses the baser passions with "Wiener Blut."[11] The place has calm, aloofness, intellectuality, aristocracy, distinction. It was the scene foreordained for the hatching of "Hedda Gabler."

But don't imagine that Munich, when it comes to elegance, must stand or fall with the Luitpold. Far from it, indeed. There are other cafés of noble and elevating quality in that delectable town—plenty of them, you may be sure. For example, the Odéon, across the street from the Luitpold, a place lavish and luxurious, but with a certain touch of dogginess, a taste of salt. The *piccolo* who lights your cigar and accepts your five pfennigs at the Odéon is an Ethiopian dwarf. Do you sense the romance, the exotic *diablerie*, the suggestion of Levantine mystery? And somewhat Levantine, too, are the ladies who sit upon the plush benches along the wall and take Russian cigarettes with their kirschenwasser. Not that the atmosphere is frankly one of Sin! No, no! The Odéon is no cabaret. A leg flung in the air would bring the Herr Wirt at a gallop, you may be sure—or, at any rate, his apoplectic corpse. In all New York, I dare say, there is no public eating house so near to the far-flung outposts, the Galapagos Islands of virtue. But one somehow feels that, for Munich, at least, the Odéon is just a bit tolerant, just a bit philosophical, just a bit Bohemian. One even imagines taking an American show girl there without being warned (by a curt note in one's serviette) that the head waiter's family lives in the house.

Again, pursuing these haunts of the baroque and arabesque, there is the restaurant of the Hotel Vier Jahreszeiten, a masterpiece of the Munich glass cutters and upholsterers. It is in the very heart of things, with the royal riding school directly opposite, the palace a block away and the green of the Englischer Garten glimmering down the street. Here, of a fine afternoon, the society is the best between Vienna and Paris. One may share the vinegar cruet with a countess, and see a general of cavalry eat peas with a knife (hollow ground, like a razor: a Bavarian trick!) and stand aghast while a great tone artist dusts his shoes with a napkin, and observe a Russian grand duke at the herculean labor of drinking himself to death.

The Vier Jahreszeiten is no place for the common people: such trade is not encouraged. The dominant note of the establishment is that of proud retirement, of elegant sanctuary. One enters, not from the garish Maximilianstrasse, with its motor cars and its sinners, but from the Marstallstrasse, a sedate and aristocratic side street. The Vier Jahreszeiten, in its time, has given food, alcohol and lodgings for the night to twenty crowned heads and a whole shipload of lesser magnificoes, and despite the rise of other hotels it retains its ancient supremacy. It is the peer of Shepheard's at Cairo, of the Cecil in London, of the old Inglaterra at Havana, of the St. Charles at New Orleans. It is one of the distinguished hotels of the world.

I could give you a long list of other Munich restaurants of a kingly order—the great breakfast room of the Bayrischer Hof, with its polyglot waiters and its amazing repertoire of English jams; the tea and liquor atelier of the same hostelry, with its high dome and its sheltering palms; the pretty little open air restaurant of the Künstlerhaus in the Lenbachplatz; the huge catacomb of the Rathaus, with its medieval arches and its vintage wines; the lovely *al fresco* café on Isar Island, with the green cascades of the Isar singing on lazy afternoons; the café in the Hofgarten, gay with birds and lovers; that in the Tiergarten, from the terrace of which one watches lions and tigers gamboling in the woods; and so on, and so on. There is even, I hear, a temperance restaurant in Munich, the Jungbrunnen in the Arcostrasse, where water is served with meals, but that is only rumor. I myself have never visited it, nor do I know anyone who has.

All this, however, is far from the point. I am here hired to discourse of Munich beer, and not of vintage wines, bogus cocktails, afternoon chocolate and well water. We are on a beeriad. Avaunt, ye grapes, ye maraschino cherries, ye puerile H$_2$O!

And so, resuming that beeriad, it appears that we are once again in the Hoftheater Café in the Residenzstrasse, and that Fräulein Sophie, that pleasing creature, has just arrived with two ewers of Spatenbräu—two ewers fresh from the wood—woody, nutty, incomparable! Ah, those elegantly manicured hands! Ah, that Mona Lisa smile! Ah, that so-graceful waist! Ah, malt! Ah, hops! *Ach, München, wie bist du so schön?*[12]

But even Paradise has its nuisances, its scandals, its lacks. The Hoftheater Café, alas, is not the place to eat sauerkraut—not the place, at any rate, to eat sauerkraut *de luxe,* the supreme and singular masterpiece of the Bavarian uplands, the perfect grass embalmed to perfection. The place for that is the Pschorrbräu in the Neuhauserstrasse, a devious and confusing journey, down past the Pompeian post office, into the narrow Schrammerstrasse, around the old cathedral, and then due south to the Neuhauserstrasse. *Sapperment!*[13] The Neuhauserstrasse is here called the Kaufingerstrasse! Well, well, don't let it fool you. A bit further to the east it is called the Marienplatz, and further still the Thal, and then the Isarthorplatz, and then the Zweibrückenstrasse, and then the Isarbrücke, and then the Ludwigbrücke, and finally, beyond the river, the Gasteig or the Rosenheimerstrasse, according as one takes its left branch or its right.

But don't be dismayed by all that versatility. Munich streets, like London streets, change their names every two or three blocks. Once you arrive between the two mediæval arches of the Karlsthor and the Sparkasse, you are in the Neuhauserstrasse, whatever the name on the street sign, and if you move westward toward the Karlsthor you will come inevitably to the Pschorrbräu, and

within you will find Fräulein Tilde (to whom my regards), who will laugh at
your German with a fine show of pearly teeth and the extreme vibration of her
195 pounds. Tilde, in these godless States, would be called fat. But observe her
in the Pschorrbräu, mellowed by that superb malt, glorified by that consummate
kraut, and you will blush to think her more than plump.

I give you the Pschorrbräu as the one best eating bet of Munich—and not
forgetting, by any means, the Luitpold, the Rathaus, the Odéon and all the other
gilded hells of victualry to northward. Imagine it: every skein of sauerkraut is
cooked three times before it reaches your plate! Once in plain water, once in
Rhine wine and once in melted snow! A dish, in this benighted republic, for
stevedores and yodlers, a coarse feed for violoncellists, barbers and reporters
for the *Staats-Zeitung*—but the delight, at the Pschorrbräu, of diplomats, the
literati and doctors of philosophy. I myself, eating it three times a day, to the ac-
companiment of *schweinesrippen* and *bonensalat*,[14] have composed triolets in the
Norwegian language, a feat not matched by Björnstjerne Björnson himself. And
I once met an American medical man, in Munich to sit under the learned Prof.
Dr. Müller,[15] who ate no less than five portions of it nightly, after his twelve long
hours of clinical prodding and hacking. He found it more nourishing, he told me,
than pure albumen, and more stimulating to the jaded nerves than laparotomy.

But to many Americans, of course, sauerkraut does not appeal. Prejudiced
against the dish by ridicule and innuendo, they are unable to differentiate between good and bad, and so it's useless to send them to this or that *ausschank*.
Well, let them then go to the Pschorrbräu and order bifstek from the grill, at M.
1.20 the ration. There may be tenderer and more savory bifsteks in the world,
bifsteks which sizzle more seductively upon red hot plates, bifsteks with more
proteids and manganese in them, bifsteks more humane to ancient and hyper-
æsthetic teeth, bifsteks from nobler cattle, more deftly cut, more passionately
grilled, more romantically served—but not, believe me, for M. 1.20! Think of
it: a cut of tenderloin for M. 1. 20—say, 28.85364273+ cents! For a side order of
sauerkraut, forty pfennigs extra. For potatoes, twenty-five pfennigs. For a *mass*
of dunkle, thirty-two pfennigs. In all, M. 2.17—an odd mill or so more or less
than fifty-two cents. A square meal, perfectly cooked, washed down with perfect
beer and served perfectly by Fräulein Tilde—and all for the price of a shampoo!

From the Pschorrbräu, if the winds be fair, the beeriad takes us westward
along the Neuhauserstrasse a distance of eighty feet and six inches, and behold,
we are at the Augustinerbräu. Good beer—a trifle pale, perhaps, and without
much grip to it, but still good beer. After all, however, there is something lack-

ing here. Or, to be more accurate, something jars. The orchestra plays Grieg and Moszkowski; a smell of chocolate is in the air; that tall, pink lieutenant over there, with his cropped head and his outstanding ears, his *backfisch*[16] waist and his mudscow feet—that military gargoyle, half lout and half fop, offends the roving eye. No doubt a handsome man, by German standards—even, perhaps, a celebrated seducer, a soldier with a future—but the mere sight of him suffices to paralyze an American esophagus. Besides, there is the smell of chocolate, sweet, sickly, effeminate, and at two in the afternoon! Again, there is the music of Grieg, clammy, clinging, creepy. Away to the Mathäserbräu, two long blocks by taxi! From the Munich of Berlinish decadence and Prussian epaulettes to the Munich of honest Bavarians! From chocolate and macaroons to pretzels and white radishes! From Grieg to "Lachende Liebe"![17] From a boudoir to an inn yard! From pale beer in fragile glasses to red beer in earthen pots!

The Mathäserbräu is up a narrow alley, and that alley is always full of Müncheners going in. Follow the crowd, and one comes presently to a row of booths set up by radish sellers—ancient dames of incredible diameter, gnarled old peasants in tapestry waistcoats and country boots: veterans, one half ventures, of the Napoleonic wars, even of the wars of Frederick the Great. A ten-pfennig piece buys a noble white radish, and the seller slices it free of charge, slices it with a little revolving blade into twoscore thin schnitzels, and puts salt between each adjacent pair. A radish so sliced and salted is the perfect complement of this dark Mathäser beer. One nibbles and drinks, drinks and nibbles, and so slides the lazy afternoon. The scene is an incredible, playhouse courtyard, with shrubs in tubs and tables painted scarlet: a fit setting for the first act of "Manon."[18] But instead of choristers in short skirts, tripping the whoopla and boosting the landlord's wine, one feasts the eye upon Münchenese of a rhinocerous fatness, dropsical and gargantuan creatures, bisons in skirts, who pass laboriously among the bibuli, offering bunches of little pretzels strung upon red strings. Six pretzels for ten pfennigs. A five-pfennig tip for Frau Dickleibig, and she brings you the *Fliegende Blätter, Le Rire,*[19] the Munich or Berlin papers, whatever you want. A drowsy, hedonistic, easy-going place. Not much talk, not much rattling of crockery, not much card playing. The mountain, one guesses, of Munich meditation. The incubator of Munich *gemüthlichkeit.*[20]

Upstairs there is the big Mathäser hall, with room for three thousand visitors of an evening, a great resort for Bavarian high privates and their best girls, the scene of honest and public courting. Between the Bavarian high private and the Bavarian lieutenant all the differences are in favor of the former. He wears no corsets, he is innocent of the monocle, he sticks to native beer. A man of amour like his officer, he disdains the elaborate winks, the complex *diableries* of that superior being, and confines himself to open hugging. One sees him, in these great beer halls, with his arm around his Lizzie. Anon he arouses himself from his coma of love to offer her a sip from his *mass* or to whisper some bovine nothing into her ear. Before they depart for the evening he escorts her to the huge sign, "*Für Damen*," and waits patiently while she goes in and fixes her mussed hair.

The Bavarians have no false pruderies, no nasty little nicenesses. There is, indeed, no race in Europe more innocent, more frank, more clean-minded. Postcards of a homely and harmless vulgarity are for sale in every Munich stationer's shop, but the connoisseur looks in vain for the studied indecencies of Paris, the appalling obscenities of the Swiss towns. Munich has little to show the American Sunday-school superintendent on the loose. The ideal there is not a sharp and stinging deviltry, a swift massacre of all the commandments, but a liquid and tolerant geniality, a great forgiveness. Beer does not refine, perhaps, but at any rate it mellows. No Münchener ever threw a stone.

And so, passing swiftly over the Burgerbräu in the Kaufingerstrasse, the Hackerbräu, the Kreuzbräu, and the Kochelbräu—all hospitable *lokale*, selling pure beer in honest measures; and over the various Pilsener fountains and the agency for Vienna beer—dishwatery stuff!—in the Maximilianstrasse; and over the various summer *keller* on the heights of Au and Haidhausen across the river, with their spacious terraces and their ancient traditions—passing over all these tempting sanctuaries of *mass* and *kellnerin*, we arrive finally at the Löwenbräukeller and the Hofbräuhaus, which is quite a feat of arriving, it must be granted, for the one is in the Nymphenburgerstrasse, in Northwest Munich, and the other is in the Platzl, not two blocks from the royal palace, and the distance from the one to the other is a good mile and a half.

The Löwenbräu first—a rococo castle sprawling over a whole city block, and with accommodations in its "halls, galleries, loges, verandas, terraces, outlying garden promenades and beer rooms" (I quote the official guide) for eight thousand drinkers. A lordly and impressive establishment is this Löwenbräu, an edifice of countless towers, buttresses, minarets and dungeons. It was designed by the learned Prof. Albert Schmidt, one of the creators of modern Munich, and when it was opened, on June 14, 1883, all the military bands in Munich played at once in the great hall, and the royal family of Bavaria turned out in state coaches, and 100,000 eager Müncheners tried to fight their way in.

How large that great hall may be I don't know, but I venture to guess that it seats four thousand people—not huddled together, as a theater seats them, but comfortably, loosely, spaciously, with plenty of room between the tables, for the 250 *kellnerin* to navigate safely with their cargoes of Löwenbräu. Four nights a week a military band plays in this hall or a *männerchor* rowels the air with song, and there is an admission fee of thirty pfennigs (7 1/5 cents). One night I heard the band of the Second Bavarian (Crown Prince's) Regiment, playing as an orchestra, go through a program that would have done credit to the New York Philharmonic. A young violinist in corporal's stripes lifted the crowd to its feet with the slow movement of the Tschaikowsky concerto; the band itself began with Wagner's "Siegfried Idyl" and ended with Strauss's "Rosen aus dem Süden," a superb waltz, magnificently performed. Three hours of first-rate music for 7 1/5 cents! And a *mass* of Löwenbräu, twice the size of the seidel sold in this country at twenty cents, for forty pfennigs (9½ cents)! An inviting and appetizing spot, believe me. A place to stretch your legs. A temple of Lethe. There, when my days of moneylust are over, I go to chew my memories and dream my dreams and listen to my arteries hardening.

By taxicab down the wide Briennerstrasse, past the Luitpold and the Odéon, to the Ludwigstrasse, gay with its after-the-opera crowds, and then to the left into the Residenzstrasse, past the Hoftheater and its café (ah, Sophie, thou angel!), and so to the Maximilianstrasse, to the Neuthurmstrasse, and at last, with a sharp turn, into the Platzl.

The Hofbräuhaus! One hears it from afar: a loud buzzing, the rattle of *mass* lids, the sputter of the released *dunkle,* the sharp cries of pretzel and radish sellers, the scratching of matches, the shuffling of feet, the eternal gurgling of the plain people. No palace this, for all its towering battlements and the frescos by Ferdinand Wagner in the great hall upstairs, but drinking butts for them that labor and are heavy laden: station porters, teamsters, servant girls, soldiers, bricklayers, blacksmiths, tinners, sweeps.

There sits the fair lady who gathers cigar stumps from the platz in front of the Bayrischer Hof, still in her green hat of labor, but now with an earthen cylinder of Hofbräu in her hands. The gentleman beside her, obviously wooing her, is third fireman at the same hotel. At the next table, a squad of yokels just in from the oberland, in their short jackets and their hobnailed boots. Beyond, a noisy meeting of Socialists, a rehearsal of some *liedertafel,*[21] a family reunion of four generations, a beer party of gay young bloods from the gas works, a conference of the executive committee of the horse butchers' union. Every second drinker has brought his lunch wrapped in a newspaper: half a *blutwurst,* two radishes, an onion, a heel of rye bread. The débris of such lunches covers the floor. One wades through escaped beer, among floating islands of radish top and newspaper. Children go overboard and are succored with shouts. Leviathans of this underground lake, *Lusitanias* of beer, Pantagruels of the Hofbräuhaus, collide, draw off, collide again and are wrecked in the narrow channels. . . . A great puffing and blowing. Stranded craft on every bench. . . . Noses like cigar bands.

No waitresses here. Each drinker for himself! You go to the long shelf, select your *mass*, wash it at the spouting faucet and fall into line. Behind the rail the *zahlmeister* takes your twenty-eight pfennigs and pushes your *mass* along the counter. Then the perspiring *bierbischof*[22] fills it from the naked keg, and you carry it to the table of your choice, or drink it standing up and at one suffocating gulp, or take it out into the yard, to wrestle with it beneath the open sky. Roughnecks enter eternally with fresh kegs; the thud of the mallet never ceases; the rude clamor of the bung-starter is as the rattle of departing time itself. Huge damsels in dirty aprons—retired *kellnerin,* too bulky, even, for that trade of human battleships—go among the tables rescuing empty *mässe.* Each *mass* returns to the shelf and begins another circuit of faucet, counter and table. A dame so fat that she must remain permanently at anchor—the venerable *Constitution* of this fleet!—bawls postcards and matches. A man in *pince-nez,* a decadent doctor of philosophy, sells pale German cigars at three for ten pfennigs. Here we are among the plain people. They believe in Karl Marx, *blutwurst* and the Hofbräuhaus. They speak a German that is half speech and half grunt. One passes them to windward and enters the yard.

A brighter scene. A cleaner, greener land. In the center a circular fountain; on four sides the mediæval gables of the old beerhouse; here and there a barrel on end, to serve as table. The yard is most gay on a Sunday morning, when thousands stop on their way to church—not only Socialists and servant girls, remember—but also solemn gentlemen in plug hats and frock coats, students in their polychrome caps and in all the glory of their astounding duelling scars, citizens' wives in holiday finery. The fountain is a great place for gossip. One rests one's *mass* on the stone coping and engages one's nearest neighbor. He has a cousin who is brewmaster of the largest brewery in Zanesville, Ohio. Is it true that all the policemen in America are convicts? That some of the skyscrapers have more than twenty stories? What a country! And those millionaire Socialists! Imagine a rich man denouncing riches! And then, *"Grüss' Gott!"*—and the pots clink. A kindly, hospitable, tolerant folk, these Bavarians! *"Grüss' Gott!"*— "the compliments of God." What other land has such a greeting for strangers?

On May day all Munich goes to the Hofbräuhaus to "prove" the new bock. I was there last May in company with a Virginian weighing 190 pounds.[23] He wept with joy when he smelled that heavenly brew. It had the coppery glint of old Falernian, the pungent bouquet of good port, the acrid grip of English ale, and the bubble and bounce of good champagne. A beer to drink reverently and silently, as if in the presence of something transcendental, ineffable—but not too slowly, for the supply is limited! One year it ran out in thirty hours and there were riots from the Max-Joseph-Platz to the Isar. But last May day there was enough and to spare—enough, at all events, to last until the Virginian and I gave up, at high noon of May 3. The Virginian went to bed at the Bayrischer Hof at 12.30, leaving a call for 4 P.M. of May 5.

Ah, the Hofbräuhaus! A massive and majestic shrine, the Parthenon of beer drinking, seductive to virtuosi, fascinating to the connoisseur, but a bit too strenuous, a trifle too cruel, perhaps, for the dilettante. The Müncheners love it as hillmen love the hills. There every one of them returns, soon or late. There he takes his children, to teach them his hereditary art. There he takes his old grandfather, to say farewell to the world. There, when he has passed out himself, his pallbearers in their gauds of grief will stop to refresh themselves, and to praise him in speech and song, and to weep unashamed for the loss of so *gemüthlich* a fellow.

But, as I have said, the Hofbräuhaus is no playroom for amateurs. My advice to you, if you would sip the cream of Munich and leave the hot acids and lye, is that you have yourself hauled forthwith to the Hoftheater Café, and that you there tackle a modest seidel of Spatenbräu—first one, and then another, and so on until you master the science.

And all that I ask in payment for that tip—the most valuable, perhaps, you have ever got from the magazines—is that you make polite inquiry of the Herr Wirt regarding Fräulein Sophie, and that you present to her, when she comes tripping to your table, the respects and compliments of one who forgets not her cerulean eyes, her swanlike glide, her Mona Lisa smile and her leucemic and superbly manicured hands!

AT LARGE IN LONDON

Macaulay's New Zealander, so I hear, will view the ruins of St. Paul's from London Bridge;[24] but as for me, I prefer that more westerly arch which celebrates Waterloo, there to sniff and immerse myself in the town. The hour is eight o'clock *post meridien* and the time is early summer. I have just rolled down Wellington Street from the Strand, smoking a ninepence Vuelta Abajo, humming an ancient air. One of Simpson's incomparable English dinners—salmon with lobster sauce, a cut from the joint, two vegetables, a cress salad, a slice of old Stilton and a mug of bitter—has lost itself, amazed and enchanted, in my interminable recesses. My board is paid at Morley's, I have some thirty-eight dollars to my credit at Brown's, a ticket home is sewn to my lingerie, there is a friendly jingle of shillings and sixpences in my pocket. The stone coping invites; I lay myself against it, fold my arms, blow a smoke ring toward the sunset and give up my soul to recondite and mellow meditation.

There are thirteen great bridges between Fulham Palace and the Isle of Dogs, and I have been at pains to try every one of them; but the best of all, for such needs as overtake a well fed and ruminative man on a summer evening, is that of Waterloo. Look westward and the towers of St. Stephen's are floating in the haze, a greenish slate color with edges of peroxide yellow and seashell pink. Look eastward and the fine old dome of St. Paul's is slipping softly into greasy shadows. Look downward and the river throws back its innumerable hues—all the coal tar dyes plus all the duns and drabs of Thames mud. The tide is out, and along the south bank a score of squat barges are high and dry upon the flats. Opposite, on the Embankment, the lights are beginning to blink, and from the little hollow behind Charing Cross comes the faint, far-away braying of a brass band.

All bands are in tune four hundred yards, the reason whereof you must not ask me now. This one plays a melody I do not know, a melody plaintive and ingratiating, of clarinet arpeggios all compact. Some lay of amour, I venture, breathing the hot passion of the Viennese Jew who wrote it. But so heard, filtered through that golden haze, echoed back from that lovely panorama of stone and water, all flavor of human frailty has been taken out of it. There is, indeed, something wholly chastening and dephlogisticating in the scene, something which makes the joys and tumults of the flesh seem trivial and debasing. A man must be fed, of course, to yield himself to the suggestion, for hunger is frankly a brute; but once he has yielded he departs forthwith from his gorged carcass and flaps his transcendental wings. . . . Do honeymooners ever come to Waterloo Bridge? I doubt it. Imagine turning from that sublime sweep of grays and somber gilts, that perfect arrangement of blank masses and sweeping lines, to the mottled pink of a cheek lately virgin, the puny curve of a modish eyebrow, the hideous madness of a trousseau hat! . . .

Clowns argue, to be sure, that London is not beautiful. You have heard them and so have I. They have composed many volumes on the subject, and they write to the newspapers incessantly. The Houses of Parliament, it appears, are defectively Gothic: here is a gargoyle with the wrong ears, there is an oriel with corbels unfit for publication. Again, Somerset House has the color of a coal hole and the shape of a Philadelphia pie woman. Yet again, St. Paul's is spoiled and made a mock of by the fact that no one has ever torn down all the houses between it and the Temple and planted the ensuing desert with alfalfa and daffodils. Yet again, Trafalgar Square is the iron dream of a man with calcareous arteries, a graphic representation of a psychic arterio-sclerosis, a delirium of hardness, a corundum nightmare. Yet again, the common statues of the town are as glyptic patent medicine advertisements, or rather say warnings—gaunt effigies of kings and queens that never were on land or sea—horrible petrifications of super-osseous field marshals—gross, lithic libels upon the angels. Yet again, and to make an end, the river Thames is the most obscene of all the world's sewers, a foul tide of slime and dead cats, a stream too narrow to have dignity and too tortuous to have repose and too drab to wake the harmonious lyre.

Alas, what a caterwauling of pedants—what a forgetting of the forest in a row over the trees! Put away the Houses of Parliament and Somerset House and St. Paul's and Trafalgar Square, and have a look at London. Feast your eyes upon the grayest, dourest, cruelest, dingiest, lordliest, loveliest town in all creation. Let your gaze sweep slowly from the towers of London Bridge, just visible on the eastern skyline, to the battlements of Lambeth, floating mistily in the west. At once those sore and dubious details drop back into the great drab picture. Now the river ceases to be a sewer and becomes a broad and beautiful curve, a magnificent "S," snaking out of the hitherto and into the yon. St. Stephen's, reduced but still dominating, is a dark mass, a blotch of greenish and diaphanous shadow, softening and mitigating that curve at its widest sweep. Somerset House is another and larger and darker mass, with hints of fathomless depths in its blackness. St. Paul's is the apex of a great convergence of majestic lines, the crown surmounting a stupendous drapery, the Matterhorn of this luminous range of hills. And there, in the foreground, are the lights of the Embankment, a string of winking topazes, and above them the staring incandescence of the Strand hotels, and beyond the eternal lights o' London, sweeping up to the stars. . . .

Ugly? Pish! If London is ugly, thus melting into the dusk of a summer evening, then there is no beauty in the world.

[II]

Afloat upon such lofty and ennobling meditations, staring into the gathering night, my cigar gone out, my coattails brushed by the passing crowd, I am reunited to the bridge and the firm ground by a hand upon my shoulder. A massive, billowy man, smoking an American cigarette in a long amber holder, introduces himself: a Mr. McDannald of Virginia. I remember the fellow: in fact, we crossed the Atlantic together, and have dined together this evening and share a modest chamber at Morley's. His proposal is that we return to the Strand, board a'bus, and proceed to Shaftesbury Avenue, there to look about for a vaudeville show. The journey is made in ten minutes, up the Strand to Trafalgar Square, around the huge lions into Cockspur Street, then up the Haymarket to Piccadilly Circus. Ten minutes—and we have come from a land of imposing lines and solemn shadows into a land of rouge and yellow light. Here, among the theaters, is where London tries to be Paris, just as she tries to be New York in Regent Street. Here is where the most moral town in Christendom discovers her native hoggishness. Here is the great slave market of the English.

But we are out for vaudeville and not for slaves, and so we pursue our virtuous way up the stream of amiable fair until we reach the Palace Music Hall, where a poster advertising a Russian dancer inspires us to part with half a dozen shillings. Luxurious seats of red velvet, wide enough for a pair of German contraltos, invite to slumber, and the juggler on the stage does the rest. Twenty times he heaves a cannon ball into the air, and twenty times he catches it safely on his neck. The Russian dancer, we find, is booked for ten thirty, and it is now but eight fifty. "Why wait?" says McDannald. "It will never kill him." So we try another hall—and find a lady with a face like a tomato singing a song about the Derby, to an American tune that was stale in 1907. Yet another—and we are in the midst of a tedious ballet founded upon "Carmen," with the music reduced to jigtime and a flute playing out of tune. A fourth—and we suffer a pair of comedians who impersonate Americans by saying "Naow" and "Amurican." When they break into "My Cousin Carus'"[25] we depart by the fire escape, guided by the red light and pursued by two young women who labor under the delusion that they know us. We have now spent eight dollars on divertisement and have failed to be diverted. We take one more chance, and pick a prize—Little Tich, to wit, a harlequin no more than four feet in his shoes, but as full of humor as a fraternal order funeral.

Before these few lines find you well, Little Tich, I dare say, will be on Broadway, drawing his four thousand stage dollars a week and longing for a decent cut of mutton. But we saw him on his native heath, uncontaminated by press agents, unboomed by a vociferous press, undefiled by contact with acquitted murderers, eminent divorcées, "perfect" women, returned explorers who never got where they went, and suchlike prodigies and nuisances of the Broadway 'alls. Tich, as I have said, is but four feet from sole to crown, but there is little of the dwarf's distortion about him. He is simply a man in miniature: in aspect much like any other man. His specialty is impersonation. First he appears as a drill sergeant, then as a headwaiter, then as a gas collector, then as some other familiar fellow. But what keen insight and penetrating humor in every detail of the picture! How mirth bubbles out! Here we have burlesque, of course, and there is even some horseplay in it, but at bottom how deft it is, and how close to life, and how wholly and irresistibly comical! You must see him do the headwaiter—hear him blarney and flabbergast the complaining guest, observe him reckon up his criminal bill, see the subtle condescension of his tip grabbing. This Tich, I assure you, is no common mountebank, but a first-rate comic actor. Given legs eighteen inches longer and an equator befitting the role, and he would make the best Falstaff of our generation. Even as he stands, he would do wonders with Bob Acres—and I'd give four dollars any day to see him play Marguerite Gautier.[26]

McDannald entered the Tich'all, whatever its name, full of the biles of hope deferred, but Tich soon had him shaking like a blanc-mange, and at the end he was in such high good humor that he proposed supper. But where? Simpson's was closed by now and the nearby restaurants were all gilded hells, inhospitable to a pair of gentlemen in brown gaiters and lavender shirts. Why not a trial of English oysters? Wasn't there an oyster house, or something of the sort, somewhere in the Strand? . . . We left the 'all of Tich and fought our way, by slow stages, through the jungle of easy ladies on the sidewalk. Mac got through with no worse damage than the thrust of a hatpin through his starboard ear, but I lost an eyebrow and a scarfpin and emerged all covered with strands of blonde and pseudo-blonde hair, like a Christmas tree with tinsel. And so, as Pepys would say, by hackney coach to the Strand, where we quickly mounted stools and ordered a couple of dozen "natives," such being the English name for oysters, apparently to distinguish them from clams.

They came on in their thin, greenish shells—slimy, saturnine, sad. Mac speared the largest with his fork and downed it at a gulp. A smile at once gallant and horrible, a smile of bitter duty, of politeness become pathological, flickered across his face. I asked the obvious question.

"Delicious," answered Mac. "I love and revere the English! Believe me, we have no such oysters at home."

Still hanging back myself, I pursued him for more specific encomiums. He swallowed a second, blinked his eyes, and made reply.

"Let me answer you," said he, "with another question. Have you ever, developing photographic films or dry plates, lifted your gross, fuzzy hand from the fixing tray to feel of a loose tooth, or to push back a wayward tonsil?"

I answered no.

"Then," pursued Mac, "you have a new experience ahead of you. Eat, my boy, and be merry! You have never tasted the hyposulphite of soda of commerce, or, more accurately, sodium thiosulphate, or, to speak symbolically, $Na_2S_2O_3$ + $5H_2O$. And never having tasted $Na_2S_2O_3$ + $5H_2O$, you have never tasted an English oyster. Feed and be hanged to you! *You* brought me here."

A palpable untruth—but I made a brave plunge, and so got that neglected knowledge. Of the hyposulphite of commerce I am now aware and wary. It is a brackish, sardonic victual, a hideous match for Philadelphia pepper pot, a blood brother to the glucose apple pie of Pittsburgh. But I ate it, or, at any rate, the English "natives" from which it is squeezed, and faced down the satirical Virginian. He, pale and staring, was in such obvious distress after the sixth that the waiter came to his aid.

"Will you have some condiment, sir? Perhaps a dash of—"

"Have you, by any chance, a few drops of fuming sulphuric acid? No? Or a pinch of quinine sulphate dissolved in dilute H_2SO_4? No? Or a couple of fingers of dry HCl? No? Then give me the ammonia bottle."

The perfect English waiter was unruffled.

"Sorry, sir; we're just out. But here is a sauce you may like—favorite here in London, sir—best of all English sauces, sir—don't hesitate to recommend it, sir."

And he pushed forward a bottle of Worcestershire—with the name of Heinz upon the label!

[III]

After all, not a novel experience in London. The Worcestershire sauce in half of the "old English" restaurants is Heinz's. So far has the American invasion gone. All Englishmen who have ever heard of America, and can afford it, wear American shoes—perhaps .0002 per cent. of the whole population. All English vaudevillians sing American songs, picking out the worst infallibly. The American garter hugs the slim legs of the nobility and gentry. American whiskey has begun to trickle down their throats, and before long, no doubt, it will rage like the Irrawaddy in flood. English newspapers are set up by American linotype machines—and printed on American presses. The white paper they use—and also the green and pink paper—is the attenuated and endless corpse of the American (or, at least, the Canadian) birch, and scores of their bright young men are Americans, or Jews, which has come to mean the same thing. American bathtubs have changed the English bawth from an esoteric debauch into a genuine bout with soap and currycomb. The trolley car, the typewriter, ragtime, the phonograph, the incandescent light, detachable cuffs, floating soap, the union suit, the sectional bookcase, the slot machine, steam heat, the gas stove, the press agent, the shoot-the-chutes, the flying machine, graft, poker, condensed milk, fake Pilsener, the Independent Order of Odd Fellows, the twostep, the crayon portrait, the canned book review, the virtuous chorus girl and the telephone—all American inventions—have been adopted and naturalized by the English. There are now, indeed, almost as many telephones in London as in Toledo, O.

But you must go down into the City proper, into the regions lying fore and aft of the Bank of England, to get the full measure of this slow and fatal Americanization. This is the quarter of manufacturers' agents—and on all sides the signs announce familiar American wares. The Yale lock, the Remington typewriter, the Globe-Wernicke filing cabinet, the Gillette safety razor, the Heinz pickle, Peruna, the Douglas shoe, the Campbell canned soup, Ivory soap, Horlick's malted milk, Huyler's chocolates, Omega oil, the Fairbanks scale, the Oliver plow, the Victor phonograph—all of these commercial commonplaces of our own fair land are fast becoming the commonplaces of England, too. But don't mistake me: there is a limit, and at times a sense of its rigidity is pressing. In all London you will not find a single American five-cent cigar. In the whole of the Strand and Fleet Street, between Trafalgar Square and Ludgate Circus, there is but one tobacconist who sells American plug tobacco—and he, as if to wring tribute for his daring, charges a shilling for a nickel plug. Search this capital of the world from center to perimeter and you will not find a single bootblack who knows his business, or a single barber who penetrates to the true technique of the hot towel, or a single real first-class soda fountain, or a single box of decent matches, or a single corncob pipe, or a single bartender with enough pride in his art to wear a diamond stud.

These great boons and usufructs of life in the United States are unknown to the Londoner. Never having been in the United States, and distrusting the sagas of those who have, he gets along without such things, just as he gets along without skyscrapers. In the same way, he still carries most of his money in heavy and inconvenient coin, instead of putting it sanely into five-, ten- and twenty-shilling bills; and he still fights for his luggage at railroad stations, instead of checking it and forgetting it; and he still wears shirts which do *not* open all the way down the façade and so have to be boarded by climbing through them from below. McDannald, greatly admiring English madrases, sought half a dozen ready-made shirts in the Strand and Regent Street, but had to give it up: his arteries are too brittle for athletics.

"Why don't you make them like coats?" he asked the haberdasher. "Why ask a man to fight his way into them?"

"You mean, in the American fashion?" replied the haberdasher. "Well, I dare say we'll come to it. In fact, I have already tried it. I made up a dozen of your coat shirts and they went like hot cakes. Quite a success, in truth."

"Then why didn't you make some more?"

"Well, it *did* occur to me, and I dare say we'll come to it. You Americans are very original."

"And why don't you put tabs over the buttonholes to protect the neck?"

The thing had to be explained in greater detail.

"A jolly good idea," said the haberdasher. "I dare say we'll come to it. You Americans are . . ."

But that wasn't the real reason why my friend from Virginia didn't buy. To find that real reason you must regard his outlines: a series of convexities, an arrangement of interrupted arcs, a maze of graceful bulges and protuberances. In brief, the fellow is somewhat bunchy, as I am myself—and the Englishmen for whom English shirts are made are as flat as so many mackerel. Walk Pall Mall from ten in the morning to five the next morning and you will not see a single paunch, leap-tick or corporation. John Bull, true enough, is always depicted as a man of girth, and some of the aldermen in the City, I suppose, have banqueted themselves into rotundity, but the normal Englishman, the average, the typical Englishman, presents an almost rectangular cross-section. Such a being, no doubt, is able to insert himself into the archaic English shirt, sinuously and without swearing. But as for Mac—! And as for me—!

[IV]

And yet, as I have hinted, the English do not repine, nor is it recorded that they gnash their teeth. A slim and resilient race, they do not miss the delights of corpulence. A race devoted for countless generations to useless endeavor, and stewing in the unruffleable self-respect it breeds, they are content to enter their clothes like felons entering the fatal noose. What is more, their contentment, if not in this case then at least in most other cases, is pretty well grounded and defended. If, for example, they have no skyscrapers, it is not because they are too stupid to build skyscrapers, or too timid, or too poor, but simply because they don't want them. Why should buildings be set on end when they might just as well be set on their sides? Why should a man travel six hundred feet into the air when it would be cheaper, quicker and safer to travel a thousand feet on the level? Do our own skyscrapers save us much time? I doubt it. Two blocks from most of them you will find vacant lots, or rows of tumbledown and useless houses. Wouldn't it be saner to utilize such waste space instead of stealing space from the archangels? And wouldn't it be easier to walk to the ensuing buildings, or even to crawl to them, than it is now to fight for a place in an elevator which stops at every floor, and is peopled to suffocation by a populace scented richly by nature and deliriously by art?

So argue the English, and the consequence is that London is one of the most spacious towns in the world. Its people are innumerable, but they are spread thin. Its streets do not run due north and south and due east and west, on the absurd theory that everybody wants to follow the parallels of latitude and longitude, but in every direction or directions the traffic of centuries has led. Half of the by-streets which open into Regent Street strike it at angles other than right angles. To get from the British Museum to Aldwych, you do not have to travel the sides of an angle, but may slide down its hypotenuse. The route from London Bridge to the Bank is not due north and then due west, but directly and gracefully north by west. That great thoroughfare which begins as Fleet Street and ends as Cannon Street is not a straight line but a long curve following the river. And so is that greater thoroughfare which begins as Cheapside and runs westward as Holborn, Oxford Street and the Bayswater Road, and runs westward as Cornhill, Leadenhall Street and the Mile End Road. Thus the difference between a city that has grown up, naturally and comfortably, out of man's quarrel with his environment, and our cities of the New World, manufactured on drawing boards by rectanglomaniacs.

Another result of this slow growing up is visible in London's enormous profusion of big and little parks—the lingering relics, nine times out of ten, of great houses which long defied the encroaching town and then tripped over it in the end. Was there ever a city with so many and so various breaks in the moraine of brick and mortar? Get out your map and have a look: the splotches of green make an almost continuous verdure from Hackney in the east to Putney bridge in the west. From the City onward to the West End they actually touch. Start in the cloistered Temple Gardens and follow the green. It takes you westward along the Embankment a good mile to the War Office, and there it leads you into a crowded Whitehall, and then it beckons you through the arch of the Horse Guards and into St. James Park. Now it stretches ahead for two miles and a half in a whole archipelago of parks, each joined to the next one. After ancient St. James's, fragrant with noble scandals and the musks of yesteryear, comes the Green Park, its brother and rival, and cheek by jowl with the Green Park are the grounds of Buckingham Palace. Then comes Hyde Park Corner, and behold, the most famous of all the parks of the world lies before, with Rotten Row showing the way through it. Follow the Row for its historic mile and you will presently find yourself in the lovely meadows of Kensington Gardens, and beyond them you will see the royal dooryard of Kensington Palace.

Four miles of green so far, but the end is not yet. A few blocks of asphalt and you are led onward and onward, now north and now north by east, by an apparently infinite series of little squares, some discreetly fenced and padlocked and some open to all who are weary—Princes Square, Leinster Square, Ladbrooke, Pembridge, Porchester, Gloucester, Cambridge, Bryanston, Montague, Portman, Manchester and Dorset squares, to say nothing of Queens Gardens, Norfolk Crescent and Westbourne Terrace. The wide grounds of Regent's Park now open before you, with their botanical gardens, their zoo and their pretty lake, and beyond them rises Primrose Hill. But still the beacons of green show a further way, this time southeasterly to the place of beginning—Mornington Crescent, Ampthill Square, Endsleigh Gardens, the interminable squares of Bloomsbury, and finally the superb old yards and gardens of the Inns of Court, Gray's, Lincoln's and the Temple. Ten miles of green—and all in the very heart of the largest city in the world!

These parks and squares of London are thrown together like the streets, upon any plan or no plan at all. No hot sweating of a landscape architect, busy with his callipers and T-square, is apparent in their arrangement. They are set down at random, often uselessly and sometimes even perversely. Not infrequently two competing squares are side by side. Gloucester Square and Hyde Park Square are no more than a stone's throw apart, and Sussex, Cambridge and Oxford squares are but a block away—and all five are within a minute's walk of Hyde Park. Euston Square and Endsleigh Gardens are on opposite sides of the Euston Road. Squares cluster about Kensington Gardens like puppies around their ma.

Nothing could be more exclusively ornamental, considering the practical uses to which green spaces are commonly put, than some of these little parks. Are they breathing spots? I fear not. Most of the people who live around them are out of London at the only time London air is breathable. Are they, then, resorts for rest and meditation, bowers of retirement in the heart of the town? Alas, most of them are surrounded by high iron rails, and one may not open the door without a key, and one may not have a key unless one owns or leases an adjacent house.

In truth, they are not public parks at all, save in a limited, visual sense, but strictly private parks, kept up at the public expense for the benefit of the few who have inherited, bought, rented or borrowed the right to enter. It is the prerogative of the owner of such and such a house, his tenants, guests, heirs and assigns, to enter such and such a square between the hours of 8 A. M. and 10 P. M. There he lies in the grass when he is so inclined (which he never is), and there he pastures his children. If, by any chance, a stranger breaks in, four threes are sounded on a large, *fortissimo* whistle and a select and indignant *posse comitatus* drives him out. The papers are full of it next morning, and the invader is lucky if he gets off with thirty days. When the owner of such a key sells his house, he turns it over to the new owner in a solemn and even grisly manner, along with the deed, the memorandum of mortgages and the studbook of the resident roaches. To lose a key is as serious an offense as to break a window of Westminster Abbey, and for the same reason. Many of them have been handed down from father to son (or from bankrupt to creditor) for three or four thousand generations, and some of them, despite the inevitable wear and tear, still weigh five pounds.

But if the squares of London, and particularly the squares of Mayfair and Belgravia, are thus sniffish and intolerant of the vulgar, the great parks make up for it by offering careless and magnificent hospitality. True enough, there is a charge of a penny for sitting on a bench, but that penny, once expended, gives the spendthrift a monopoly of the bench for the rest of the day or night. Besides, the lawns are wholly free—and it is on the lawns that the weary Londoner prefers to do his lolling. Walk along the Ring road in Hyde Park on a summer day and you will fancy that you are at Gettysburg after the battle. Almost as far as the eye can reach are sprawling figures, some lying flat upon their faces, some on their backs with newspapers or caps over their eyes, some hunched into grotesque and startling shapes, some hideously grouped and commingled, like squads brought down by the vast blast of a field piece or machine gun. Now and then a sleeper rolls over, flinging his arms and legs—for all the world like a man wounded and in pain. At rarer times some fellow with a conscience sits up, stricken, it would seem, by a sense of time wasting, and meditating a move.

But I myself have never seen one rise to his legs and depart. It is done, I have no doubt, in the autumn, and perhaps every night, but though I have watched for hours and then circled the Serpentine and come back to watch again, I have not beheld it with these eyes. Once down on that grim field, a man is down for more than a cat nap.

The likeness to a battlefield is reinforced by the constant procession of nurses in their elaborate uniforms—long blue or purple cloaks, little round bonnets and flapping streamers of white. I mean hospital nurses and not the idle hussies who guard and torture the young. A dozen great hospitals are within a few minutes' walk of Hyde Park and the fair Samaritans use it for taking the air. Put red crosses on their arms and send them out into the field to disinfect the sleepers, and you would have your shambles to the life.

Shambles? After all, why not give this Inkerman[27] of peace the name? These men are the killed and wounded of civilization, butchered and blown to pieces by the shells of industry, mowed down by the withering fire of competition, poisoned and blanched by bad rations, hacked and ground to pieces in the struggle for existence. These are the sub-Englishmen, the by-products of England's greatness, the anthropoid brothers of the pink and fit Englishmen you see in Pall Mall and the Strand. Christian charity has evolved a new and fearful race in this tight little island. Because it wrung tender hearts to see their grandfathers starve, they themselves, now increased and multiplied enormously, wallow here in the grass, useless, helpless, hopeless. In every hundred of them, there are not four with honest trades to excuse their living. In the best of imaginable times starvation is but three days behind them; in these hard and parlous days they are frank pensioners upon the castes above. Close the workhouses and souphouses of London and a hundred thousand of them would die before Wednesday week. Here they lie, by the flow of the inland river, mentally wounded, physically dying, socially dead. You may see their brothers at night on the Embankment, dodging about Covent Garden, swarming in the filthy lanes of the East End. Their wives are at the doors of the "pubs," cadging pennies from passersby, a pack of blowzy, frowzy old harridans, the brood animals of this degraded and godforsaken species. Their daughters, if it be night, are in Piccadilly Circus.

[V]

But enough of this solemn stuff, this mad mixture of fashionable gossip and eugenics. Let us go back to Waterloo Bridge and look at the river. It is night, and a red theatrical moon is hanging over the towers of St. Stephen's. There below us, a crinkling tapestry of gilts, silvers and coppery pinks, is ancient Father Thames, the emperor and archbishop of all earthly streams. There are the harsh waters (but now so soft!) that the Romans braved, watching furtively for blue savages along the banks, and the Danes after the Romans, and the Normans after the Danes, and innumerable companies of hardy seafarers in the long years following. At this lovely turning, where the river flouts the geography books by flowing almost due northward for a mile, bloody battles must have been fought in those old, forgotten, far-off times—and battles, I venture, not always ending with Roman cheers. One pictures some young naval lieutenant, just out of the Tiber Annapolis, and brash and nosey like his kind—one sees some such youngster pushing thus far in his light craft, and perhaps going aground on the mud of the south bank, and there fighting to the death with Britons of the fog-wrapped marshes, "hairy, horrible, human." And one sees, too, his return to the fleet so snug at Gravesend, an imperfect carcass lashed to a log, the pioneer and prophet of all that multitude of dead men who have since bobbed down this dirty tide.

Dead men—and men alive, men full of divine courage and high hopes, the great dreamers and experimenters of the race. Out of this sluggish sewer the Anglo-Saxon, that fabulous creature, has gone forth to his blundering conquest of the earth. And conquering, he has brought back his loot to the place of his beginning. The great liners, flashing along their policed and humdrum lanes, have long since abandoned London, but every turn of the tide brings up her fleet of cargo ships, straggling, weather-worn and gray, trudging in from ports far-flung and incredible—Surinam, Punta Arenas, Antofagasta, Port Banana, Tang-Chow, Noumea, Sarawak. If you think that commerce, yielding to steel and steam, has lost all romance, just give an idle day or two to the London docks. The very names upon the street signs are as exotic as a breath of frankincense. Mango Wharf, Kamchatka Wharf, Havannah Street, the Borneo Stores, Greenland Dock, Sealers' Yard—on all sides are these suggestions of adventure beyond the sky-rim, of soft, tropical moons and cold, arctic stars, of strange peoples, strange tongues and strange lands. In one Limehouse barroom you will find sailors from Behring Straits and the China Sea, the Baltic and the River Plate, the Congo and Labrador, all calling London home, all paying an orang-outang's devotions to the selfsame London barmaid, all drenched and paralyzed by London beer . . .

The *kaiserstadt* of the world, this grim and gray old London! And the river of rivers, this oily, sluggish, immemorial Thames! At its widest, I suppose, it might be doubled upon itself and squeezed into the lower Potomac, and no doubt the Mississippi, even at St. Louis, could swallow it without rising a foot—but it leads from London Bridge to every coast and headland of the world! Of all the pathways used by man this is the longest and the greatest. And not only the greatest, but the loveliest. Grant the Rhine its castles, the Hudson its hills, the Amazon its stupendous reaches. Not one of these can match the wonder and splendor of frail St. Stephen's, wrapped in the mists of a summer night, or the cool dignity of St. Paul's, crowning its historic mount, or the iron beauty of the bridges, or the magic of the ancient docks, or the twinkling lights o' London, sweeping upward to the stars . . .

REMINISCENCES OF 1917

When I read of the bombardments and slaughter in the Basque country the picture simply refuses to register. It seems as outlandish and impossible as a camp meeting in the gardens of the Vatican, or a Bach festival in Mississippi. For my only memory of that lovely region is a memory of the profoundest imaginable peace, to wit, peace after war. I came into it on a smiling day in early spring, *anno* 1917, after two months of a wartime journey that had taken me as far north as the Orkney Islands and as far east as the River Dvina, and had left me covered with frostbites and full of woe.

The frostbites were acquired in what is now Lithuania, along the German front running above a little town called Novo Alexandrovsk. This, at the beginning of 1917, was the spearhead of the great German *Vormarsch* into Russia, and the show it offered was certainly exciting enough to a novice. The outfit I was a part of included two other newspaper reporters—a Swiss and a Hollander—and two officers of the German General Staff. The job of these officers was to take us over the works, and they pursued it with great industry. All day we tramped the trenches, and every evening we were put up in some officers' mess.

There were *Polizeistünde*[28] for all ordinary officers, including even generals; they had to shut down their meager revels at 10 P. M., but the young flying officers were allowed to carry on as late as they pleased, for it was understood that all of them would soon be dead anyhow, and everyone wanted to be nice to them. We pilgrims proceeded to their quarters at 10 o'clock, and there helped them to get down their evening ration of half French champagne and half English porter—both stolen goods, and hence extra sweet.

The General Staff brethren were under orders to bring their charges back alive if practicable, but their colleagues at the front, after more than two years

197

in the field, were somewhat inured to flying missiles, and in consequence there were occasions when we were conducted to seats that, to me at least, seemed rather too near the stage. I recall, for example, having dinner one evening with a division commander whose quarters were within point-blank range of the Russian artillery. He was an amiable old *Junker,* and he entertained us by propounding banal riddles out of some German almanac. I enjoyed them in a pallid, sneaky way, but there were undoubtedly moments when my mind wandered from them, speculating as to the probable effects of a shell landed in the middle of the dinner table.

But all this is now fading, and I no longer shiver when I think of it. Wars, indeed, are soon forgotten, else there would not be so many of them. The thing I remember most clearly of those brief days is not the risk of colliding with hog-wild metal, but the appalling and incomparable cold. It was far beyond anything in my previous experience, and even beyond anything I could imagine. It seemed to have almost a solid quality, like a downpour of gravel, and at the same time it was as penetrating as X-rays.

I had been warned about it in Berlin, and got to the front dressed almost like an Arctic explorer, but after the first day I began to lay on more and more furs. When the wind blew, which was often, there was simply no getting warm—that is, in the open. The quarters behind the line, mainly log houses built by Russian prisoners, were cozy enough, but in the field one froze and despaired. The precise temperature I never found out. Some said it was 10 below zero, and some said 40, 50, 100, 500, 1,000. The more impossible the guess, the more probable it seemed.

I got back to Berlin one dismal winter night, determined to hole in at the Adion Hotel for a week, with four feather pillows under me and six or eight on top. But the first news I heard when I reached the hotel was of the Zimmerman U-boat note,[29] and thus my week of rest blew up, and I was on the go day and night. The cold of Lithuania seemed to have followed me. Horrible blasts roared down Unter den Linden. The Friedrichstrasse was an icehouse. I swelled in all directions, and my hide turned a dark purple. I was stiff in every joint, and began to wheeze and choke up.

When Ambassador Gerard was recalled he went to Switzerland, and I went along. Zürich was deep in snow. Basel was buried in a dense white fog, as clammy as grave-clothes. On to Paris! A night on an unheated train, curled up on the floor. Paris was dark, damp and dismal. No lights in the streets. None in the hotels save one blue lamp to a floor. My teeth kept on chattering.

All ocean traffic was blockaded north of Spanish waters, so I decided to go to Madrid. It turned out to be surprisingly easy. A $20 American gold note, discreetly planted, got me a bootleg berth on a train leaving for the south that very night, and I turned in as soon as the gates opened. The car was like a refrigerator, and there was but one thin blanket. I began to believe that a new Ice Age had dawned. But somehow I fell asleep—and when I awoke in the morning it was to gape at the beautiful Bay of Biscay, with a row of palms along the shore and the good red sun beating down.

Where this was I don't know precisely—probably somewhere near St. Jean de Luz. All I recall is the immense, the almost unbearable joy of seeing the sun again. I had not had a clear look at it for at least six weeks. When the train stopped somewhere I rushed out to wallow in it. It seemed so big that it half filled the sky, and it glared down with all the hospitable ferocity of the gates of Hell. When I got back on the train I threw up my window and leaned out. It was infinitely warm and comfortable and soothing. It was like opium after pain.

We got to Hendaye on the border before noon, and were presently at Irun and on Spanish soil, with the war far behind and already half forgotten. Irun, I believe, is now a wreck—battered to pieces in one of the earlier battles of the Spanish revolution. But I can think of it only as it was that balmy winter day—a charming toy town, seemingly made of cardboard, with some of the houses painted red, and some blue, but most of them yellow, and the whole bathed in golden sunlight. The sun seemed to be shifting on both sides of the streets. There were no shadows. It was a world all light, and warmth—and peace.

I had lunch somewhere in the town—outdoors, of course—and afterward took a stroll. I recall the Basques sitting quietly before their Christmas-garden houses, snoozing away the lazy afternoon. Compared to the armed men I had been living with for weeks, they looked as harmless as so many tabby cats. Here and there a couple of children played somberly in a gutter. Now and then a housewife ambled along, burdened with marketing. I recall encountering a bookshop. The window was full of Spanish translations of the works of Orison Swett Marden and Upton Sinclair. Another war had been forgotten.

Toward the end of the afternoon the train for Madrid set out, and by dusk we were at San Sebastien. As the evening cool came down I was astonished to find that I liked it. The day before I had believed that I'd never be happy again save in front of a blast furnace. As I thawed out my chilblains began to abate, and I returned to my normal contours. It was a placid, dreamy, almost boozy feeling. Joint after joint lost its stiffness, and began to function.

At San Sebastien there was a longish wait, and a good deal of pother on the platform. I went out to see what was up, and found that the private car of King Alfonso XIII was being attached to the train. We started up through the high, romantic Basque country in the late twilight, and as the darkness gathered I observed that there were armed sentries all along the track, with a corporal and his guard at every bridge.

Some time before this the anarchists of Barcelona had tried to bomb Alfonso, and the show of troops was to let him sleep. Another war was casting its shadows before. But I didn't know it. The Basque country that I saw was as peaceful as a bankrupt church, soldiers or no soldiers. I find it almost impossible to think of it as shot to pieces.

THE BLACK COUNTRY

The other, day, coming out of Pittsburgh by train, I rolled eastward for an hour through the coal and steel towns of Westmoreland county. It was familiar ground: I had been over it often before. But somehow I had never quite sensed its appalling desolation. Here was the very heart of industrial America, the richest and greatest nation ever seen on earth—and here was a scene so dreadfully hideous, so intolerably bleak and forlorn that it reduced the whole aspiration of man to a sort of joke. Here was wealth beyond computation, almost beyond imagination—and here were human habitations so abominable that they would have disgraced a race of alley cats.

I am not speaking of mere filth. One expects steel towns to be dirty. What I allude to is the unbroken and agonizing ugliness, the sheer revolting monstrousness, of every house in sight. From East Liberty to Greensburg, a distance of twenty-five miles, there was not one in sight that did not offend the eye. Some were so bad, and they were among the most pretentious—churches, stores, warehouses and the like—that they were downright startling: one blinked before them as one blinks before a man with his face shot away. It was as if all the more advanced expressionist architects of Berlin had been got drunk on vodka, and put to matching designs.

I recall a few masterpieces, horrible even in memory—a crazy little church just west of Jeanette, set like a dormer-window on the side of a bare hill; the headquarters of the Veterans of Foreign Wars at Irwin; a steel stadium like a mouse rat-trap somewhere farther down the line. But most of all I recall the general effect—of hideousness without a break. There was not a single decent house from the Pittsburgh suburbs to the Greensburg yards. There was not one that was not misshapen and there was not one that was not shabby.

The country itself is not uncomely, despite the grime of the endless mills. It is, in form, a narrow river valley, with deep gullies running up into the hills. It is thickly settled, but not noticeably overcrowded. There is still plenty of room for building, even in the larger towns, and there are very few solid blocks. Nearly every house, big and little, has space on all four sides. Obviously, if there were architects of any sense in the region, they would have perfected a chalet to hug the hillside—a chalet with a high-pitched roof, to throw off the heavy winter snows, but still essentially a low and clinging building, wider than it was tall.

But what have they done? They have taken as their model a brick set on end. This they have converted into a thing of dingy clapboards, with a narrow, pinched roof. And the whole they have set upon thin, preposterous brick piers. And what could be more appalling? By the hundreds of thousands these ghastly houses cover the bare hillsides, like gravestones in some gigantic and decaying cemetery. On their deep sides they are three, four and even five stories high; on their low sides they bury themselves in the mud. Not a fifth of them are perpendicular. They lean this way and that, hanging on to their bases precariously. And one and all they are streaked in grime, with dead and leprous patches of paint peeping through the streaks.

Now and then there is a house of brick. But what brick! When it is new it is the color of a fried egg. When it has taken on the patina of the mills it is the color of an egg long past all hope or caring. Was it necessary to adopt that shocking color? No more than it was necessary to set all of the houses on end. Red brick, even in a mill town, ages with some dignity. Even when it has become downright black it is still sightly, especially if its trimmings are of white stone, with soot in the depths and the high spots washed by the rain. But in Westmoreland they prefer that uremic yellow, and so they have the most loathsome towns and villages ever seen by mortal eye.

I award this championship only after laborious research and incessant prayer. I have seen, I believe, all of the most unlovely towns of the world; they are all to be found in the United States. I have seen the mill towns of decomposing New England and the desert towns of Utah, Arizona and Texas. I am familiar with the back streets of Newark, Brooklyn, Chicago and Pittsburgh, and have made bold scientific expeditions to Camden, N. J., and Newport News, Va.

Safe in a Pullman, I have whirled through the gloomy, God-forsaken villages of Iowa and Kansas, and the malarious tidewater hamlets of Georgia. I have been to Bridgeport, Conn., and to Thomas, W. Va.

But nowhere on this earth, at home or abroad, have I seen anything to compare with the villages that huddle along the line of the Pennsylvania Railroad from the Pittsburgh yards to Greensburg. They are incomparable in color, and they are incomparable in design. It is as if some titanic and aberrant genius, uncompromisingly inimical to man, had devoted all the ingenuity of hell to the making of them. They show grotesqueries of ugliness that, in retrospect, become almost fabulous. One cannot imagine mere human beings concocting such dreadful things, and one can scarcely imagine human beings bearing life in them.

Are they so frightful because the valley is full of foreigners—dull, insensate brutes, with no love of beauty in them? Then why didn't these foreigners set up similar abominations in the countries that they came from? You will, in fact, find nothing of the sort in Europe—save perhaps in a few putrefying parts of England. There is scarcely an ugly village on the whole continent. The peasants, however poor, somehow manage to make themselves graceful and charming habitations, even in Italy and Spain. But in the American village and small town the pull is always toward ugliness, and in that Westmoreland valley it has been yielded to with an eagerness bordering on passion. It seems incredible that mere ignorance should have achieved such masterpieces of horror. There is a voluptuous quality in them. They look deliberate.

On certain strata of the human race, indeed, there is a libido for the ugly, as on other strata there is a libido for the beautiful. It is impossible to put down the wallpaper that defaces the average American home of the lower middle class to mere inadvertence, or the obscene humor of the manufacturers. Such awful designs, it must be apparent, give a positive pleasure to a certain type of mind. They meet, in some unfathomable way, its obscure and unintelligible demands. The taste for them is as enigmatical and yet as common as the taste for jazz, soda fountain drinks, dogmatic theology and the poetry of Edgar A. Guest.

I suspect (though confessedly without knowing) that the vast majority of the people of Westmoreland, and especially the 100 per cent. Americans among them, actually admire the houses they inhabit. For the same money they could get vastly better ones, but they prefer what they have got. Certainly there was no pressure upon the Veterans of Foreign Wars at Irwin to choose the dreadful edifice that bears their banner; they might have chosen other and less unsightly houses in the town, or built a better one of their own. But they chose that incredible clapboarded horror on the hillside, and having chosen it, they let it mellow into its present dingy depravity. In the same way the authors of the rat-trap stadium I have mentioned, after painfully designing and erecting it, made it perfect in their own sight, by putting a wholly impossible pent-house, painted a staring yellow, on top of it.

Here is something the psychologists have hitherto neglected—this love of ugliness for its own sake, the lust to make the world intolerable. It shows itself brilliantly in the whole race of wowsers: they police the fine arts, not because the fine arts are bawdy, but because beauty itself is offensive to them. The better the picture, the greater their delight in turning it to the wall. The nobler the book, the more it charms and caresses them to hand it over to the *Polizei*. On lower levels the thing is even plainer and more pathetic. Those sad Pennsylvania steel towns are constantly beset by fires. The very forests of the adjacent hills are full of black stumps. But when a town burns down its people do not thank God on bended knee. Instead, they gather together with heroic fortitude, and proceed to build it anew—and worse.

WEST INDIAN NOTES

IN THE CARIBBEAN IN JANUARY [1932].

Regarding Young Teddy Roosevelt, that busy fellow, opinion in Porto Rico seems to be divided. One faction, it appears, holds that he made the best Governor the island had seen since the death of Ponce de Leon; another views him far more critically, and inclines to the suspicion that he never really liked either his job or his lieges, and used the former only as a springboard to reach the Philippines. But both sides agree that he did very little loafing during his term of service. Either he was touring the island, listening to woes and running down deviltries, or he was whooping up Porto Rico back home. Most American politicians, when they are sent to the tropics, spend half their time boozing away their livers and the other half snoring. But Young Teddy was on the jump day and night, and if he did not actually restore Porto Rico to complete solvency and felicity, then he at least made something of an attempt.

The island is poor, and no wonder, for its 3,350 square miles, largely waste-land, try to support a million and a half people. This works out to a density of population three times that of Maryland, even with Baltimore city counted in. Take out the city, and Maryland has no more than one-fifth as many people to the square mile. The birth rate must be immense, for on the streets of San Juan one sees at least twice as many children as adults. At intervals of three or four blocks there are public schools, many of them very elaborate buildings, with the windows wide open and long ranks of boys and girls buzzing over their books within, learning the principles of American idealism.

But the noblest gift of the American *Kultur* to the Porto Ricans is a new and stupendous jail. It stands on a hill just outside San Juan, and is so vast that it is almost incredible. No other building in the town, not even the new Capitol, is so large. In the days of the Spaniards the cool, lizardy dungeons of the Morro were used for jail purposes, and they were seldom crowded, for the Spanish police were lazy and the Spanish laws were light. But now that Porto Rico is Americanized much more jail space is needed. The new building stands in the middle of a lot of perhaps fifty acres. Presently, no doubt, it will begin to sprout wings.

The last country I ever expected to see in this world was Venezuela. It was more remote from my thoughts than Korea or Iceland. But it turned out to be on the route of the *Columbus,* and so I found myself contemplating its shores the other morning. Seen through a porthole, they made a very pretty picture. In front was the pea-green inshore water of the Caribbean. Then a couple of rows of pink and yellow houses, with a few palms sprouting from them. Then a background of bare brown mountains, with their peaks lost in clouds. The port was La Guaira, founded twenty-five years before Jamestown. Beyond the mountains lay Caracas, the *Kaiserstadt* of the once famous Cipriano Castro, now as cruelly forgotten as Benjamin Harrison or Jake Kilrain.

La Guaira turned out to be two streets wide—the width of the beach. There were houses above, but no streets. I saw a few ladders, but in the main the uptown people appeared to go home on all fours, like shingles climbing a roof. All the automobiles in sight were bound for Caracas, but finally a driver was found who agreed to drive up the coast. For a couple of miles there was an excellent concrete road, with the sea on one side and the first step of the mountains on the other. Then, for ten miles more, there was a sound dirt road. Then it began to grow vague, and suddenly it ended in a swamp. So we came back.

On the way out we had observed a hotel at a village called Miramar—a very sightly and even pretentious building, with a vast veranda overlooking the sea. It turned out, on investigation, to be run by Germans, and on further investigation, to be as good as it looked. We had an excellent lunch, washed down by a bottle of pale Pilsnerish beer from Caracas. I have been wondering ever since what suggested opening such a hotel at such a place. What inducement brought the Germans there? Who put up the capital? Where do the guests come from? These questions, I confess, worry me strangely. There is in them the exigent futility of How Old Is Ann? If the weather were cooler I think I'd give them some really serious consideration.

Visiting Curaçao seemed more natural. Its name has been kept green by the booticians,[30] who have also done so much to make an increasingly skeptical and worldly nation remember the celebrated Rule of St. Benedict. But I had had long labored under an absurd misapprehension, inculcated by idiot pedagogues: I thought Curaçao was an island somewhere near Martinique. It turned out to be off the coast of Venezuela, somewhere near the mouth of the Orinoco. At first glance it appeared to consist of a group of oil tanks and a crumbling old fort. But this, it quickly developed, was only the back alley. The town of Curaçao was twelve miles away, hidden by sand dunes. Its harbor was too shallow for so large a ship as the *Columbus,* so we were tied up at the oil dock, and the rest of the journey had to be made by automobile.

It was full of surprises. In fact, it was downright astonishing. For Curaçao, when reached at last, appeared as alien to that desolate and sinister coast as a metaphysician would be to Congress. In the midst of the Venezuelan squalor it shone like a pearl. What prim and lovely houses, row on row! What clean and well-paved streets! What gorgeous gardens! What buxom and rosy Dutch girls! Every vista was a backdrop for an old-time musical comedy, *circa* 1895. Every house was a blaze of color—red, green, blue, yellow, heliotrope, even purple. And the roofs ran from the most brilliant golden orange all the way through the scarlets and vermilions to a palpitating, flame-licked brown.

A bit of Holland? Scarcely. Holland is a foggy country, and even the blaze of its tulip fields is somewhat subdued. But in Curaçao every color is developed and exaggerated by the tropical sun, and the result is an optical conflagration that would bring the police of Amsterdam on the run. It was like entering a dark cave to go into a shop. And it was a good deal like applying for the benefit of the bankruptcy laws to open negotiations with one of the ever so suave and accommodating clerks. The women of the ship's company came back carrying tons of perfumes. For Curaçao is a free port, and scents that sell for $25 a bottle in Baltimore may be had there for $24.65. It was a saving.

Life on so large a ship as this one, plying in such quiet and balmy waters, is infinitely caressing and restful. I came aboard with five different malaises, all of them apparently fatal, but in two days four of them were gone: in fact, they flew away the instant we struck the blue water. The fifth was more resistant, but it too yielded before we saw land. I took no medicine save a single soda-mint tablet, broken into six pieces, and each washed down with half a liter of Pilsner. The sea air did the rest.

It took me two whole days to read a book—a job I ordinarily knock off between 10 P. M. and bedtime. I fell asleep four or five times in the first chapter, and had to start all over again. A notice was posted announcing a series of deck sports. I slept through them. The Rotarians called a meeting, apparently to stop the Japanese-Chinese War. I slept through it. There was some sort of show in the evening. I was asleep when it began, while it went on, and after it ended. Not until late of an evening did I revive. Then I took some exercise in the smoke-room—and returned to bed, lulled by the wash of water along the ship's side and a singularly narcotic breeze.

All the ports we touch on this voyage, save poor San Juan, lie outside the range of the Wesleyan *Kultur,* and the ship itself, of course, is magnificently wet. I naturally expected to see some wide and handsome boozing, for at least nine-tenths of the passengers are Americans, and many of them come from presumably dry areas. But at the end of a week and a day at sea I have not seen a single case of alcoholic inflammation. The stuff is on tap, and, as the saying goes, they take it or leave it. Wine bottles are on half of the tables at dinner and lunch, and glasses of beer are on most of the rest. All the drinkables aboard are of truly magnificent quality. There is plenty of time for drinking, and the stewards are skilled at Red Cross work. But not a soul goes over the edge. What the moral may be here I do not know. Perhaps I had better leave it to Dr. Kelly and Dr. Crabbe.

OUR FOOTLOOSE CORRESPONDENTS

HAMBURG, APRIL [1934]

With good beer again on tap and the value of the *Reichsmark,* in baloney dollars, hoisted from around twenty cents to nearly forty, thousands of Germans are discovering a yearning to see America, and both of the big German transatlantic lines prepare to accommodate them. The North German Lloyd has arranged seven tours, the first of which will arrive in New York by the Bremen on May 24th, and the Hamburg-American Line will start two from Hamburg every week, one to last three weeks and the other four. The Lloyd tours will all be for about a month. The Hamburg-American Line price, first class on the *Albert*

Ballin, Deutschland, Hamburg, and New York, ranges from $376 to $400, with an $8.50 *Saisonaufschlag*[31] between June 11th and July 9th. The North German Lloyd is asking somewhat higher rates, but its customers will have the felicity of traveling on the *Europa, Bremen,* and *Columbus.* All these prices, rather cunningly, are published in American money. It is when the German begins to figure how cheap they are in marks that his *Wanderlust* really bubbles in his veins.

In New York the visitors will see all the sights that stagger strangers from the provinces, including the Empire State Building (which turns out to be 380 *m. hoch*), the Aquarium, Grant's Tomb, and the Cathedral of St. John the Divine. They will tour Broadway, Fifth Avenue, Wall Street, the Bowery, and Riverside Drive. They will go through the N.B.C. studios, and visit what the prospectuses describe as "the Ghetto." One night they will see a show at the *Roxykinopalast* and the next they will go to the celebrated *Vergnügungspark und Seebad,* Coney Island. In the intervals of ah-ing and oh-ing by day they will be free to roam through Columbia University and the department stores. There will be no need for interpreters, for Germans always prepare for a strange country by studying its language. Moreover, nearly all those with money enough to travel speak English anyhow.

It is rather curious to note what the German Cooks consider worth showing to their clients in the United States outside New York. No doubt Hollywood would be on their list if they were going beyond the Mississippi, but on all these tours they are turning back at Chicago. The name of Boston does not appear in their literature, and neither do they mention a stop at Baltimore, or Cincinnati, or Cleveland, or even Milwaukee. Pittsburgh is offered on only one tour out of the lot: its chief attraction turns out to be the Heinz pickle factory. But each and every tour includes Buffalo, for Niagara Falls, and each and every one includes Detroit, for the Ford works at Highland Park. Here is a typical itinerary:

> First day: Leave Bremen or Hamburg.
> Second day: Stops at Southampton and Cherbourg.
> Third to eighth days: At sea (visits to the engine-room and kitchens).
> Ninth day: Arrival in New York.
> Ninth and tenth days: Seeing its wonders, followed by a trip by Pullman *Schlafwagen*[32] to Buffalo.
> Eleventh day: Niagara Falls.
> Twelfth and thirteenth days: Detroit and the Ford works.
> Fourteenth to seventeenth days: Chicago and the *Weltausstellung,*[33] ending with a jump by *Schlafwagen* to Washington.

Eighteenth day: Washington, including the White House, the Capitol, the Treasury, the Library of Congress, the Smithsonian, the National Museum, the Washington Monument, the Lincoln Memorial, Mount Vernon, and Arlington. [A busy day!]

Nineteenth day: To New York again, with a brief stopover at Philadelphia.

Twentieth day: Off for home.

Twenty-fifth day: Cherbourg and Southampton.

Twenty-sixth day: Bremerhaven or Cuxhaven.

Obviously, it is the Ford factory that takes them all to Detroit; nevertheless, the literature shows that the town has many other marvels, unknown to most Americans. For example, there is the Campus Martius. It must be worth seeing, for the tours mention it ahead of even the Masonic Temple, the Penobscot Building, the Public Library and Belle Isle Park. In Philadelphia, of course, the chief show spot is Independence Hall, but it is crowded closely by the United States Mint and the Eastern Penitentiary. In Pittsburgh the only considerable rival to the Heinz pickle works is the Carnegie Institute. In Chicago the World's Fair will occupy nearly the whole four days, but there will still be time to see the stockyards and the Loop.

The latest edition of Baedeker's United States is somewhat out of date, but there is a recent edition of Grieben, its briefer and cheaper rival, and no doubt most of the pilgrims will have Grieben in their pockets. Unfortunately, it warns them against coming to New York in summer. We translate literally: "The great, damp heat during the day, and the sultry nights that no cooling-off bring, work a prostration on everyone who to the New York summer climate is not accustomed." But this will seem mild when they get to Washington. One of the tours will land there on July 6th and another on August 2nd! Certainly this is something that couldn't have happened before It Came Back.[34]

FOREIGN PARTS

[ATHENS]

It will take Athens years to get over Insull—maybe even centuries. While he was in residence, Socrates dropped out of the local papers, and the Sunday family trade of the Acropolis fell to a new low. . . . His old G.H.Q., the Hôtel de la

Grande-Bretagne, basks in the lemon-yellow sunshine at the end of the Place de la Constitution, between the Royal Palace and the Ministry of Justice. A wide, cool, matronly hotel, with an American bar and a competent bartender. His Old-Fashioneds have a name throughout the Mediterranean world. . . . More-over, there is a good local beer, called the Fix in honor of its founder. He began brewing in 1864, and Charles Fix, Inc., now operates four breweries. There is a rivalry between them, but judicious men refuse to choose; they all do their best, and it is very good. . . . Like the Rock of Gibraltar, the Parthenon surprises everybody. They expect it to be white, as they expect the Rock to be black, and it turns out to be a beautiful old ivory with blue halftones. . . . The Greeks have begun to repair some of the crumbling columns and friezes. Extremely neat work, but the effect is that of china inlays in eye-teeth. . . . Hoofing over the Acropolis is heavy exercise, for it covers the area of a good-sized race track and is very bumpy. The visitors console themselves by cabbaging small frag-ments of marble. There seems to be no objection; thousands of tons are left. . . . The guides spout the history of Greece to the winds which roar down from Marathon. Their customers begin to move away the moment they begin, and in the end only a few deaf valetudinarians are left. . . . The souvenir stands sell embroidered bags, alabaster figurines, Japanesy-looking vases, frescoed sea shells and dolls. The dolls are dressed in short flaring skirts, and gaudy bob-tailed jackets. The women are horrified to discover that a neat mustache has been painted on each. An inquest develops the fact that they are supposed to be effigies of Greek soldiers in the native costume. This native costume, on a further search, turns out to be not Greek at all, but Albanian. . . . Back in town someone discovers a soldier so dressed, but he is smooth-shaven, which some-how seems a joke. The rest of the military do their prancing in imitations of German uniforms. . . . In the Place de la Constitution are a hundred bootblacks, each with a box covered with polished coins. They are forbidden by the police to grab a passerby, but they are free to yell at him as he passes. The price of a shine *parfait,* including a brush-down, is five cents American. Did I forget to say that beer is five cents a large glass, with no false bottom? Insull lived softly here! . . . Everyone seems to have at least a little English, and especially all the beggars. Little girls towing still littler ones gallop alongside the stranger, bellowing "No papa, no mamma!" The parents of these orphans keep watch from doorways: children must be brought up to be honest in money matters. . . . A large bunch of lovely violets, powerfully scented, for ten cents. . . . The National Museum is disappointing. Most of the best sculptures of Athens were stolen a century ago by the heroes who delivered Greece from the Turk, and are now in London, Berlin, Paris or Rome. But there are some pieces of the Archaic Period, all of males, that attract a lively custom. They lack fig leaves, and show a virile and even boastful spirit. . . . The ancient jewelry would do well in any American ten-cent store. The Greeks were metaphysicians, not jewelers. . . . Mars Hill lies just below the Acropolis—a bare, rugged slope covered with loose stones. It is a marvel that Paul escaped alive when he lectured here. . . . The jail of Socrates is nearby. It looks comfortable, considering the climate, but it wouldn't hold a Dillinger. . . . The Near East Relief maintains a shoppe for the sale of its clients' work. They make everything from lace handkerchiefs to suites of furniture. In the courtyard a couple of porters are crating a huge table; the crate is marked New York. But the women decline to buy, on the ground that nearly everything on sale is obtainable in Fifty-seventh Street, and much cheaper. . . . Aside from the marble glories of the Acropolis there is curiously little to see, and next to nothing that Pericles ever saw. Most of the ruins date from Roman times, and those that are older show Roman repairs. . . . The modern town has nothing on Buffalo. . . . A new four-lane boulevard runs down to The Piræus, where the ships dock. The taxi-drivers rush it like hearsemen returning from a funeral. They arrive ahead of time, leaving an hour to kill. What better way to kill it than to find out if Fix's beer has improved since yesterday? . . . It turns out to be no better. But it is just as good.

[ISTANBUL]

It is a serious *faux pas* to say Constantinople; the Turks are trying to forget that their metropolis once bore the name of a Christian emperor. But the teachings of the schoolma'm stick in the mind like cockleburs, and so the American visitor usually starts off with "Constanti-" and then adds "-bul" as an apologetic afterthought, making it Constantibul, pronounced "bool," not "bull." The Turks still frown. . . . They have been more successful in getting rid of another relic of ancient shame—the Arabic alphabet. It is a misdemeanor to show a street sign in it; they are all in the new Roman alphabet designed by Kemal the Liberator. So are all the newspapers. Penalty for the first offence: 1,000 piastres. For the second: the bastinado. . . . But the authorities of the Mint seem to be exempt, for all the coins are still stamped in Arabic letters, and it takes a couple of days to learn that a bold-face o is 5, and an exclamation point followed by a little diamond 10. . . . The German influence is still visible. The old German Embassy, on a high hill overlooking the Bosporus, remains a landmark, and the branch of the Deutsche Bank has elegant quarters downtown. But on its bronze doorplate "Deutsch" has become "Doyçe." Every hotel is now an oteli. . . . It is rather startling to see shop windows full of Oriental rugs: one harbored the impression that they were made only for the innocent American trade. Their tomato reds and morgue blues are just as hideous here as at home. . . . An excellent lunch at the Pera Palace, including crabs that might have come out of the Chesapeake. The hotel business, alas, is not so hot. The politicians have all gone to the new capital, Angora (more correctly, Ankara), and many of the merchants have moved to Smyrna or Salonika. . . . But Istanbul, despite its miseries, is still a *Kaiserstadt*. It may be sick, but it is sick in a Large Way. The indefinable air of a great city hangs about it. It spreads out over its hills lavishly, embracing the narrow and shabby but romantic Golden Horn, and it is studded with vast, bumpy domes, and sharp, wicked-looking minarets. For two thousand years it held the pass between East and West, taking toll of every ship and caravan. A good deal of this money seems to linger. Many swell villas along the Bosporus. Good cars waiting outside high-toned shops. Young Turks in Savile Row clothes. The mosques sweat porphyry, lapis and alabaster, and at the Imperial Treasury in the Old Seraglio is an emerald as big as a ham sandwich. . . . A pleasant atmosphere of good-humored skepticism. Christianity is too feeble to be a nuisance, and Moslemism has been adjourned. All the public jobholders have to work on Friday, the Moslem Sabbath, and there is no time off for the five daily prayers. Priests are registered like taxi-drivers. . . . In the Mosque of Suleiman the Magnificent there are exactly thirty customers for the midday service. A kind of Low Mass, with the priest chanting passages from the Koran. The customers bow, kneel, touch their heads to the floor. All of them seem to be poor men. Only one wears a boiled collar. Very dignified proceedings, and humanely short. . . . No fezzes. Penalty for the first offence: fifty piastres and a warning. Penalty for the second: the third degree in Insull's jail. Kemal stands no nonsense. . . . In Santa Sophia his agents are scratching the plaster off the priceless sixth-century mosaics concealed from pious eyes for thirteen hundred years. Priceless they may be, but their beauty remains to be argued. . . . Santa Sophia itself has the shape of a Philadelphia pie-woman, and the same patchy exterior. Inside, it is vast, dim, silent and spookish. . . . Now ho for a trip up the Bosporus, and a glimpse of the Black Sea! Robert College on the heights above the mediæval castle of Roumeli

Hissar: the former a huge, depressing, jailish-looking pile in the style of 1865. Villas and villas, most of them with large gardens. A trolley line along the beach. . . . The Constantinople Woman's College. Some of the gals are aboard. They are of every region from the Dardanelles to the Tigris, are mainly dark and dumpy, and not many would qualify as catechumens in Hollywood. They chatter in Turkish, Armenian, Syrian, Greek, Arabic and English. One of them is deep in a book; it turns out to be Willa Cather's "Lost Lady." Outfitted with their A.B.'s, these ladies will disperse over Asia Minor, teaching, uplifting, marrying. . . . An idle day, loafing about Istanbul. A walk along the old walls, built by Theodosius. Two or three mosques, all empty. The bazaars. Rugs. Stilettos. Flintlock muskets. Old silver. The rattly old bridge across the Golden Horn. The Serpent Column from Delphi, *circa* 475 B.C. . . . A free reading notice for a good guide, Ahmet Hamdi. He may be reached in care of the American Express Company.

[GRANADA]

The trip down from the north is long and full of grief; it is much easier to approach the Alhambra from Malaga. Easier, but certainly something short of voluptuous. The upholstery in the first-class compartments of the train dates from the days of Maria Christina, and the carpets on the floors are antiques out of the dark backward and abysm of time. . . . The little locomotive takes five hours to drag the train over the Sierra Nevada. Sometimes it slows down to four miles an hour. A dog running along the tracks beats it. . . . But the scenery is worth the puffing. High gray crags with dizzy ravines between. Sometimes, in a tunnel, there is a break in the wall, and a tortured, improbable landscape by Gustave Doré flashes by. Bridges one hundred feet long and three hundred high. . . . Once over the mountains, the train skis down into Granada, but not without some tedious halts at way stations, during which the boozers aboard rush the station *bodegas*, and gulp down a pale, sourish native wine at one peseta twenty-five a bottle. . . . Once there is a stop between towns, precisely athwart a farmstead. A traveling butcher happens along, and the farmer's wife brings him a lamb. While she holds it up by the tail, he kills and skins it. He performs the job with many flourishes, and one eye on his audience. Done, he washes his hands at the pump, loads the skin on his donkey, raises his hat and departs. A gifted technician, and a man of airs. . . . But here is the flat Vega de Granada at last, and ahead lie the town and the Alhambra. First something to cut the dust and quiet the nerves; the bartender at the Alhambra Palace Hotel has it in the form of large, cold, sweaty bottles of Alhambra *cerveza*, which is to say, drinking beer. Down goes one, hooray, hooray, and then another! Now for the Alhambra! . . . It turns out to be on a high hill, and from the Puerta de las Granadas, where the taxis stop, to the main buildings is quite a step, and on cobblestones. The guide is an elderly gentleman with the manners of an ambassador—Spanish, of course, not American. His English is exact, and runs largely to names and dates. . . . Away with such statistics; where are the crown jewels? Alas, they were taken to Madrid in 1562. Well, then, let us see the mummies of Ferdinand and Isabella. Alas again, they are down in the town, lying under eight feet of granite in the cathedral. . . . The Court of the Lions. What! *This?* Are you sure you are right, Mr. Gonzalez? . . . *Ciertamente, Señor.* I was born only a step down the road. . . . Figures cannot lie. The Court of the Lions is ninety-two feet long, which is just fourteen feet longer than a Pullman car. It is fifty-two feet wide, which is less than the width of Forty-fifth Street. The lions all have club feet and the heads of Towser. The Hall of the Ambassadors—even smaller, but much more impressive. One must, of course, imagine the alabaster that used to pave the floor, and the jasper, porphyry and mother-of-pearl that once adorned the ceiling, but even so it is still something to look at, gray and ragged though it may be today. In the plaster of the ceiling are a hundred and fifty-two patterns, no two alike. Have they been counted lately? Are they all there? They are counted annually at Michaelmas. The check tallies. But from the floor only a dim, spooky chaos is visible. . . . And so to the Hall of the Abencerrages, with a roof that has somehow cheated Time, and remains brilliant with reds, blues and old golds. A fountain in the center, with the marble coping showing splotches of rusty brown. The blood of nobles butchered by the wicked King Boabdil in 1483. Believe it or not. . . . The Hall of Justice, entered through a really magnificent arch, swathed in gorgeous filigree . . . . The Hall of the Two Sisters . . . . The Court of the Myrtles. . . . The Patio of the Council. . . . The baths downstairs, still damp after six hundred years. The guide explains how the water was brought in and let out. It is complicated, and he must go over it four or five times. It remains complicated. . . . So farewell to the Alhambra, and back to the Alhambra Palace Hotel, and another shot of that Alhambra *cerveza*. An extremely comfortable inn. The reading-room is upholstered in leather and velvet, both a brilliant scarlet. A long and excellent Spanish dinner—soup, fish, eggs, entrée, roast, cheese, fruit. . . . The sun goes down over the Picacho de

Veleta—11,148 feet high. The view from the hotel terrace is superb. But suddenly it turns cold, and the customers come in, shivering. . . . No night life. To the hay at once. Tomorrow the Generalife, the Sacro Monte, the Cabildo, the house where Washington Irving lived, the Cathedral.

[GIBRALTAR]

Gibraltar looks infinitely old, and it is. There were men here in Early Paleolithic times, and there have been men here ever since. The Rock is covered with mangy bald spots, and is full of huge zigzag cracks. One night of frost would bring down a million tons of it. But there is no frost, and so the English arrive copiously on ten-day excursions, and bask in the blinding sunlight at the Rock Hotel. The round trip from London or Liverpool costs £18 and is well worth it, for Gibraltar not only has a soothing climate but is the safest place on earth. If a pirate came across the straits from Barbary, he would be confronted by two hundred twelve-inch cannon, not to mention three battleships, five cruisers, twenty destroyers and ten submarines. . . . This protection, of course, carries its inconveniences. Even Britons may not climb the Rock beyond a certain point. As for Americans and other such lower fauna, they are halted far below. Every day the Gibraltar *Chronicle and Official Gazette* carries notices like this: "On Wednesday Gun Practice of a Heavy Nature will take place from the Spur and Levant Batteries, commencing at about 10 A. M. In order to avoid danger windows near the line of fire *must* be kept open." . . . The *Chronicle* is heavy with shipping notices. Ships are about to sail for Port Said, Shanghai, Colon, Bombay, Buenos Aires, Kingston, the Azores, the Persian Gulf, Oslo, Cardiff, the Cape. The *Gibel Dersa*, a neat packet, runs to Tangier three times a week, "subject to weather and other conditions." To Algeciras, across the bay in Spain, there is a ferry five times daily. One way, two pesetas. The round trip, three fifty. . . . The Rock is loveliest at dawn, with the sun coming up behind it. For a quarter of an hour it is coal-black, as in the Prudential advertisements. Then, of a sudden, it turns a luminous gray, and when the sun pops over the top it burns with every color of the rainbow. . . . The bumboats, with English precision, are labeled "Bumboat" in large letters, and numbered. Their commanders address themselves mainly not to passengers but to the gentlemen of the crew. The stewards and engineers negotiate with them out of the ports of G Deck, and the sailors up forward heave lines to them over the foredeck, and haul up socks, boots, accordions, tobacco and baskets of oranges. . . . On the tender going ashore the passengers encounter dealers in postcards, postage stamps, walking sticks and flowers—flowers gaudy beyond words, and immensely cheap. A whole basket, large enough to make a funeral piece for a Grand Exalted Ruler of the B.P.O.E.,[35] for a dollar, with the basket thrown in—and no churlish mention of the baloney in the dollar. . . . The main and only street starts at the dock and runs uphill to the Alameda, a tropical garden halfway up the Rock. Palms. Crotons. Nurse-maids of all shades, mainly Spanish. Baby buggies of every reign since George IV's. Retired sergeants drowsing in the sun, dreaming of the booze in Calcutta, the gals in the Malay States. . . . The upper classes mount a step higher to the Rock Hotel. A decorous, well-turned-out house, with a competent chef and an enlightened bartender. The guests seem to be nearly all English. Sir Marma-duke Beasley, Bart., nursing his hereditary sinus infection. Lady Vi Snodgrass recovering from a hound's bite. They are no great shakes here, for every season sees three or four head of dukes, and even Royalty is not uncommon. A some-what swanky place. Coats and pantaloons never match. The duchesses wear out their clothes. On Saturday and Tuesday nights there is the sound of viols and hautboys, and a unanimous shaking of legs. The Super Five Dance Band. Now and then a Fancy Dress Ball, with Great Fun. . . . Down in the town the rival Bristol Hotel announces a *Ladies'* Super Five Dance Band, with a Dinner Dance every Friday. . . . The one street swarms with military, but the naval brethren are quartered on the other side of the Rock, and seem to keep to themselves. By night they are busy with their red, green and white signals, and early in the morning they go out in their gray craft for mysterious operations in the straits. At intervals it is reported briefly in the *Chronicle* that a gunner's mate has fallen overboard or that two destroyers have bumped. . . . But the chief news in the *Chronicle* is about the weather. The daily weather story, in fact, stretches across the top of Page 1, like a murder at home. It is so important that the temperature is reported both in the shade and in the sun. A sample day: 61° maximum in the shade and 106° in the sun. . . . To the north stretch the lush hills of Andalusia, with the Sierra Nevada for backdrop. Southward, across the narrow straits, lies the coast of Africa, dour, dangerous and excessively romantic.

[JERUSALEM]

Why do all the guide books omit the most salient fact about the Holy City—that the streets and alleys within the walls are as slippery as glass? Almost every visitor, prancing in unwarned, comes down furiously upon his *tokus*, to the damage of his health and faith. Some day the English overlords will tear up the ancient cobbles, worn and polished by a hundred generations of sandals, and lay asphalt. . . . For the present they are too busy policing the town. At the Wailing Wall sits a stout cop in his shirt sleeves, patiently waiting for trade. Any bloodshed today? No, sir, but there's no telling when an Arab may heave a dead rat over the wall, or two Jews may begin to fight for the same spot. . . . Nor is all of the rough-house theological. The Mount of Olives and the Garden of Gethsemane swarm at night with Arab torpedoes from down Jericho way. Tourists who go out to the Garden to see the moon are often stuck up and robbed. Now and then one of them, resisting, is carved. . . . The Jaffa Gate is the main entrance. Inside the way leads straight to the Church of the Holy Sepulchre, the headliner of the show; outside lie the King David Hotel, the tourist agencies, and the chief souvenir stands and antique shoppes. . . . Across Julian's Way from the hotel is the new million-dollar Y.M.C.A., a huge pile nearly a block long, pseudo-Byzantine in design. Within, troops of young Moslems disport in the swimming pool, and diligent Zionists study advertising layout, business correspondence and advanced corporation accounting. . . . The hotel itself, four years old, is the finest in the Levant. The gentlemen of the staff, all Swiss professionals, wear cutaways, striped pantaloons and gardenias. The *portière*, a local boy, speaks ten languages; some say twenty; a few make it twenty-five. The waiters are Soudanese—handsome blackamoors in long white nightshirts with red sashes and rakish fezzes. . . . The tourists pile into automobiles and go scooting down the Hebron road to Bethlehem, five miles away. A dirty-gray, dried-up village on a steep hillside, unanimously devoted to the souvenir business. Camels carved out of olive wood. Arab outfits in gaudy colors for the kiddies at home. Postcards. . . . The Church of the Nativity is operated jointly by Latin, Greek Orthodox and Armenian monks, all of them heavily whiskered. One must duck through a low stone doorway to get in; a little way along there is another doorway, at least fifteen feet high, but the low one is more romantic. A monk has tapers ready for the descent to the crypt; silver of any coinage thankfully received. The nave is hung with red, blue, green and gold Christmas-tree balls. . . . Back to Jerusalem and the Church of the Holy Sepulchre. Here the Latins, Orthodox and Armenians have had to make room for a Copt. The division of interest is shown by the lamps hanging in the Chapel of the Angel—five Latin, five Orthodox, four Armenian and one Copt. Another descent underground. The monk in charge stands a four-hour watch, and admits only five visitors at a time. Some give a dollar, some less. . . . One of the chapels has begun to crack, and union men on high scaffolds are knocking the plaster off its ceiling. Much dust and a horrible noise. The plaster was put up in 1846, but the pieces make cheap and handy souvenirs. . . . The shoppes near the hotel do a lively trade in knitted caps: no native seems to wear them, but they show all the colors of the rainbow, and look like good value at a quarter. Presently the price comes down to two for a quarter, and then to ten cents apiece, and then to five. The tourists who have paid a quarter howl "Heil Hitler!" . . . But there is a one-price shoppe nearby—Oman's at the Jaffa Gate—perhaps the only one east of Gibraltar, save Ahmed Soliman's perfume palace in Cairo. Oman sells antiques—silver jewelry, brass candlesticks, old tiles and so on. Each customer receives gratis a charm against the evil eye—a useful weapon in these parts. . . . No night life. The tourists, save for a few Presbyterians, try jazz at the King David Hotel, but their legs are too stiff after all day on the cobblestones. . . . Two bold fellows go out to see what is what. They stumble home in an hour, reporting that the cops have just sent the last convoy of girls back to Port Said. They found an Arab guide who described what seemed to be a parlor-house, out beyond the American School of Archeology, but the neighborhood looked too dark for safety. . . . Good rye in the bar: a highball, since the balonization of the dollar, works out to 27.34562 cents. . . . And so to bed, and sweet dreams of Abraham, Jeremiah, Micah, Elijah and company. Jerusalem would be a swell place for sleep if it were not for the church bells.

[VENICE]

Venice is the movie gal among the cities: it photographs beautifully, but is freckly and fossilized face to face. The way to get on to its deceptions is to approach it from the sea. The ship lies far out, and coming in by tender is a matter of nearly an hour. At the start the city is only a thin, dim line on the horizon, and even when it begins to rise out of its marsh it seems to rise only a few feet. One never gets over that sense of dismal flatness. . . . The landing is on the Riva, with the Bridge of Sighs directly ahead. A few steps through the Piazzetta, and the Piazza of Saint Mark's is revealed. The same old head shops, unchanged since the Turkish Wars. The same old cafés with tinkly pianos playing inside. The same old pigeons doing their stuff for the same old hat-cleaners. . . . But here is something new: on every pillar of the Doges' Palace is a one-sheet hearing the brief words "Viva Il Duce." The eye moves to the pillars of the Palazzo Reale—and each hears the same sign. It proceeds to those of the Procuratie Vecchie—and there are more. In the whole square, perhaps two hundred. . . . Between them are stickers setting forth the latest apothegms of the Great Man. In one he allows that there is no substitute for Service. In another that the first thought of every patriot must be for the State. In a third that Italy has a glorious destiny, and will face it bravely. In a fourth that the hope of the world is Peace with Honor. No sign of running out of ideas here; he seems to have millions in reserve. . . . Can this gray and squatty pile be Saint Mark's? And this sad silo the Campanile? Somehow, they seemed larger, grander, nobler the last time. Within the portals of the cathedral the same old dingy portières entangle the visitor. A priest with a powerful tenor voice is chanting the office for the day. The metallic echoes turn his strophes into an amazing, and even alarming, roaring. . . . Outside in the square two flocks of pigeons swoop down at once, colliding and tussling in mid-air. Someone has broached a sack of corn. The pigeons depart, leaving three men examining their hats with wild surmise, and a little girl crying over her spoiled pinafore. . . . At the western end of the Piazza something is afoot. There is a platform with chairs on it, and people are crowding up. Presently a band of music files out from the dark arcade behind. Every member wears a huge black hat with a green feather. While they tune up, a boy comes out toting a velvet banner covered with medals, and carries it slowly across the front of the platform. The professor's trophies. . . . The boys look silly in those feathers, but play divinely. The trumpets produce a tone that is all gold and molasses. The clarinets whinny like angels. But what are they playing? They are playing a potpourri from "Aïda"! It is like putting the Brain Trust to swapping penknives. The music stops. A hurricane of applause. An encore. More "Aïda." The audience pants with joy. . . . One escapes into the Via XXII Marzo, searching for the Bauer-Grünwald. In the old days it tapped a perfect Pilsner, golden, pungent, and swimming with cunning little *Bierfisch*. But no more. Pilsner, for some reason unfathomable, appears to be going out. All around the Mediterranean one must drink Münchener, or the Amsterdam Amstel. So down with a *Seidel* of Pschorr, and back to the Piazza. . . . Outside the Church of San Moisè is an American priest carrying a satchel, three large books and an umbrella. He is hunting for a way to get into the church, but all the doors are locked. Evidently the theological internes have shut up shop for the day and gone to hear the band. But why should anyone want to see the banal baroque of San Moisè? . . . A couple of billstickers at work on the Doges' Palace, putting up more copies of "Viva Il Duce." The band has got to "Rigoletto." Ah, for a bust of honest *band* music, say the "Radetzky March" or "El Capitan"![36] But to the Venetians music is only opera, opera is only Verdi, and Verdi is only his worst. . . . The bead-sellers announce a *novità*, a necklace made of fifteen or twenty strands of very small beads, plaited like a rope. A German woman buys two dozen; the sisters of the *Damenverein* are not forgotten. . . . Two Americans talking at a café table. "The motor boat has killed the gondola." A bit further on, two at a bar. "The motor boat has killed the gondola." At the next bar two more. "The motor boat has killed the gondola." The melancholy word, it appears, has been passed along; indeed, it has got into Baedeker. . . . One cuts through narrow back streets to the Grand Canal. In five minutes forty-eight gondolas pass—and two motor boats.

[MADEIRA]

The tires of the automobiles make a horrible roar on the little round cobble-stones. Rather curiously, the heavy sleds drawn by oxen—every visitor is expected to try a ride—kick up very little noise. . . . Twenty thousand tourists a year, mainly English. Dinner at Reid's Hotel, buried in green on a melodramatic bluff west of Funchal. The waiters move so fast that they seem like figures in a movie film. Retired colonels. Oxford dons. Lady Augusta Leigh-Basingstoke in her pearls. Very good chow. . . . The wine warehouses are all near the waterfront. They are dark, ancient, and romantic, and smell heavenly. The dealers are full of optimism. They hope to run Madeira against sherry in succession to the cocktail in post-prohibition America. . . . The peasants who descend from the hills, driving their meager donkeys, look dyspeptic and despondent. Many Irish faces, as in northern Spain. Sad old bucks with young and buxom wives. . . . Latitude 32° 37′ 45′′ N—on a level with Savannah and Montgomery. But the flora is tropical, and the whole landscape is gorgeous with roses, mimosa, calla lilies, geraniums and purple bougainvillea. . . . Mobiloil signs everywhere, but so far no Coca-Cola. . . . The poor come down to the beach, lay a circle of wave-worn stones, somehow fill it with dirt, and cultivate market gardens—onions, radishes, cabbages, even potatoes. Twenty feet away the long rollers thunder in from the Atlantic. . . . Between the gardens and the surf the week's wash is spread out to dry. A rooster treads it solemnly, searching for spiders, beached

minnows and the larvae of whales. . . . Two men sifting sand—a gloomy business, full of grunts and panting. They fill a small sieve with handles at each end,
and then wobble it to and fro. When a bushel of sand accumulates it is scooped
into a bag and hung upon the back of a donkey. . . . The moment a ship casts
anchor in the roads fifty bumboats surround it. Genuine handmade lace—"Two
yearrrs wurrk!" Fifty dollars for a starter. Then down quickly to eighteen. Then
seven. Then three and a quarter. . . . But most of the bumboats sell nothing, and
offer nothing. Rowed out laboriously, they simply wallow in the swell, hour on
hour. The oarsman, exhausted, takes a nap, and his brother keeps watch. What
are they up to? No one seems to know. Perhaps they hope that a rich passenger
will fall overboard, and need service. Or that a beefsteak will somehow bounce
out of the galley. . . . Cross-examined in loud pidgin English, they turn out to
be unhappy. Times are hard. They have been hard since 1419. The highest birth
rate in the Western World. . . . The passengers go ashore and buy wicker porch-
chairs, to the scandal of the deck stewards. Before the ship gets to Gibraltar the
stewards will report that all these chairs have washed overboard in the night. . . .
Also, the brethren and sisters bring back bottles of Madeira in wicker baskets, to
the scandal of the wine stewards. Madeira averages nineteen per cent of alcohol.
The two fat widows at the captain's table are visibly corned at dinner. . . . The
residents, tiring of wine, turn to beer. The Atlantic Brewery offers a *Helles* called
the Diamond. Not bad. . . . Everyone tries the trip up the funicular railway to
Terreiro da Lucta, three thousand feet in the air. Vineyards all the way. The
peasants tramp out the grapes with their bare feet, and rush it down to Funchal
by ox sled and donkey train before it can ferment. The dealers do the rest. . .
. Some of the firms go back two hundred years. The head of such a firm ranks
locally as a duke, and all other partners as marquises. Even the bookkeeper is
a kind of baronet. . . . The ship's bore returns on the last tender, loaded with
statistics. There are three hundred and sixty-three genera of native wild flowers.
At the age of fifteen the trunk of a palm is five feet in diameter. The highest
peak lifts itself sixty-one hundred feet. There are five islands, and their total
area is 314 square miles, exactly 5.14 miles more than that of Greater New York.
. . . After the World War the Emperor Karl of Austria was banished to Madeira.
Pretty soft—or so it seemed. But though the English have been trooping here to
cure their catarrh since Charles I's time, Karl soon came down with pneumonia
and passed away. . . . No night life. The girls are all earnest Christians. There
is a movie parlor, but no place in town to dance. At Reid's Hotel a trio plays
at meals. A Punch-and-Judy show in the main street would make a sensation

and suspend the communal life. There is also a swell opening for the Salvation Army. . . . Two thousand, seven hundred and sixty-five miles from New York. Three hundred and sixty to the African coast. A quiet spot.

[RÂBAT]

Nobody stays long enough at Casablanca to do more than bolt a few drinks and buy some native leather work, made in Japan. The hot spot is Râbat, sixty miles away, one of the four capitals of His Heavenly Gloriousness, Sidi Mohammed, Sultan of Morocco by grace of the French. . . . The road is good, and the third-hand jitneys make lightning time. There is a guide standing up in one of them, howling out the names of the villages along the way; they all sound like Oriental rugs. He wears a red fez, a green raincoat, horn-rimmed spectacles and a toothbrush mustache. . . . At a halt for stretching legs, he allows that if their luck holds out the pilgrims may see the Sultan. But it turns out otherwise. The new palace, straight from Hollywood, is duly found, and inquiry at the gate proves that His Gloriousness is within, but he is busy searching the Koran in the harem, and can't be induced to do his stuff. . . . The guide explains that he is a member of the strictest of all the Moslem sects—what, in America, would be called a Presbyterian—and has only one wife. The law allows him four, but one is enough. . . . The Al Smith Building of Râbat is the Hussein Tower, on a hill overlooking the harbor, and perhaps two hundred feet high. Everyone must climb it. Fortunately, there are no steps; instead, an inclined plane like a gigantic corkscrew—easy going. . . . Two French soldiers loll against the coping at the top, gabbling to one another in German. *Aber was! . . . Warum nicht? Bin ich nicht Deutsch?* . . . To be sure, the Foreign Legion. Well, *Kamerad,* how do you find things? . . . Not so bad, *danke.* It is a life like any other. Americans? Only a few. The French don't like them. Whenever one of them is sent to the guardhouse to be groomed for hanging, he howls for the American consul, the American ambassador at Paris, the Secretary of State at Washington. The French prefer politer necks. . . . A pretty fair lunch at the hotel, but no butter. Can it be a kosher house? Yells for the headwater, the manager, the American consul, the French resident-general. The butter comes on, looking somewhat sheepish. . . . Well, now, who is for a walk? First some good open-air cigars; then let us head for the *souks,* which are what the Moors call what the guidebooks call bazaars. The *souks* run for blocks. Narrow alleys. Merchants squatting on their hind quarters. More Japanese souvenirs—in leather, wood, mother-of-pearl, celluloid. Antiques from the High Atlas. Amber, brasses, pottery, brocades. *Entrée libre.* But *sortie* is something else again. A dealer in sheepskins with a dial telephone. Next door to him a Moorish butcher. His cuts suggest that he uses a garden hoe. Sheep's heads with sad eyes. The smells are really not so bad. Fulton Market is worse. Black boys in long gowns demanding *bucksheesh*—but only stealthily. Signs everywhere: *La mendicité est interdite.* Cops on the prowl. . . . Back to the Sultan's Palace. Maybe he will show himself. But no, he is still busy with his studies. At his gates linger other students of the same instructive book—mainly old men in long beards, squatting in the shadows. They accept silver. . . . The soldiers on guard are coal-black, and wear gorgeous uniforms. They face the palace, with their backs to the universe, and carry their rifles at parade rest. . . . Seen again, the palace looks even more Hollywoodish than before. The stone turns out to be mainly stucco. There is no grass in the courtyard. Someone discerns an eye peeking through the jalousies of the harem windows. Great excitement. Movie cameras begin to click. But all they record is a somewhat frayed MGM set. . . . Back to Main Street. Buses loading for Fez, Casablanca, Marrakech. When they are packed inside, the surviving customers climb to the roofs. The buses start off to the time of a wild hullabaloo, their horns tooting and donkeys, camels and goats leaping out of the way. . . . The Moors, like all dark folk, love to travel. Outside the town the road back to Casablanca is crowded. The careening buses plunge through long trains of donkeys, laden beyond belief. Now and then a Ford bangs along, with a native driving and his whole family bouncing around among the household goods behind. . . . A fine farming country. Wide fields of alfalfa. The farmhouses are always on hilltops, and nine-tenths of them are fortified. The farmers take no chances: some day the French may leave. . . . Camps of desert Bedouins in every hogwallow. They are nuisances, but must be handled tenderly. . . . Casablanca, reëxamined, turns out to be only a French provincial town. The Café Foch. The Café Verdun. Maxim's. The Compagnie Générale de Transport et Tourisme au Maroc. . . . Back to the ship!

[CAIRO]

During the Big Winter of 1929–30, 30,000 Americans visited Egypt. This year: less than 5,000. . . . A dragoman: "But how can Americans be poor too? You had sense enough not to go into the war." One wobbles around in the vast spaces of the hotels, all of them with expensive and empty gardens. . . . Dressing for dinner is adjourned, even at the immensely swanky Shepheard's. . . . Across the Shâri' Kâmil from the Continental-Savoy, fifty dragomans pant and hope. Their official wage is $2 a day, but they have all heard of the baloney dollar, and it is now $3. . . . Is the local water safe? Some say one thing and some another. Most visitors drink Évian—or beer. All the bars stock Amstel in quart bottles—a thin brew out of Holland, faintly Pilsnerish. . . . No one seems to exult over the hotel chow, but there is a good restaurant in the Shâri' Elfi Bly, around the corner from Shepheard's—the St. James's, run by a Greek. Superb *crevettes* fresh from Alexandria daily, with vintage mayonnaise. A carafe of the house wine, red or white, for 9 piastres. . . . The peddlers in the Shâri' Kâmil are operated by despair: it is a kind of bum's rush for every white passerby. A Chicago man claps on a fez, and stalks out to fool them. They detect the disguise at 200 yards. They sell postcards (both archeological and pornographic), tin jewelry, bogus scarabs, walking sticks, fezes, perfumery, riding whips, Sudanese spears (made in Japan), cigarettes, newspapers, fly-swatters, brass pots and pans, blue goggles, veils. They offer cut-rate trips to mosques, museums, pyramids, bawdy houses. . . . All the women go to Ahmed Soliman's in the Khan el Khalili to buy perfumes. His atelier is the last gasp in Oriental magnificence—a Hollywood dream of Araby. Soliman himself sits gravely at a desk, pondering the glories of his clientele—H.R.H. the Princess Mary, the Lady Helen Brocklehurst, Police Commissioner L. M. Rubens, Sir Moh Ahmed Said, Lord Charles Cavendish, Adolph S. Ochs, J. Kindleberger, Edgar Wallace, Jr.[37] The full list is in a little blue pamphlet: copies are passed around. Also, glasses of tea flavored with ambar paste—"the perfume of which makes old men young again." Waiting husbands are fetched in from the street to hear, sotto voce, that it is the world's most reliable aphrodisiac. The polished salesmen, each a sheik, recommend Black Narcissus, "the scent for moonless nights of love"; Harem, "compiled from a secret process of the harems"; Fotna, "which means temptation." The bottles are small, and the bill runs into money. Each bottle is elaborately wrapped and boxed by a black functionary in a costume by Joseph Urban. Whispers: "Is he a eunuch?" Nay, he is a family man with six children in school. . . . Who is for a night on the Nile, under the eternal stars? They come back complaining that it was dark out there: they could see only the lights of Cairo. . . . Who is for a night in the desert, by camel and jackass, with a Bedouin's tent to sleep in? It appears next morning that the desert is full of fleas. . . . Everyone wants to see Tut-ankh-amen's 350-pound gold coffin in the Museum. The authorities talk of moving it out: it kills the rest of their show. . . . Many go to the Pyramids twice. Scared the first time, they return to prove that they have mastered camel-riding.

The cameleers complain in very good English that the sheik hogs all the money: they reach for their tips behind their camels, so that the greedy fellow won't see. Anything less than a dollar insults sheik, cameleer, and camel. . . . On sailing day a great gang flocks to Port Said. A fast train, for Africa—148½ miles in 4 hours flat. One Pullman, with a porter in a red fez and a flowing white nightshirt. . . . It is two blocks from the Port Said station to the dock. Two-horse hacks of the XII dynasty, horses of the early Mousterian. The drivers demand $2 for the trip. Pressed, they come down to $1, but at the dock they demand $2—and usually get it. They are not above slugging a passenger who resists: Port Said is as tough as Sing Sing. . . . The scoundrel who hands the baggage down demands $1, and takes 50 cents. His brother, who carries it to the dock, refuses 50 cents, but takes 75. His five cousins rush up yelling for cuts. Two of them drive the other three away, and demand $1 apiece for doing it. The other three come back, and demand $1 apiece for the time lost. A couple of *colorado maduro* cops look on. . . . Aboard ship, the women storm the studio of the *Damenfriseur:* their hair needs washing. The men make for the bar.

THE ADRIATIC: EAST SIDE

The western shore of the shallow Adriatic has been a tourist stamping-ground for centuries, but it is only since the World War that the other bank has come under the fire of the kodak. On a gorgeous morning last Spring, when the *Columbus* dropped anchor off Durazzo, the Albanians saw a great tour-ship for the first time. What they thought of it, and of the Americanos who swarmed ashore in the ship's boats, must remain unrecorded, for though the whole population of the town turned out to gape and gabble, only two of its members could speak anything even remotely resembling English, and they were both politely reticent. Nevertheless, some lively trading went on, mainly in the sign language, but helped out with French, Italian and German, and when the visitors reëmbarked they were loaded with sheepskins, Albanian cutlasses and bead necklaces made in the form of gaudy snakes, with yellow fangs, red eyes and blue tails.

Durazzo, it must be confessed, is no great shakes. It is the chief seaport of a sovereign State nearly twenty-two years old, with a King named Zog, a Premier named Evangeli,[38] and a finger in the hot Balkan pie, but it remains somewhat backward, and even Paleolithic. Not until April 2, 1929, did most of its heads of families adopt surnames, and then it was only under pressure from a new and drastic law, supported by King Zog's stranglers. About that time the

Moslem faithful of the town decided to flaunt their piety by building a Grade A mosque—indeed, the finest west of Istanbul. They employed an Italian architect of advanced ideas, and he drew up plans for something that would enchant all Islam, and at the same time have a sound inner core of steel I-beams. Unluckily, the money ran out soon after the I-beams were erected, and so they now entreat Heaven in all their piteous nakedness, with only a thin skin of concrete to save them from the leprosy of rust.

The chief trade of Durazzo is in sheep, and it is carried on in the public square, a large space in the center of the town, unpaved, bumpy and dirty, with the skeleton of the fossil mosque on one side and rows of sickly shops and cafés on the other three. The herdsmen come down from the mountains driving their flocks, and their customers lurk coyly in the shade of the shops, waiting to be wooed. When a trade is joined there is a loud hullabaloo, with the sheep at issue prodded from nose to tail, and each side putting expert witnesses on the stand. Not infrequently the debate comes to fisticuffs, and one of King Zog's soldiers rushes into it, and the whole market falls into chaos, with sheep running away, lambs trampled, and a universal rowdy-dow. It ends in anti-climax, with the customer marching off and the sheep slung about his neck. The smell dismays him no more than it would dismay a polecat, and for the same reason.

Durazzo, despite its touch of structural steel, has changed little since the Eleventh Century, when it was stormed by Robert the Norman. At that remote time it was already eighteen centuries old. It has been Greek, Roman, Venetian, Serbian and Turkish, but preserves no traces of any of its masters save a few fragments of crumbling wall, a superannuated viaduct, and the trash-piles of 2700 years. Since November 28, 1912, it has been the Liverpool and Hamburg of a marionette kingdom that blew up in anarchy in 1914, became an Italian protectorate in 1917, a regency in 1920, and a republic in 1925, and then went back to being a kingdom in 1928. Durazzo passed through all these changes unscathed, sticking to the sheep business. It has no more sights than a prairie town, but there is charm in it for the visitor who wants to know what the Adriatic coast looked like to a crusader in the year 1100.

A hundred miles to the northward, over the border of what used to be Montenegro and is now Jugoslavia, there is the great show place of the coast, Kotor Bay. It is a Norwegian fjord torn loose from its moorings and flung clear across Europe. Its loveliness is immense, theatrical, incredible. Narrow at the entrance, it bulges out at intervals like a cobra swallowing a litter of guinea-pigs, and every bulge is a mad riot of beauty—gnarled, green-gray rocks rising from blue water, with vast white peaks above, and villages out of picture-books every mile or so. At the head of the fifth, largest and final bulge is the ancient town of Cattaro, a nest of pirates in the old days, but now chiefly devoted, like Durazzo, to the sheep trade. It has been, in its time, Roman, Venetian, Turkish, Spanish, Serbian, Hungarian, Bulgarian, Russian, French, English and Austrian, and all the while it was really Montenegran. But some conqueror or other was always strong enough to chase the Montenegrans off the shore and up the hills, and they got possession of their frontyard at last only by abandoning their independence and joining Jugoslavia.

The general aspect of the Bay is one of profound peace. Indeed, it looks far more operatic than warlike, and its gory history is hard to believe. In front of Cattaro lie three little islets, and on each is a church. One of these islets is thick with tall cypresses; it might have served as a model for Arnold Boecklin's "Toteninsel," a picture once almost as popular as Whistler's portrait of his mother, or "His Master's Voice."[39] The ship goes very near it, waving a fan of long ripples toward the tiny shore. Not a soul is in sight. Nor does Cattaro send out any bumboats to seduce the passengers with sheepskins, daggers and native leather-work made in Japan. The Cattarese have given up piracy for good.

Another brief step up the coast and we are in the harbor of Ragusa, now called Dubrovnik by its Jugoslav overlords. But they hang on precariously, and it will probably go back to being Ragusa, as it was for more than a thousand years, after the next war. We are out of the wilds now, and get the smell of an ancient civilization. Ragusa was the chief rival of Venice for centuries, and accumulated a vast wealth. In this wealth nested poets, theologians, jurists, metaphysicians and other such parasites, and their benign festering gave Ragusa the intellectual leadership of the whole Balkan peninsula. Its Homer was Gjivo Gundulic, whose epic, "Osman," is still studied by all Eastern Adriatic schoolboys. And there was a lady poet, Cvijeta Zuzoric, who wrote in Serbo-Croatian, Italian and Latin, and made such a stir that Tasso dedicated a sonnet to her.

Ragusa is now a placid watering-place with bathing-machines along the shore and an excellent hotel. The main street of the old town is the Placa Kralja Petra—two blocks of the most charming little shops ever seen, full of Croatian needlework in all the colors of the rainbow and manned by staffs of sales engineers speaking Italian, French, German, Serbian, Spanish, English, Greek and Turkish, and making them all sound alike. The Placa Kralja Petra is paved with square stones, and makes a pleasant promenade. Up to a few years ago no automobiles were permitted to enter it, but now, thanks to the protests and petitions of the *Kurgäste*[40] from Belgrade, Budapest, Rome and Vienna, they may come in if they keep in low gear. But Ragusa itself sticks to shank's mare, and does its hauling in pushcarts.

At the landward end of the Placa is the Franciscan monastery, and opening from its cloisters is the oldest drugstore in the world. It opened in 1307 and has been in continuous operation ever since. The monk who now manages it looks much less than 627 years old, but some of his stock is so plainly ancient that it must have been second hand when it was first laid in. But today there is only one call for powdered frog's eyes or graveyard moss to a hundred for aspirin, and on some near tomorrow a counter for chewing-gum may be added, such is the rate of human progress in Ragusa. Meanwhile, the town remains a lovely souvenir of the almost immemorial past. It is, indeed, a museum piece of the first caliber—but it also has good cafés, and the Croatian cooking is very well spoken of.

The whole coast of the Eastern Adriatic is studded with such gems. It has almost as many good harbors as the Italian shore has banks of sand. Islands without number string along it—some of them mere lonely rocks, but others covered with vineyards and olive groves, and gay with white and yellow towns. It was at its best in Roman times, but it kept going valiantly during the long night of the Middle Ages, beating off both Western conquerors and Saracen pirates. Only in the modern age has it slipped back. But that slipping back is not likely to last; already it shows signs of a revival, with visitors roaring in, umbrellas on every beach, golf in the foothills, and jazz in the hotels. If you want to see it before it turns Lido altogether, now is the time to take ship.

EPILOGUE

HENRY LOUIS MENCKEN (1936)

I was born in Baltimore on September 12, 1880, and have lived there ever since. For twenty years on end my office was in New York, and I have at all times had frequent business there, but I prefer living in Baltimore. It is, save for a few bright spots, a somewhat shabby town, but it is full of honest and amusing people, and its bores are appreciably less virulent than those who infest New York. I went to a private school until I was twelve, and then transferred to the Baltimore Polytechnic. That transfer was my father's choice, not mine. A business man all his life, he carried about with him a secret weakness for engineering, and I suppose he hoped that it would develop in me. But it didn't, and neither did a taste for business. One week after his death in 1899, I applied for a job on the old Baltimore *Herald,* and in another week I was at work on the street, covering the remoter suburbs. I remained on the paper until it blew up in 1906—one of the first victims of the intensive competition that has disposed of so many other American newspapers since. When the ship went down, I was its captain. This is to say, I was the chief editor, with a private office, a secretary, and passes on all the railroads.

All the other Baltimore papers offered me jobs, and I chose the Sunday editorship of the Baltimore *Sun.* A little while later I was put to writing editorials, and in 1910, when an evening edition was started, I went to work on its editorial page. After a few months I had a department of my own, called "The Free Lance," and this I operated until the end of 1916.[1] Then I went to Germany for the two *Suns* and a group of other newspapers. Unfortunately, the United States got into the war soon afterward, and I had to come home. For a year or so, with the censorship in full operation, I was debarred from any sensible newspaper work, but in 1918 I rejoined the *Evening Sun,* and have been on its staff ever since. I commonly write an article for its editorial page every Monday, and do various other jobs from time to time. I am greatly interested in the paper, and like to think that I have had some small hand in its extraordinary success. It is probably the best evening paper in the United States, and it is certainly one of the most prosperous.

My chief interest has always been in daily journalism. For twenty years I also edited magazines, but that was only a sideline, and in 1933 I concluded that I had had enough of it. My books, in the same way, have also been by-products. The largest of them, 'The American Language,' began as a series of articles in the Baltimore *Evening Sun,* and much of the matter in the rest came out of the columns of the same paper. It is my belief that writing for a daily paper offers much more agreeable opportunities than writing for the magazines—that is, if the paper is solvent, and is run by men of intelligence and independent spirit. One gets one's notions into print much more quickly, and, though many will not believe it, one often has more freedom. I print things in the *Evening Sun* almost every week that not four magazines in the United States (save, of course, some of the bankrupt propaganda organs) would dare to publish. If any of it is good, one may make books of it later.

My books have covered a wide range—perhaps too wide a range. I have done volumes on religion, on morals, on language, on the woman question, on politics, and on a great variety of social matters. All of them, save one, have sold sufficiently to bring me good profits. I was a literary critic for twenty-five years, and enjoyed it more or less, but it always seemed to me to be a vain trade, and so I was glad to forsake it when the chance came. I am much more interested in what people do than in what other people write about it. I'd rather go to a national convention, or cover a great fire or earthquake, or look in upon the mountebanks at London, Berlin, or Washington than listen to all the literary gabble ever loosed on earth. My acquaintance among authors is naturally large, and I have some close friends among them, but taking one with another they seem to me to be dull fellows, and, in some aspects, hard to distinguish from eunuchs.

My plans for the future are always vague, so I don't know what enterprise I'll be tackling next. But I have always wanted to do a book about my early youth—say from the dawn of consciousness to adolescence—and I may get to work upon it anon. I had a happy infancy, for I lived in a pleasant home in a very pleasant town. It might be a good idea to set some account of it alongside the tales of privation and frustration that so often get into print. Frustration is something that I know of only by report. I have always managed to get anything that I really wanted, and have never suffered any of the oppressions that proletarian authors tell of. Thus I am almost completely free of envy, and can't pass the examination for democrats.

NOTES

INTRODUCTION

1. Fred Hobson, *Mencken: A Life* (New York: Random House, 1994), 430–31.

2. Hobson, 445.

3. A good many of these reports can be found in *The Impossible H. L. Mencken*, ed. Marion Elizabeth Rodgers (New York: Doubleday, 1991).

4. "Treason in the Tabernacle" (1931), in *H. L. Mencken on Religion*, ed. S. T. Joshi (Amherst, NY: Prometheus Books, 2002), 285.

5. See Hobson, 349–50.

6. See HLM to Katharine Sergeant White (an editor at the *New Yorker*), 27 April [1934], in *The New Mencken Letters*, ed. Carl Bode (New York: Dial Press, 1977), 311.

7. John W. Larner, "'The Libido for the Ugly': H. L. Mencken versus Western Pennsylvania," *Western Pennsylvania Historical Magazine* 7 (January 1988): 84–94.

PROLOGUE

1. HLM had published in none of these papers, although he had had an article in the *Pittsburgh Press* in 1900, published under the pseudonym "J. D. B. Jarvis."

2. This is of course an exaggeration at this juncture in HLM's career, but toward the end of his life he estimated that he had published 10 to 15 million words. The total is probably closer to the first of these figures.

MEMORIES OF A LONG LIFE

1. Library catalogs date the anonymous *Story of Simple Simon* (New York: McLoughlin Brothers) to the 1860s. The book is 8 pages long.

2. Justin H. Howard, *A Peep at Buffalo Bill's Wild West* (New York: McLoughlin Brothers, 1887). 20 pp.

3. Mercantile Trust Co. of Baltimore, *The Early Eighties: Sidelights on the Baltimore of Forty Years Ago* (Baltimore: Mercantile Trust & Deposit Co., 1924). 24 pp. The illustrations are reproductions of engravings from the second edition (1889) of George W. Howard's *The Monumental City: Its Past History and Present Resources* (1873–76).

4. *Die Gartenlaube* ("The Arbor") was a popular German periodical (1853–1944) that fostered a distinctive style of family-oriented illustration.

5. HLM refers to the Haymarket riot in Chicago in 1886, a riot involving striking laborers. The Knights of Labor, a powerful labor organization, was falsely implicated in the deaths of police officers during the riot, and their influence declined significantly thereafter.

6. The title ("The deaf hear") is taken from the Vulgate (Matt. 11:5; Luke 7:22).

7. Both the mother and wife of Alexander Graham Bell (1847–1922) were deaf, and he devoted a considerable part of his early career to educational aids for the deaf.

8. A fourflusher is a bluffer, or one who makes false claims. See HLM's humorous sketch, "The Science of Four-Flushing," *Smart Set* 44, no. 2 (October 1914): 81–85 (as by "Owen Hatteras").

9. The German Aged People's Home of Baltimore.

10. In another article, "Baltimore's Wild West," *Baltimore Evening Sun* (7 November 1927): 19, HLM admits that he was one of the boys who had been robbed. In that article he states that he only had two cents in coins, so presumably the other boy had the other two cents.

11. HLM refers to Philip Danforth Armour (1832–1901), American businessman who in 1867 established the meatpacking firm of Armour and Company in Chicago.

12. The father of George Herman "Babe" Ruth, Jr., was George Herman Ruth, Sr., a Baltimore tavern keeper.

13. Winfield Scott Schley (1839–1911), admiral of the United States Navy who gained both celebrity and notoriety during the Spanish-American War, sported a full goatee and moustache.

14. A Dayton-wagon is a wagon that forms part of the equipment of a fire-fighting force.

15. *Puck* (1871–1918) was a humor magazine. "Bonner's *Ledger*" refers to the *New York Ledger* (1856–98), a weekly story paper established by Robert Bonner. *Godey's Lady's Book* (1830–98) was a celebrated magazine for women. *Bow Bells* (1862–87) was a British magazine "for family reading."

16. *Ben-Hur: A Tale of the Christ* (1880), an immensely popular historical novel by General Lew Wallace. It was later turned into a stage play and filmed twice (1925, 1959).

17. A Great Incohonee is a high functionary in the Improved Order of Red Men, a fraternal patriotic organization purportedly dating to 1765.

18. *Krausmeyer's Alley* (1903) was a burlesque show about a Jewish father who objects to his son marrying a young Irish woman. It was composed by Billy Watson (1866–1945), an American singer, comic, and producer.

19. *Growler* is a slang term referring to a keg of beer.

20. HLM refers to the New York Society for the Suppression of Vice, a private organization established by Anthony Comstock for the purpose of censoring publications that he deemed obscene or immoral. Upon Comstock's death, the organization was taken over by John S. Sumner (1876–1971). Under Sumner, the society launched a furious attack on Dreiser's novel *The "Genius"* (1915).

21. Frank Norris had strongly praised Dreiser's *Sister Carrie* (1900) when he was a reader-editor with Doubleday, Page & Co.

22. Heliogabalus (more properly Elagabalus) was a Roman emperor (r. 218–222) who gained a reputation in antiquity for decadence and sexual irregularities. HLM and George Jean Nathan wrote a full-length comic play about him (see 116).

23. Huneker's essays on (Richard) Strauss and Brahms are in *Mezzotints in Modern Music* (1899); the essay on Nietzsche is in *Egoists: A Book of Supermen* (1910); the book on Chopin is *Chopin: The Man and His Music* (1900).

24. The essays on Ibsen and Maeterlinck are in *Iconoclasts: A Book of Dramatists* (1905).

25. The *Musical Courier* (1880–1962) was a journal of musical and, occasionally, dramatic criticism published in New York.

26. HLM refers to the purchase in 1916 of the *New York Sun* by Frank A. Munsey (1854–1925), owner of a number of popular fiction magazines.

27. *M'lle New York* (1895–99) was a literary magazine of which Huneker was coeditor (with Vance Thompson).

28. Huneker's chapter on "Roosevelt and Brandes" in the volume *Variations* (1921) recounts his meetings with Theodore Roosevelt and Roosevelt's praise of Huneker's work.

29. The Austrian composer Franz von Suppé (1819–1895) composed the incidental music to *Dichter und Bauer* (Poet and Peasant), a play by Karl Elmar.

30. The reference is to A. H. McDannald. See n. 23 to "World Traveler."

31. HLM refers to the Hungarian Josef Gung'l (1810–1889), the Austrian Karl Michael Ziehrer (1843–1922), and the Czech Karel Komzák (1850–1905).

32. *Don Juan* (1889), a tone poem by Richard Strauss.

AUTHOR AND JOURNALIST

1. The column in question was called "Rhyme and Reason." Three installments appeared (28 October, 4 November, and 11 November 1900). The following week, HLM began another column, "Knocks and Jollies," which comprised twelve installments from 18 November 1900 to 17 February 1901.

2. As of 1999, of the approximately one hundred copies printed, forty-six were known to exist, sixteen in private hands. See Richard J. Schrader, *H. L. Mencken: A Descriptive Bibliography* (Pittsburgh: University of Pittsburgh Press, 1999), 4. Schrader has since identified a total of 53 copies in existence (see his online list of Mencken bibliographical addenda, http://www2.bc.edu/~schrader/mencken.pdf).

3. There was in fact a second edition, by Smith's Book Store (Baltimore) in 1960, a 250-copy facsimile reprint of the 1903 edition.

4. *Poeta nascitur, non fit* (A poet is born, not made). A Roman proverb.

5. HLM refers to the unsigned editorials (averaging about four hundred words) that appeared on the far left-hand columns of the editorial page, not the signed op-ed pieces (averaging about fifteen hundred words) that HLM later wrote once a week for the *Evening Sun.* He actually began writing unsigned editorials for the *Sun* in August 1906, producing approximately four hundred of them down to the spring of 1910.

6. HLM wrote approximately 825 unsigned editorials for the *Evening Sun* during the period 1910–12.

7. In fact, HLM wrote several wrote several editorials for the *Evening Sun* about airships. See "The First Passenger Airship Line" (23 June 1910), "The Airships to the Fore" (9 July 1910), "The Aerotaxi Next" (3 November 1910), and "The Airship in Actual War" (29 November 1911).

8. HLM and Nathan founded three periodicals—the *Parisienne* (1915), a fiction magazine with stories set in France; *Saucy Stories* (1916), a purported rival to the pulp magazine *Snappy Stories* and featuring tales with a sexual undercurrent; and *Black Mask* (1920), a detective pulp magazine—for the purpose of raising money. They soon ceased to have any direct editorial involvement in these magazines. *Black Mask* went on to become a celebrated venue for the writers of hard-boiled crime fiction, including Dashiell Hammett, Raymond Chandler, and Erle Stanley Gardner.

9. A novelette usually led off each issue of the *Smart Set.* HLM himself wrote one of them: "The Charmed Circle" (August 1917), a 16,500-word story published under the pseudonym William Drayham.

10. These stories appeared, respectively, in the issues of April 1921, August 1920, and May 1919.

11. These articles appeared, respectively, in the issues of November 1920, January 1911, and February 1922. "The Rural Soul" was published prior to HLM's assuming the coeditorship of the *Smart Set*.

12. The editors of the *Smart Set* were Arthur Grissom (1900–1901), Marvin Dana (1902–4), Charles Hanson Towne (1904–7), Fred C. Splint (1907–8), Norman Boyer (1909–11), Mark Lee Luther (1911–12), Willard Huntington Wright (1913–14), Mark Lee Luther (1914), and HLM and George Jean Nathan (1914–23). After 1923 the magazine changed its focus radically and became a popular magazine of fiction and features.

13. In this article, HLM refers to the following books (listed in the order in which they are mentioned): *Ventures into Verse* (1903); *George Bernard Shaw: His Plays* (1905); *The Philosophy of Friedrich Nietzsche* (1908); *The Artist: A Drama without Words* (1912), a one-act play; *A Little Book in C Major* (1916), a collection of aphorisms; *A Book of Burlesques* (1916; rev. 1920), humorous sketches; *Damn! A Book of Calumny* (1918), short extracts of articles from the *Smart Set; In Defense of Women* (1918; rev. 1922), a tongue-in-cheek discussion of the relations between men and women; *The American Language* (1919); *A Book of Prefaces* (1917), a volume of lengthy essays on Theodore Dreiser, Joseph Conrad, James Huneker, and "Puritanism as a Literary Force"; *Prejudices* (1919–27; 6 volumes), HLM's most celebrated series of critical essays; *Men vs. the Man: A Correspondence between Rives La Monte, Socialist, and H. L. Mencken, Individualist* (1910), a letter exchange between La Monte and HLM; *Europe After 8:15* (1914), a whimsical tour of Europe, cowritten with George Jean Nathan and Willard Huntington Wright; *The American Credo* (1920; rev. 1921), a collection of conventional beliefs of Americans, with a long preface by HLM; *A Doll's House* (1909) and *Little Eyolf* (1909), new translations of Ibsen's plays (with Holger A. Koppel) with prefaces by HLM; *The Gist of Nietzsche* (1910), a slim collection of extracts from Nietzsche; and *Heliogabalus: A Buffoonery in Three Acts* (1920), a play cowritten with Nathan.

14. HLM apparently refers to the article "The Two Englishes" (*Baltimore Evening Sun,* 10 October 1910).

15. The Free Lance Series was a series of six books published by Alfred A. Knopf between 1920 and 1922. The third book in the series was HLM's translation of Nietzsche's *Antichrist* (1920), and the sixth book was the second revised edition of *In Defense of Women* (1922). The other books contained introductions by HLM.

16. There was no magazine of the period with the exact title *True Stories* (or *True Story*). HLM is either referring erroneously to *True Confessions* or generically to the pulp magazines, which published genre stories (romance, western, adventure, horror, mystery, science fiction) for a popular audience.

17. This was the celebrated "Hatrack" case. In the April 1926 issue of the *American Mercury* HLM published Herbert Asbury's story "Hatrack," about a small-town prostitute. The Watch and Ward Society of Boston attempted to ban the sale and distribution of the issue in Boston, but HLM challenged the society in court and prevailed.

18. Americana was a long-running column, extending over the entirety of HLM's editorship of the *American Mercury* (1924–33), which printed humorous or absurd items from newspapers around the country, arranged by state.

19. Ernest Booth's "We Rob a Bank" appeared in the *American Mercury* for September 1927.

20. Robert J. Tasker's articles "The First Day" and "A Man Is Hanged" appeared in the *American*

Mercury for March and June 1927, respectively. *Grimhaven,* an account of prison life written while Tasker was serving his sentence at San Quentin, was published by Alfred A. Knopf in 1928, presumably on HLM's recommendation.

21. In 1936, HLM published the fourth edition of *The American Language* (1919), radically revised and expanded from the third edition of 1923. He then compiled *The American Language: Supplement I* (1945) and *The American Language: Supplement II* (1948).

22. HLM ran a monthly book review column in the *Smart Set* from November 1908 to December 1923 (a total of 182 columns) and another review column, The Library, in the *American Mercury* from its inception in January 1924 to December 1933 (a total of 118 columns [no columns for January 1927 and April 1930]).

23. Francis, Lord Jeffrey (1773–1850), cofounder with Sydney Smith of the *Edinburgh Review* and its editor from 1802 to 1829.

24. *The Charlatanry of the Learned (De Charlataneria Eruditorum),* by Johann Burkhardt Mencken (1674–1732), translated by Francis E. Litz and containing an eleven-thousand-word introduction by HLM.

THINKER

1. The *Landsturm* (literally, "country storm") was a corps of irregular military forces, including all able-bodied men between the ages of forty and forty-four, set up in Prussia in 1813 to defend the nation in the event of invasion. This article was published five days prior to HLM's forty-fifth birthday.

2. HLM wrote this article only two months after publishing his scathing reports on the Scopes trial.

3. HLM misquotes the Vulgate (John 18:38): *Quid est veritas?* (What is truth?)

4. HLM refers to the date of the United States' entry into World War I, a conflict in which he largely took the side of the Germans.

5. The governor Maryland in 1928 was Albert Ritchie, who was in office from 1920 to 1935 and whom HLM consistently supported. Alvan T. Fuller was governor of Massachusetts (1925–29) at the time when Nicola Sacco and Bartolomeo Vanzetti were executed on 23 August 1927; Warren T. McCray was the governor of Indiana (1921–24) who resigned after he had been convicted of mail fraud.

6. Webster Thayer (1857–1933) was the presiding judge in the Sacco-Vanzetti case, who was widely accused of prejudice against the defendants.

7. *Sáorstat* is the Irish term for "free state."

8. The Industrial Workers of the World, a radical labor organization founded in 1905.

9. Hebrews 11:1 (King James Version).

10. HLM refers figuratively to Richard Croker (1843–1922), a leader of Tammany Hall; HLM is suggesting that Methodist leaders conduct themselves in his corrupt manner. Charles F. Murphy (1858–1924) succeeded Croker as leader of Tammany Hall in 1902, becoming the most powerful boss in Tammany Hall's history.

11. *Pollyanna* (1913) was an immensely popular bestseller by Eleanor H. Porter (1868–1920), about a young girl who cheers herself up by thinking how much worse her life could be. It was widely ridiculed for advocating an irrational optimism.

12. "Definition of the truth: something somehow discreditable to someone." HLM, *A Little Book in C Major* (New York: John Lane, 1916), 24.

13. HLM refers to vice president John Nance Garner (1868–1967), who had had increasing disagreements with President Franklin D. Roosevelt during Roosevelt's second term and sought to win the Democratic presidential nomination in 1940. Garner was seventy-one at the time HLM delivered the text of this essay as a speech (4 January 1940).

14. HLM evidently refers to the presidential campaign of 1904, the first that he covered. Although he covered both the Republican and Democratic national conventions of that year (in which Theodore Roosevelt and Alton B. Parker, respectively, were nominated), there is no evidence that he accompanied either nominee on his campaign tour.

15. Carl Sandburg wrote a six-volume biography of Lincoln (1926–39). HLM reviewed the first two volumes (*American Mercury*, July 1926).

WORLD TRAVELER

1. Admiral William Penn (father of William Penn, settler of Pennsylvania); General Robert Venables, who led a force that seized the island in 1655.

2. Barmaids.

3. HLM refers to the operas *Hänsel und Gretel* (1893) by Engelbert Humperdinck; *Elektra* (1909) by Richard Strauss; *Parsifal* (1882) by Richard Wagner; and *Les Huguénots* (1836) by Giacomo Meyerbeer.

4. Alehouses or pubs.

5. *The Rosary* (1909) is a sentimental novel by Florence L. Barclay. The "Elsie books" are a series of twenty-eight Sunday-school novels featuring Elsie Dinsmore, published between 1868 and 1905, by Martha Farquharson (pseudonym of Martha Farquharson Finley).

6. *Tristan und Isolde* (1865), an opera by Richard Wagner.

7. *Todesursachen* means "causes of death." The *Statistischer Monatsbericht der Stadt München* is the monthly statistical report for the city of Munich.

8. After having spent seven years in Dresden, Ibsen settled in Munich in 1875. He remained there until 1891. *Hedda Gabler* was written in 1889–90, *Rosmersholm* in 1886, *The Lady from the Sea* in 1888.

9. Dr. Adolf Himmelheber is fictitious. His last name would mean "Heaven-raiser."

10. The German statements can be translated as follows: "Is there any fire in this goddamn tavern? My feet are as cold as icicles!" "The fellow is crazy!" "It is as stupid as an actor!"

11. "Wiener Blut" ("Vienna Blood"), a waltz and operetta by Johann Strauss II (1825–1899).

12. "Munich, how lovely are you?"—a play on the song "O Jugend, wie bist du so schön," by Franz Wilhelm Abt (1819–1885).

13. "The dickens!"

14. Pork chops and bean salad (the latter term now spelled *bohnensalat*).

15. HLM apparently refers to Friedrich von Müller (1858–1941), a German internist who was a professor in Munich from 1902 until his death.

16. *Backfisch* is a slang term referring to a young woman. In other writings HLM notes that this word is the closest that German comes to the American slang term "flapper."

17. "Lachende Liebe" (Laughing Love) is a song by Henri Christiné and Charles Lion.

18. *Manon* (1884), an opera by Jules Massenet. Act 1 is set in the courtyard of an inn in Amiens.

19. The *Fliegende Blätter* (1845–1944) was a long-running humorous/satirical paper published in Munich. *Le Rire* (1894–1949) was a comic paper published in Paris.

20. *Gemüthlichkeit*, a word much favored by HLM, means comfort or coziness (now spelled *Gemütlichkeit*).

21. A glee club.

22. A *Zahlmeister* is a paymaster. A *Bierbischof* (lit., "beer bishop") is a bartender.

23. HLM refers to A. H. McDannald, a political reporter for the *Baltimore Sun* and a nonplaying member of the Saturday Night Club. He figures extensively in HLM's travelogue of London, "At Large in London" (p. 187).

24. HLM alludes to Thomas Babington Macaulay's famous remark that the Catholic Church "may still exist in undiminished vigour when some traveller from New Zealand shall, in the midst of a vast solitude, take his stand on a broken arch of London Bridge to sketch the ruins of St. Paul's." Macaulay, "Von Ranke" (1840), in *Critical, Historical, and Miscellaneous Essays* (Boston: Houghton Mifflin, 1860), vol. 4, 201.

25. "My Cousin Carus'" (1907), a song about Caruso, was written by Gus Edwards and Edward Madden. It was featured in the Ziegfeld Follies of 1909.

26. Bob Acres is a coward in Richard Brinsley Sheridan's comic play *The Rivals* (1775). Marguerite Gautier, a courtesan, is the heroine of Alexandre Dumas's play *La Dame aux Camélias* (1852), based on his 1848 novel. It was the basis for Verdi's opera *La Traviata* (1853).

27. HLM alludes to the Battle of Inkerman (5 November 1854), a battle of the Crimean War, in which a combined force of English and French soldiers defeated the Russian army.

28. Curfews.

29. HLM refers to German foreign minister Arthur Zimmerman and to Germany's resumption of unrestrained submarine (U-boat) warfare.

30. The term *bootician* was HLM's coinage for a high-class bootlegger. See *The American Language: Supplement I* (New York: Knopf, 1945), 584.

31. A seasonal rate increase.

32. A sleeping car.

33. A world's fair. The Chicago World's Fair of 1934, a reprise of the Century of Progress Exhibition (27 May–12 November 1933), ran from 26 May to 31 October 1934.

34. By "It Came Back" HLM probably refers to the renewed availability of legal liquor in the wake of the repeal of Prohibition.

35. The Benevolent and Protective Order of Elks.

36. The "Radetzky March" (1848) is by Johann Strauss the Elder. "El Capitán" (1896) is a march by John Philip Sousa, included in an operetta of that title.

37. HLM refers to Princess Mary (1897–1965), daughter of George V; Lady Helen Brocklehurst (1890–1973), wife of Henry Courtney Brocklehurst (1888–1942), a decorated British soldier; Lord Charles Cavendish (1905–1944), British soldier and businessman; Adolph S. Ochs (1858–1935), owner of the *New York Times;* Jacob Kindleberger (1875–1947), German-American salesman and aphorist. L. M. Rubens, Sir Moh Ahmed Said, and Edgar Wallace, Jr., are unidentified. (The British

detective novelist Edgar Wallace [1875–1932] did not have any children named Edgar.) Some of these names may be fictitious or distorted.

38. Zog I (1895–1961), king of Albania (1928–39); Pandeli Evangeli (1859–1939), prime minister (1921, 1930–35).

39. Arnold Böcklin (1827–1902), *Toteninsel* (1880; The Island of Death); James McNeill Whistler (1834–1903), *Whistler's Mother* (1871; properly titled *Arrangement in Grey and Black: The Artist's Mother*); Francis Barraud (1856–1924), *His Master's Voice* (1898).

40. Visitors.

EPILOGUE

1. The Free Lance column ended on 23 October 1915.

GLOSSARY OF NAMES

ABELL, WALTER W. (1872–1941), American newspaper owner whose grandfather Arunah S. Abell (1806–88), had founded the *Baltimore Sun* in 1837. As a young man Walter worked in the business and editorial departments of the paper; he became director of the A. S. Abell Company in 1894 and was president from 1904 to 1909. A year after his retirement, control of the paper passed out of the Abell family for the first time.

ADAMS, JOHN HASLUP (1871–1927), American journalist who worked for the B. & O. Railroad before joining the staff of the *Baltimore News* in 1899, becoming managing editor in 1904. In 1910 he became managing editor of the newly established *Baltimore Evening Sun*. He and HLM worked closely on the editorial policy of the paper.

ANDERSON, SHERWOOD (1876–1941), novelist and poet whom HLM regarded as one of the leading writers of the day. His most celebrated works—all reviewed by HLM—are *Windy McPherson's Son* (1916), *Marching Men* (1917), *Winesburg, Ohio* (1919), *Poor White* (1920), *The Triumph of the Egg* (1921), *Many Marriages* (1922–23), *Horses and Men* (1923), and *Dark Laughter* (1925). See also his autobiography, *A Story Teller's Story* (1924).

ANDERSON, WILLIAM H. (1874–1959), long associated with the Anti-Saloon League in Illinois, New York, and Maryland, and a member of the executive and legislative committee of the Anti-Saloon League of America (1912–24). HLM battled with him repeatedly in print, especially in his Free Lance columns (1911–15).

ARCHER, WILLIAM (1856–1924), Scottish-born drama critic who, having spent much of his childhood in Norway, became the leading advocate for the work of Henrik Ibsen in the English-speaking world. His translation of *The Pillars of Society,* performed in 1880, was the first of Ibsen's plays to be staged in London. His translation of *A Doll's House* was staged in 1897. He assembled a collected edition of Ibsen's plays in 1906–7. He also championed the work of George Bernard Shaw.

ASBURY, HERBERT (1891–1963), American journalist who wrote several popular historical works, including *The Gangs of New York* (1928; rev. by HLM in *American Mercury,* July 1928) and *Life of Carry Nation* (1929; rev. by HLM in *American Mercury,* December 1929). His autobiographical work dealing with his renunciation of his Methodist upbringing, *Up from Methodism,* was published in 1926; a segment had appeared in the *American Mercury* (February 1925). HLM reviewed the book in the *Baltimore Evening Sun* (20 September 1926) and *American Mercury* (November 1926).

BELASCO, DAVID (1853–1931), American playwright, director, and producer who wrote many successful plays for Broadway. He also wrote the libretto to Puccini's opera *Madame Butterfly.*

BJØRNSON, BJØRNSTJENE (1832–1910), Norwegian playwright and novelist who won the Nobel Prize for literature in 1903.

BOK, EDWARD W. (1863–1930), longtime editor of the *Ladies' Home Journal* (1889–1919). HLM charitably reviewed his autobiography, *The Americanization of Edward Bok* (1920; rev. in *Smart Set,* January 1921), but found less interest in Bok's biography of the publisher Cyrus H. K. Curtis, *A Man from Maine* (1923; rev. in *Baltimore Evening Sun,* 26 May 1923, and *Smart Set,* August 1923).

BONHEUR, ROSA (1822–99), French painter and sculptor who enjoyed high critical acclaim as a female artist during and shortly after her lifetime. One of her most famous paintings, *The Horse Fair,* was purchased by Cornelius Vanderbilt and later donated to the Metropolitan Museum of Art in New York.

BOOTH, EDWIN (1833–93), celebrated American actor noted for his Shakespearean roles. He was the brother of John Wilkes Booth, the assassin of Abraham Lincoln.

BORAH, WILLIAM EDGAR (1865–1940), U.S. senator (Republican) from Idaho (1907–40). He gained a reputation as an isolationist and anti-imperialist, opposing the United States' entrance into the League of Nations.

BRANDES, GEORG (1842–1907), Danish critic whose works of literary criticism were highly influential in Europe and the United States.

BRISBANE, ARTHUR (1864–1936), American journalist who was hired by Charles Dana as a reporter for the *New York Sun* in 1883. In 1890 he joined Joseph Pulitzer's *New York World.* In 1897 he left the *World* to join its bitter rival, William Randolph Hearst's *New York Journal,* where he was instrumental in drumming up popular support for the Spanish-American War. He was given his own column, To-day, in 1917, and became one of the most widely syndicated journalists in the United States. He continued writing prolifically until his death.

BRYAN, WILLIAM JENNINGS (1860–1925), leading Democratic politician of the late nineteenth and early twentieth centuries. He was a Democratic candidate for president in 1896, 1900, and 1908, and secretary of state under Woodrow Wilson (1912–15). His role in the prosecution of the Scopes trial in 1925 is notorious.

BRYANT, WILLIAM CULLEN (1794–1878), poet who attained celebrity with the early poem "Thanatopsis" (1817) and continued to write poetry prolifically for the remainder of his long career. From 1829 until his death he was part owner and editor in chief of the *New York Evening Post*.

CABELL, JAMES BRANCH (1879–1958), Virginia novelist whom HLM regarded as one of the leading authors of his day. HLM reviewed almost every one of his works from 1909 to the late 1920s; he also helped to defend Cabell when his novel *Jurgen* (1919) came under attack from the New York Society for the Suppression of Vice. See HLM's brief monograph, *James Branch Cabell* (1927).

CALLAHAN, PATRICK H. (1865–1940), American businessman and Catholic layman. He established the successful Louisville Varnish Company in 1915. He advocated the repudiation of religious bigotry but supported Prohibition and William Jennings Bryan's fundamentalism at the Scopes trial.

CANNON, JAMES (1864–1944), perhaps the leading American Methodist clergyman of his time, was elected bishop in 1918. He was a vigorous proponent of temperance, being the leading lobbyist for the Anti-Saloon League both before and after the passage of the Eighteenth Amendment.

CARTER, BERNARD (1834–1912), Baltimore lawyer who began his practice in 1855. He later became a professor at the University of Maryland Law School and provost of the University of Maryland. He was also Baltimore city solicitor (1883–89).

CASTRO, CIPRIANO (1858–1924), Venezuelan soldier known as the Lion of the Andes. He ruled Venezuela as a dictator from 1899 to 1909, during which time he embezzled immense sums of money and lived a dissolute life. He was deposed by his lieutenant, Juan Vicente Gómez.

CATHER, WILLA (1876–1947), novelist and poet whom HLM considered the best American woman writer of her age. She won the Pulitzer Prize for *One of Ours* (1922). Aside from numerous reviews of her novels, HLM also wrote a brief essay, "Willa Cather" (in *The Borzoi 1920* [1920]).

COMSTOCK, ANTHONY (1844–1915), founder of the New York Society for the Suppression of Vice in 1873. Attaining tremendous power and influence, Comstock and his allies carried on numerous campaigns to prevent the distribution of "obscene" books and other matter. He was one of HLM's bêtes noires. See HLM's review of Charles Gallaudet Turnbull's *Anthony Comstock, Fighter* (1913; rev. in *Smart Set,* April 1914).

CRABBE, GEORGE WILLIAM (1875–1951), attorney for the Anti-Saloon League in Ohio, West Virginia, Maryland, and Delaware.

CRANE, FRANK (1861–1928), American clergyman and journalist and one of the most widely read columnists of his day. HLM regarded his work as trite and naïvely optimistic.

CURTIS, CHARLES (1860–1936), U.S. representative (1892–1907) and senator (1907–29) from Kansas (Republican) and vice president under Herbert Hoover (1929–33).

CZERNY, CARL (1791–1857), Austrian pianist, composer, and teacher whose books of etudes for the piano continue to be used in moderate to advanced piano instruction.

D'ANNUNZIO, GABRIELE (1863–1938), Italian poet, novelist, and dramatist whose works achieved both popularity and critical acclaim in the two decades preceding World War I.

DORÉ, GUSTAVE (1832–1883), French painter and illustrator whose illustrations of such works as Dante's *Divine Comedy* (1861–68), Milton's *Paradise Lost* (1866), the Bible (1866), and Coleridge's *Rime of the Ancient Mariner* (1875) were immensely popular and influential.

DREISER, THEODORE (1871–1945), pioneering novelist; HLM became his chief advocate. HLM reviewed most of his major works, including *Sister Carrie* (1900), *Jennie Gerhardt* (1911), *The Titan* (1914), *The "Genius"* (1915), and *An American Tragedy* (1925). For their tortured personal relationship see *Dreiser-Mencken Letters* (1977, 2 vols.) as well as HLM's *My Life as Author and Editor* (1993).

DREW, JOHN (1853–1927), American actor and son of the actor and manager John Drew (1827–62). He began performing in the mid-1870s and won acclaim in both popular and serious roles.

DUNSANY, LORD (Edward John Moreton Drax Plunkett, 1878–1957), Anglo-Irish novelist, short story writer, and playwright whose tales and plays of fantasy enjoyed a tremendous vogue in America in the 1910s and 1920s and remain central works in modern fantastic literature. HLM reviewed them enthusiastically in *Smart Set,* July 1917, and published much of Dunsany's work in *Smart Set.* HLM refers to Dunsany's play *The Gods of the Mountain* (erroneously cited as *The Green Gods from the Mountains*) in *Five Plays* (1914).

DUSE, ELEONORA (1858–1924), Italian stage actress who first toured the United States in 1893. In 1895 she began a romantic relationship with Gabriele D'Annunzio; he wrote four plays for her.

ERLANGER, ABRAHAM L. (1860–1930), American theatrical producer and manager. Along with Charles Frohman and others, he formed the Theatrical Syndicate in 1896 to coordinate theatrical bookings in New York and later in other parts of the country. He produced the early Ziegfeld Follies.

FISKE, CHARLES (1868–1941), rector of St. Michael and All Angels Church (Episcopal) in Baltimore (1910–15) and later a bishop. HLM refers to his article "Bringing In the Millennium" (*American Mercury,* August 1925).

FITZGERALD, F. SCOTT (1896–1940), novelist and short story writer whose early work HLM published in the *Smart Set* and whose novels HLM held in high esteem. See his reviews of *This Side of Paradise* (1920; rev. in *Smart Set,* August 1920); *The Beautiful and Damned* (1922; rev. in *Smart Set,* April 1922); and *The Great Gatsby* (1925; rev. in *American Mercury,* July 1925, and *Chicago Sunday Tribune,* 3 May 1925). HLM's complex involvement with Scott and Zelda Fitzgerald is chronicled in *My Life as Author and Editor* (1993).

FROHMAN, CHARLES (1860–1915), American theater producer who, with his older brother, Daniel (1851–1940), began producing plays on Broadway in the late 1880s, including works by Oscar Wilde, Clyde Fitch, and Arthur Wing Pinero. He was killed in the sinking of the *Lusitania* on 7 May 1915.

GALLAUDET, EDWARD MINER (1837–1917), American educator who pioneered the education of the deaf by the establishment in 1857 of the Columbia Institution for the Deaf and Blind (later Gallaudet University).

GARLAND, HAMLIN (1860–1940), novelist and essayist. HLM poked fun at his study of spiritualism, *The Shadow World* (1908; rev. in *Smart Set,* February 1909) but was more charitable toward Garland's autobiography, *A Son of the Middle Border* (1917; rev. in *New York Evening Mail,* 29 September 1917).

GATES, JOHN W. (1855–1911), American businessman who pioneered the use of barbed-wire fencing in the West. He later formed the American Steel & Wire Company and several other companies that challenged Andrew Carnegie's control of the steel industry.

GERARD, JAMES WATSON (1867–1951), American diplomat and U.S. ambassador to Germany (1913–17). He and HLM left Berlin together when the United States broke off diplomatic relations with Germany in February 1917.

GIBBONS, CARDINAL JAMES (1834–1921), archbishop of Baltimore and later a cardinal (1886). He was one of the leading Catholic theologians of his day and author of the popular volume *The Faith of Our Fathers* (1876). Early in his career, HLM wrote a flattering article about him: "James, Cardinal Gibbons" (*Leslie's Monthly Magazine,* May 1904 [as by "John F. Brownell"]).

GILMAN, DANIEL COIT (1831–1908), American educator who, after founding the Sheffield Scientific School at Yale and serving as the president of the University of California (1872–75), became the first president of Johns Hopkins University (1876–1902).

GÓMEZ Y BÁEZ, MÁXIMO (1836–1905), Cuban military leader who became its military commander during the War of Independence (1895–98). After the war he retired to Havana, refusing the presidential nomination in 1901.

GRASTY, CHARLES H. (1863–1924), American journalist who was editor and proprietor of the *Baltimore Evening News* (1892–1908) and an editor at the *Baltimore Sun* (1910–14). He was later the treasurer (1916–20) and editorial staff correspondent (1916–21) of the *New York Times.*

GRUNDY, JOSEPH RIDGWAY (1863–1961), founder and president of the Pennsylvania Manufacturers' Association (1909–47) and U.S. senator (Republican) from Pennsylvania (1929–30).

GUEST, EDGAR A. (1881–1959), English-born journalist and poet whose endless array of sentimental and homiletic poems, syndicated widely in newspapers, earned him great popularity among the masses but scorn from critics as a prototypical hack. His *Collected Verse* appeared in 1934.

GULDULIĆ, IVAN (1589–1638), Croatian poet and dramatist. He was the author of the epic poem *Osman* (written 1626; published 1826), which deals with the Ottoman sultan Osman II's defeat by the Poles in Bessarabia.

HARRIS, FRANK (1855–1931), Irish-born literary critic and essayist who settled in London and wrote prolifically for British magazines. His biography *Oscar Wilde: His Life and Confession* was self-published in 1916 and enthusiastically reviewed by HLM (*Smart Set*, September 1916). HLM also thought highly of other works by Harris, including *The Man Shakespeare* (1909; rev. in *Smart Set*, January 1910) and *Bernard Shaw* (1931; rev. in *American Mercury*, February 1932).

HAYES, THOMAS GORDON (1844–1915), American politician who was U.S. district attorney in the first Grover Cleveland administration (1885–89) and mayor of Baltimore (1899–1903). At various times he was also a state senator and city solicitor.

HAZLITT, HENRY (1894–1993), American author and editor. He was an editorial writer for several New York City newspapers in the 1920s before becoming literary editor of the *Nation* (1930–33). He edited the *American Mercury* in 1934, then joined the editorial staff of the *New York Times*. He wrote a number of influential books on economics, generally from a conservative or anti-Keynesian perspective.

HECHT, BEN (1894–1964), prolific Chicago journalist, novelist, and playwright. His novel *Erik Dorn* (1921) was both hailed and condemned as a representative of iconoclastic modernism. *Fantazius Mallare* (1922), a sexually explicit fantasy novel, was banned for obscenity. Hecht later achieved celebrity for the stage play *The Front Page* (1928, with Charles McArthur) and for numerous Hollywood screenplays.

HENRY, O. (pseudonym of William Sydney Porter, 1862–1910), short story writer who attained tremendous popularity in the first decade of the twentieth century. HLM generally considered his work facile and hackneyed. See HLM's reviews of *Cabbages and Kings* (1904; rev. in the *Baltimore Sunday Herald*, 18 December 1904); *Roads of Destiny* (1909; rev. in *Smart Set*, July 1909); and *Strictly Business* (1910; rev. in *Smart Set*, May 1910). See also "O. Henry" (*Chicago Sunday Tribune*, 25 October 1925).

HOLMES, OLIVER WENDELL, JR. (1841–1935), son of the author Oliver Wendell Holmes, Sr., and justice of the U.S. Supreme Court (1902–32). His book *The Dissenting Opinions of Mr. Justice Holmes*, arranged by Alfred Lief (1930), was reviewed by HLM (*American Mercury*, May 1930).

HUGHES, CHARLES EVANS (1862–1948), governor of New York (1907–10), member of the U.S. Supreme Court (1910–16), and Republican candidate for president in 1916. He later became secretary of state under Warren G. Harding and Calvin Coolidge (1921–25), and in that capacity he led the U.S. delegation at the Washington Naval Arms Conference (1921–22), covered by HLM. Still later he became Chief Justice of the United States (1930–41).

HUNEKER, JAMES GIBBONS (1860–1921), critic, novelist, and memoirist who befriended HLM in the 1910s and exercised a considerable influence on his critical manner. HLM considered Huneker a pioneering American critic, especially in the realm of music criticism, and admired the vigor and iconoclasm of his writing. He regularly reviewed Huneker's works as they appeared: *Egoists* (1909; rev. in the *Baltimore Sun*, 11 April 1909 and *Smart Set*, June 1909); *The Pathos of Distance* (1913; rev. in *Smart Set*, October 1913); *Old Fogy* (1913; rev. in *Smart Set*, July 1914); *New Cosmopolis* (1915; rev. in *Smart Set*, July 1915); *Ivory, Apes and Peacocks* (1915; rev. in *Smart Set*, December 1915); *Unicorns* (1917; rev. in *Smart Set*, December 1917); the autobiography *Steeplejack* (1920; rev. in the *Literary Review [New York Evening Post]*, 2 September 1920, and *Smart Set*, December 1920); etc. HLM devoted an extensive chapter to Huneker in *A Book of Prefaces* (1917) and edited a selection of Huneker's *Essays* (1929). See also *Painted Veils* (1920).

HUXLEY, THOMAS HENRY (1825–95), British naturalist and vigorous opponent of religious orthodoxy. HLM thought his essays a model of English prose. Huxley engaged in celebrated debates with William Wilberforce and William Ewart Gladstone over the issue of science and religion. HLM spoke of him highly in the article "Huxley" (*Chicago Sunday Tribune*, 2 August 1925). HLM refers to Huxley's *The Crayfish: An Introduction to the Study of Zoology* (1880).

INGERSOLL, ROBERT G. (1833–99), voluminous American author and one of the most popular lecturers of the late nineteenth century. His pungent attacks on religion and his espousal of agnosticism were embodied in numerous volumes, including *The Mistakes of Moses* (1879) and *The Christian Religion* (1882). See HLM's "Editorial" (*American Mercury*, November 1924), speaking of the need for a new Ingersoll to challenge religious orthodoxy.

INSULL, SAMUEL (1859–1938), American businessman who, after being Thomas Alva Edison's personal secretary, made a fortune as an executive in several immense electric companies. He was ruined by the Depression, and facing an indictment on mail fraud and antitrust charges, he fled to Greece, but was later extradited to the United States. In the ensuing trial he was found not guilty.

IRWIN, WILL (1873–1948), American journalist and writer who served on the staffs of the *San Francisco Chronicle*, the *New York Sun*, *McClure's Magazine*, and *Collier's*. He was a war correspondent during World War I and wrote several books about the war. He also wrote fiction and plays.

JANVIER, MEREDITH (1872–1936), longtime bookseller in Baltimore. HLM reviewed Janvier's reminiscent volume *Baltimore in the Eighties and Nineties* (1933; rev.

in *Baltimore Evening Sun,* 15 April 1933) and wrote the preface to Janvier's *Baltimore Yesterdays* (1937).

JOHNSON, JAMES WELDON (1871–1938), African American lawyer, poet, and songwriter who also wrote the novel *The Autobiography of an Ex-Colored Man* (1917) and the autobiography *Along This Way* (1933). HLM reviewed Johnson's *The Book of Negro Spirituals* (1925; rev. in *American Mercury,* December 1925). HLM refers (erroneously) to Johnson's poem "Go Down, Death!" (*American Mercury,* April 1927).

KELLY, HOWARD A. (1858–1943), American gynecologist and surgeon who taught at Johns Hopkins Hospital (1889–1919) and Johns Hopkins Medical School (1893–1919). Aside from many works on medicine, he wrote *A Scientific Man and the Bible* (1925; reviewed by HLM in *American Mercury,* February 1926), in which he proclaimed his literal belief in the Bible.

KEMAL ATATURK, MUSTAFA (1881–1938), the founder of modern Turkey. After World War I he drove out the Ottoman sultan and established a secular republic in 1923. He was the country's autocratic president from that date until his death.

KENT, FRANK R. (1877–1953), American journalist who joined the *Baltimore Sun* as a reporter in 1898 and served as managing editor (1911–21) and London correspondent (1922–23). With HLM, Gerald W. Johnson, and Hamilton Owens, he cowrote *The Sunpapers of Baltimore* (1937), a comprehensive history of the paper.

KILRAIN, JAKE (1859–1937), American bare-knuckle and glove boxer who turned professional in 1883. He was recognized as heavyweight champion of the world in 1887 but lost a bare-knuckle fight to John L. Sullivan in 1889 in the seventy-sixth round.

KNOPF, ALFRED A. (1892–1984), American publisher who established the firm bearing his name in 1915. He published the great majority of HLM's books during and after the latter's lifetime. He was significantly assisted in his enterprise by his wife, Blanche, who became president of the company in 1957.

LAGERLÖF, SELMA (1858–1940), Swedish novelist and the first woman to win the Nobel Prize for literature in 1909. HLM reviewed only the short story collection *The Girl from the Marsh Croft* (1910; rev. in *Smart Set,* August 1910), noting that "the short stories here printed are, in the main, of an exceedingly commonplace sort."

LANDON, ALF (1887–1987), governor of Kansas (1933–37) and Republican candidate for president in 1936. He lost to Franklin D. Roosevelt in a landslide. HLM, by that time disgusted with FDR's New Deal, supported Landon and accompanied him on a campaign tour.

LATROBE, FERDINAND C. (1833–1911), Maryland politician who was elected mayor of Baltimore seven times during the period 1874–95. He also served in the Maryland House of Delegates and held other state offices.

LYON, HARRIS MERTON (1883–1916), American short story writer. HLM published his story "The Pact" in *Smart Set* (December 1914). His tales were collected in *Sardonics* (1908) and *Graphics* (1913).

MABIE, HAMILTON WRIGHT (1845–1916), American editor and critic whose work HLM always regarded as prototypical of conventional, moralizing, unimaginative criticism.

MACHADO, GERALDO (1871–1939), general during the Cuban War of Independence (1895–98). He took the side of the Liberals against President Mario García Menocal in the rebellion of 1917; although Menocal prevailed in that conflict (some of which was witnessed by HLM when he went to Cuba after leaving Germany), Machado later defeated Menocal to become the fifth president of Cuba (1925–33).

MACREADY, WILLIAM CHARLES (1793–1873), well-known British actor who gained celebrity playing roles from Shakespeare, Racine, Sheridan, and others.

MCDOUGALL, WALT (1858–1938), American artist and cartoonist who worked for the *New York Graphic, Puck,* and other magazines before being hired by the *New York Herald* in 1896. He became the first syndicated newspaper cartoonist and produced an immense body of work. HLM refers to McDougall's article "Pictures in the Papers" (*American Mercury,* September 1925).

MARDEN, OLIVER SWETT (1850–1924), American author of inspirational and motivational books. He was associated with the New Thought (a spiritualist and self-help movement of the late nineteenth and early twentieth centuries), contributing to the New Thought journal *Nautilus* and founding his own magazine, *Success,* in 1897. HLM regularly poked fun at his elementary homilies.

MASON, GREGORY (1889–?), American novelist, historian, and social critic. HLM refers to Mason's article "Chautauqua: Its Technic" (*American Mercury,* March 1924).

MELLON, ANDREW (1855–1937), American banker and industrialist who made a fortune in oil, steel, shipbuilding, and construction. He was secretary of the treasury in the Harding, Coolidge, and Hoover administrations (1921–32).

MELTZER, CHARLES HENRY (1853–1936), British-born playwright and drama and music critic who wrote for the *New York Herald,* the *New York World,* the *New York American,* and other newspapers and magazines.

MILLIKAN, ROBERT A. (1868–1953), American scientist who became one of the leading physicists of his day, known chiefly for his work on cosmic rays. He won the Nobel Prize in 1923. In the 1920s he devoted his efforts to reconciling science and religion in such works as *Science and Life* (1924) and *Evolution in Science and Religion* (1927).

MITCHELL, DONALD G. (1822–1908), American journalist, essayist, and editor who became the first editor of The Easy Chair department of *Harper's Magazine.* Of his many books, *The Reveries of a Bachelor* (1850) is the best known.

MOORE, GEORGE (1862–1933), Anglo-Irish novelist and memoirist whom HLM regarded as one of the leading writers of his age. He gained celebrity with such works as the novels *A Mummer's Wife* (1885), *Esther Waters* (1894), and *The Brook Kerith* (1916) and the autobiographical work *Confessions of a Young Man* (1888). HLM sympathetically reviewed the three volumes of Moore's autobiography, *Hail and Farewell: Ave* (1911), *Salve* (1912), and *Vale* (1914), as well as *A Story-Teller's Holiday* (1918) and *An Anthology of Pure Poetry* (1924; rev. in *American Mercury,* October 1925).

MOSZKOWSKI, MORITZ (1854–1925), Polish-German pianist and composer, best known for his piano pieces and songs.

NATHAN, GEORGE JEAN (1882–1958), American editor and theater critic who became one of HLM's closest friends and colleagues. He assisted HLM in editing *Smart Set* (1914–23) and for a time was a coeditor of *American Mercury* (1924–25). His pungent theater reviews (beginning in *Smart Set* in 1909) provoked much controversy. He collaborated with HLM on *Europe After 8:15* (1914), the play *Heliogabalus* (1920), and other works. He continued writing reviews for the next forty years, attaining celebrity with the annual *Theatre Book of the Year* (1943–51).

NIETZSCHE, FRIEDRICH (1844–1900), revolutionary German philosopher whose anticlericalism and theories of the superman significantly influenced HLM. See HLM's *The Philosophy of Friedrich Nietzsche* (1908), his slim selection *The Gist of Nietzsche* (1910), and his translation of *The Antichrist* (1920). HLM wrote frequently of Nietzsche in *Smart*

Set (see the issues of November 1909, March 1910, March 1912, August 1913, and August 1915). See also "Nietzsche" (*Chicago Sunday Tribune,* 23 August 1925).

O'CONNELL, CARDINAL WILLIAM HENRY (1859–1944), Roman Catholic clergyman who was made archbishop of Boston (1907) and subsequently a cardinal (1911). He aggressively exercised both religious and political influence during much of his tenure.

O'NEILL, EUGENE (1888–1953), leading American dramatist whose early one-act plays HLM published in the *Smart Set.* HLM did not, however, formally review any of his plays.

OSLER, WILLIAM (1849–1919), Canadian-born physician and professor of medicine who taught at Johns Hopkins Medical School (1888–1904) and then emigrated to England, becoming the Regius Professor of Medicine at Oxford. His textbook, *The Principles and Practice of Medicine* (1892), long remained standard.

PAINE, THOMAS (1737–1809), British-born pamphleteer who wrote in support of American independence in the tract *Common Sense* (1776) but whose religious skepticism, exhibited in *The Age of Reason* (1795–96), earned him notoriety as an "infidel."

RAULSTON, JOHN TATE (1868–1956), judge in the Eighteenth Judicial Circuit in Tennessee and presiding judge in the Scopes trial.

ROOSEVELT, THEODORE, JR. (1887–1944), son of President Theodore Roosevelt. He served as assistant secretary of the navy (1921–24), governor of Puerto Rico (1929–32), and governor-general of the Philippines (1932–33) and later became a brigadier general in the U.S. Army.

SALTUS, EDGAR (1855–1921), American novelist and essayist whose works were considered the height of fashionable literature in the late nineteenth and early twentieth centuries, notably the novel *The Truth about Tristrem Varick* (1888). HLM, however, considered his only enduring work to be a cynical account of the Roman emperors, *Imperial Purple* (1892): see "Edgar Saltus" (*Chicago Sunday Tribune,* 11 October 1925).

SANGER, MARGARET (1879–1966), founder of the birth control movement in the United States. She founded and edited the *Birth Control Review,* for which HLM wrote a brief article on Havelock Ellis, "Man of Science, Artist and Gentleman" (February 1926). HLM wrote an extensive review of one of her tracts on birth control, *The Pivot of Civilization* (1922; rev. in *Smart Set,* February 1923), saying that it was "lyrical and sometimes almost hysterical." HLM refers to her article "The Bias against Birth Control" (*American Mercury,* June 1924).

SCHWAB, CHARLES (1862–1939), president of the Carnegie Steel Company and the first president of the United States Steel Corporation (founded 1901). In 1904 he formed the rival Bethlehem Steel Corporation. Although at one time having assets of $200,000,000, he died insolvent.

SEIDL, ANTON (1850–1898), Hungarian conductor and colleague of Richard Wagner. He conducted at the Leipzig State Theater, the German Opera Company in New York, and the New York Philharmonic (1891–98).

SHAW, MARY (1860?–1929), American actress who made her debut in Boston in 1878. She subsequently became famous for playing roles in the plays of Henrik Ibsen and George Bernard Shaw.

SINCLAIR, UPTON (1878–1968), American novelist, journalist, and political activist whose numerous and multifarious attempts at social and economic reform (chiefly of a socialist variety) earned HLM's continual scorn and amusement. He attained celebrity with the novel *The Jungle* (1906), exposing the appalling conditions of the Chicago stockyards. HLM took note of many of his subsequent works, including the novel *The Moneychangers* (1908; rev. in *Smart Set,* November 1908); *The Brass Check: A Study of American Journalism* (1919; rev. in *Smart Set,* April 1920); *The Book of Life, Mind and Body* (1921; rev. in *Smart Set,* July 1922); *The Goose-Step: A Study of American Education* (1923; rev. in *Smart Set,* May 1923); *Money Writes!* (1927; rev. in *American Mercury,* February 1928); and *The Wet Parade* (1931; rev. in the *Nation,* 23 September 1931). HLM actually agreed with many of Sinclair's criticisms of American journalism, education, and politics, but his congenital distaste for anything smacking of "uplift" prevented him from envisaging that any of Sinclair's reforms would have any effect.

STARRETT, VINCENT (1886–1974), American journalist and bookman best known for his account of obscure literary figures, *Buried Caesars* (1923), and his reviews in various Chicago newspapers, gathered in *Books Alive* (1940) and other volumes.

STEDMAN, EDMUND CLARENCE (1833–1908), American poet, critic, and editor best known for such anthologies as *Poets of America* (1885) and *An American Anthology* (1900). Although an early champion of Walt Whitman, he nonetheless symbolized for HLM an attitude of Victorian rectitude still prevailing in the literary criticism of the early twentieth century.

STEVENS, JAMES (1891–1972), American folklorist who contributed extensively to the *American Mercury* during the years 1924–28. Some of the articles were gathered in the book *Paul Bunyan* (1925). He also wrote the autobiographical novel *Big Jim Turner* (1948).

STIRNER, MAX (pseudonym of Johann Kaspar Schmidt, 1806–56), German philosopher, significantly influenced by Hegel, best known for the treatise *Der Einzige und sein Eigentum* (1844), usually translated as *The Ego and His Own*. Stirner's work fell into obscurity after his death but was revived toward the end of the nineteenth century.

STRATON, JOHN ROACH (1875–1929), American Baptist clergyman who served as pastor in Chicago (1905–8); Baltimore (1908–13); Norfolk, Virginia (1914–17); and the Calvary Baptist Church in New York (1918–29), where he introduced the innovation of regular radio broadcasts. He was a frequent butt of HLM's attacks.

SUNDAY, BILLY (1862?–1935), American itinerant evangelist who became immensely popular in the first two decades of the twentieth century through his histrionic outdoor sermons. HLM discussed him at length in a *Smart Set* column of July 1916 and also recorded his impressions of one of Sunday's lecture tours in the *Baltimore Evening Sun* (17 February, 14 and 27 March, and 2 May 1916).

TASCHERAUD, HENRI (?–?), author about whom nothing is known. HLM refers to Tascheraud's article "The Art of Begging a Meal" (*American Mercury,* June 1925).

TETLOW, HENRY (?–?), American author of several books on farming. Tetlow had five articles in the *American Mercury* between 1925 and 1927.

THAYER, WEBSTER (1857–1933), American judge who presided over the Sacco-Vanzetti trial in 1920. Both during the trial and in statements made outside the courtroom, Thayer exhibited clear prejudice against the defendants' purported involvement in anarchist organizations. After the trial Thayer was the target of bomb threats; his house in Worcester, Massachusetts, was bombed, and he thereafter lived the rest of his life in a club in Boston.

TICH, LITTLE (1867–1928), the stage name of Harry Relph, a British music hall comedian who was four feet six inches tall. He began performing at the age of twelve and continued until a year before his death.

TOWNSEND, FRANCIS E. (1867–1960), American physician who gained celebrity in the 1930s by proposing an old-age pension program called the "Townsend Plan." Townsend's activities in part led Franklin D. Roosevelt to propose the Social Security

Act, passed in 1935. Townsend was a significant figure in the presidential election of 1936, supporting a third-party candidate, William Lemke, as mouthpiece for his views.

TULLY, JIM (1891–1947), American hobo whom HLM discovered and whose work he encouraged. Tully went on to become a prolific novelist. He went to Hollywood in the mid-1920s and became a colorful personality there, although he did very little work as a screenwriter and actor. Tully contributed eleven articles and stories to the *American Mercury* between 1925 and 1928.

URBAN, JOSEPH (1872–1933), Austrian architect and theatrical designer who emigrated to the United States in 1912 and became art director of the Boston Opera House. He subsequently worked with the Ziegfeld Follies and the Metropolitan Opera. He continued his work as an architect, designing many hotels, theaters, department stores, and apartment buildings across the United States.

VENABLE, RICHARD M. (1839–1910), professor of law at the University of Maryland (1870–1905) and member of the Baltimore City Council (1899–1903).

WAGNER, FERDINAND (1856–?), California artist.

WATSON, JAMES ELI (1864–1948), U.S. representative (1896–97, 1899–1909) and senator (1916–33) from Indiana (Republican). He was known for his conservative views, his flamboyant speeches, and his devotion to party orthodoxy.

WHEELER, WAYNE B. (1869–1927), superintendent of the Anti-Saloon League of Ohio (1904–15), general counsel for the Anti-Saloon League of America (1915–27), and vigorous supporter of Prohibition.

WHITE, ANDREW D. (1832–1918), first president of Cornell University (1868–85) and author of the landmark treatise *A History of the Warfare of Science with Theology in Christendom* (1895).

WHITE, OWEN (1879–1946), American journalist who worked for the *El Paso Herald* before moving to Long Island in 1925, where he wrote for *Collier's,* gaining notoriety for writing critically about the oil industry and political corruption in Texas. He had several articles in the *American Mercury* between 1925 and 1928; HLM refers specifically to "Reminiscences of Texas Divines" (*American Mercury,* September 1926).

WHITE, STANFORD (1853–1906), American architect and member of the celebrated form of McKim, Mead and White. He designed numerous structures in New York

City (including the Washington Square Arch) as well as the First Methodist Episcopal Church in Baltimore (1887) and many other homes and buildings. He was murdered by millionaire Harry K. Thaw.

WHITNEY, CHARLOTTE ANITA (1867–1955), radical American labor organizer who was a member of the Socialist Party and the American Communist Party. In 1920 she was convicted of belonging to a party that advocated violence in seeking political change, but was later pardoned by California governor Clement Calhoun Young.

WHYTE, WILLIAM PINKNEY (1824–1908), Baltimore politician who held a number of offices in Baltimore and Maryland, including U.S. senator (1868–69, 1875–81), governor (1873–75), and mayor of Baltimore (1881–83).

WRIGHT, WILLARD HUNTINGTON (1888–1939), prolific American journalist and novelist and friend of HLM. He worked extensively for the *Los Angeles Times* early in his career and also edited the *Smart Set* in 1913–14. He collaborated with HLM and George Jean Nathan on the travel volume *Europe After 8:15* (1914). Among many other volumes on literature, art, and philosophy, he wrote *What Nietzsche Taught* (1915). As S. S. Van Dine, he published a dozen popular novels in the 1920s and 1930s featuring the detective Philo Vance.

YORKE, DANE (1899–?), American author of books and articles on manufacturing and insurance. Yorke had five articles in the *American Mercury* between 1926 and 1928.

ZANGWILL, ISRAEL (1864–1926), Anglo-Jewish dramatist and novelist whose novel *Children of the Ghetto* (1892) was a striking portrait of the Jewish colony in London. Also noteworthy is the play *The Melting Pot* (1909), in which that phrase was coined.

ZORN, ANDERS (1860–1920), the most celebrated artist in Sweden, best known for his nudes and his portraits. He painted the portraits of three American presidents.

ZUZORIĆ, CVIJETA (1555?–1600?), poet from the Republic of Ragusa (now Dubrovnik) who wrote in Croatian and Italian. Torquato Tasso mentioned her in several sonnets, although he never met her.

BIBLIOGRAPHY OF
ORIGINAL APPEARANCES

PROLOGUE

"Henry Louis Mencken." In *The Vagabonds: Autobiographies and Sketches of the Vagabonds.* Baltimore, 1905, 16.

MEMORIES OF A LONG LIFE

"Early Days." *Borzoi Battledore* (May 1945): 1–2, 4–5.

"Old Days." *Baltimore Evening Sun* (19 January 1925): 15.

"Surdi Audiunt." *New Yorker* 19, no. 17 (12 June 1943): 19–22.

"The Passing of 'The Hill.'" *Baltimore Evening Herald* (15 March 1905): 7.

"West Baltimore." *Baltimore Evening Sun* (27 June 1927): 19.

"Mr. Kipling." *New York American* (14 January 1935): 15.

"Man of Means." *New York American* (4 April 1935): 17.

"Tale of a Traveller." *New Yorker* 21, no. 36 (20 October 1945): 48–53.

"Christmas Story." *New Yorker* 20, no. 46 (30 December 1944): 17–21 (as "Stare Decisis"). Reprinted in *Christmas Story* (New York: Alfred A. Knopf, 1946).

"An Evening on the House." *Esquire* 20, no. 6 (December 1943): 63, 233–34, 236, 238–39.

"Baltimoriana." *Baltimore Evening Sun* (15 February 1926): 15.

"Obsequies in the Grand Manner." *Esquire* 21, no. 1 (January 1944): 43, 133–35.

"Love Story." *New Yorker* 23, no. 48 (17 January 1948): 23–26.

"The Life of an Artist." *New Yorker* 24, no. 8 (17 April 1948): 64, 66–71.

"James Huneker." *Century Magazine* 102, no. 2 (June 1921): 191–97.

"The Life of Tone." *New Yorker* 19, no. 32 (25 September 1943): 21–25.

AUTHOR AND JOURNALIST

"A Footnote on Journalism." *Optimist* 2, no. 1 (March 1901): 39–44.

["Reminiscences of the *Herald*."] "Reminiscence." *Baltimore Evening Sun* (10 January 1927): 17.

"On Breaking into Type." *Colophon* 1, no. 1 (February 1930): 1–8.

["Walter Abell and the *Sun*."] "Walter Abell and The *Sun*." *Baltimore Sun* (26 January 1941): 10.

["Twenty-five Years of the *Evening Sun*."] "Twenty-five Years." *Baltimore Evening Sun* (15 April 1935): 17.

["A Word about the *Smart Set*."] *A Personal Word.* [New York: Privately printed, 1921.]

Foreword to *A Bibliography of the Writings of H. L. Mencken,* by Carroll Frey, 3–6. Philadelphia: Centaur Book Shop, 1924.

["Five Years of the *American Mercury.*"] "Editorial." *American Mercury* 15, no. 4 (December 1928): 407–10.

["Ten Years of the *American Mercury.*"] "Ten Years." *American Mercury* 30, no. 4 (December 1933): 385–87.

"Memoirs of an Editor." *Vanity Fair* 41, no. 6 (February 1934): 16, 54, 60.

"The Worst Trade of All." *Liberty* 19, no. 4 (4 April 1942): 19–20.

"Why I Am Not a Book Collector." In *For Loving a Book,* by Charles Honce, xvii–xx. Mt. Vernon, NY: Golden Eagle Press, 1945.

THINKER

"Off the Grand Banks." *Baltimore Evening Sun* (7 September 1925): 13.

"Meditations at Vespers." *Baltimore Evening Sun* (12 December 1927): 21.

"What Is This Talk about Utopia?" *Nation* 126 (13 June 1928): 662–63.

"What I Believe." *Forum* 84, no. 3 (September 1930): 133–39.

["On the Meaning of Life."] In *On the Meaning of Life,* [edited by] Will Durant, 30–36 (untitled). New York: Ray Long & Richard R. Smith, 1932.

"Generally Political." [New York: Columbia University, 1940.]

WORLD TRAVELER

"At the Edge of the Spanish Main." *Baltimore Sunday Herald* (26 August 1900): 22.

"The Beeriad." *Smart Set* 39, no. 4 (April 1913): 103–11.

"At Large in London." *Smart Set* 40, no. 2 (June 1913): 99–107 (as by "George Weems Peregoy").

["Reminiscences of 1917."] "Reminiscence." *Baltimore Evening Sun* (21 June 1937): 17.

"The Black Country." *Chicago Sunday Tribune* (23 January 1927): Part 1, 1.

"West Indian Notes." *Baltimore Evening Sun* (25 January 1932): 19.

"Our Footloose Correspondents." *New Yorker* 10, no. 12 (5 May 1934): 87 (as by "M. R. C.").

"Foreign Parts: Athens." *New Yorker* 10, no. 13 (12 May 1934): 39–40.

"Foreign Parts: Istanbul." *New Yorker* 10, no. 14 (19 May 1934): 72–73.

"Foreign Parts: Granada." *New Yorker* 10, no. 16 (2 June 1934): 68–69.

"Foreign Parts: Gibraltar." *New Yorker* 10, no. 18 (16 June 1934): 71–72.

"Foreign Parts: Jerusalem." *New Yorker* 10, no. 19 (23 June 1934): 52.

"Foreign Parts: Venice." *New Yorker* 10, no. 20 (30 June 1934): 37–38.

"Foreign Parts: Madeira." *New Yorker* 10, no. 22 (14 July 1934): 50.

"Foreign Parts: Râbat." *New Yorker* 10, no. 23 (21 July 1934): 51–52.

"Foreign Parts: Cairo." *New Yorker* 10, no. 24 (28 July 1934): 34.

"The Adriatic: East Side." *Seven Seas* 13, no. 4 (June 1934): 9–10.

EPILOGUE

["Henry Louis Mencken (1936)."] In *Portraits and Self-Portraits,* collected and illustrated by Georges Schreiber, 103–7 (untitled). Boston: Houghton Mifflin, 1936.

INDEX